From the Farm to the Electric Chair
The Truth Behind the John Wallace Story

By

Ivey Nance

This book is being dedicated to all those who knew him, who loved him and who stood behind him during his darkest hour and who are still standing sixty one years later.

Special acknowledgment to an Angel named Debbie and to all those who shared their stories and their photos with me.

Foreword

If anyone had told me during this time last year that I would be writing a book to vindicate a convicted killer, I probably would have called them crazy. But here I am, writing this one. The awful truth weighs so heavy on my heart that I have to write it. As much as I have tried, I cannot get the facts out of my head. So much poppycock has been written that the real story about John Wallace needs to be told. His actions caused the death of a man but he should not have been sentenced to the electric chair. It was not murder. It was manslaughter. A huge difference. One has the intent to kill. The other one doesn't.

Once you remove all the sensationalism, the theatrics, the facts will speak for themselves. John Wallace was convicted of murder in 1948 and sentenced to the electric chair in Coweta County, Georgia. If he had been given a fair and impartial trial, the outcome would have been very different. Most any other state would have looked at the facts and charged him with manslaughter or at the very maximum guilty with mercy. The verdict would have meant prison but not the chair.

Let's just suppose for one instant that sound minded, and intelligent people believe in ghost, witches, warlocks, vampires, fortunetellers and the all powerful mystics and beyond. This includes any self-proclaimed Oracle of the Ages. Then let us hope if any of these things are real that John Wallace's spirit has found solace in the knowledge that his family knows the truth and hereby sets his soul free.

Many, many years ago back when I first started getting into genealogy, I heard about John Wallace and the book, 'Murder in Coweta County'. Naturally I couldn't wait to read all about him. I purchased this book and bought several copies of the movie and gave them to my brothers one year. I told them not to be so cocky that it just might get them the electric chair. Well, of course, I was just joking with them at the time. I didn't really believe that having a cocky attitude would get anyone the electric chair but that was my impression from reading the book.

I'm also a big Sherlock Holmes fan and there were parts in the book exactly written like an old 1950s television episode I own. Ms. Barnes wrote Sheriff Potts as if he were Sherlock and Hancock was Inspector Lestrade out to get all of Potts' glory. After I realized what she was doing, I just took everything she said with a grain of salt. Knowing full well that I was not going to get accurate information about the person John Wallace really was. She was just out to write a good book and didn't really care what damage she did to those involved or to their families, the ones who were left behind. The problem is that outsiders believed what she wrote and accepted it as fact, without question.

Last year I started work on The Strickland Family History, particularly focusing on the Descendants of John Milledge Gilbert Strickland. Although this book is not ready for publication, another story developed during my search of gathering pictures for the family history book.

The real John Wallace story started to unfold. It appears that there are several people still living who actually knew him and broke bread at his table. They state very emphatically that he was not the man so many of the Coweta county people claim he was. It perked my interest enough to start asking a few more questions and before I knew it the real John Wallace story was born.

I have included his 1948 statement to the jury. I have seen it written as long winded and babbling but I find it in character with the man. It tells us who he was. It gives us insight into the real man. His words have been twisted and turned to serve the purpose that others wanted to give. They had their owns reasons for making him out to be something that he wasn't. I'm not privy to those reasons and have no desire in trying to guess at their motives. This book is simply to present you with the true facts in an attempt to give you the correct image of the man, the trial and the news reporting done at the time. For some reason, John Wallace was made out to be a ruthless, wealthy dairyman and that misconception continues to be perpetrated years later. I've read his statement and I've read the court file.

There are many discrepancies in the case that are unexplainable. We have no way of knowing what really happened that day or what was in the heart of John Wallace. The record is all we have to go by and the record shows that there is, and was, plenty of room for doubt. It was definitely not an open and shut case. For anyone to say "there was no question is a ridiculous and absurd statement. There were plenty of questions, plenty of doubt. Very odd, very strange things took place during this court case. Things that lawmen don't usually do, were done. It's disturbing but it's true.

This book is about John Wallace and who he really was. He took full blame for the tragic loss of life for one William H., alias Wilson Turner. He claimed to his death that his cohorts were innocent of any wrong doing. He also claimed that the killing was an accident. This is his story. It was important to him that people know the truth. Enclosed are his words about the accident that caused a man to lose his life. I believe he spoke from the heart and I believe he spoke the truth. Hence the book about the real John Wallace.

Table of Contents

John Wallace's statement to the Jury broken up into three parts

Timeline

June 12, 1896 - John Wallace born on a farm in Chambers County, Alabama

April 20, 1948 - Tuesday - death of William, aka Wilson Turner occurs.

April 23, 1948 - Friday - arrested - seven men charged with one murder.

April 27, 1948 - Commitment hearing of John Wallace and Herring Sivell
                    held in Newnan, Coweta County Georgia. Lasted two hours.

April 28, 1948 - 200 to 500 men comb the country in a day long search looking for
     Turner's body. They searched all around Wallace's estate and adjacent Meriwether
     County yet nothing was found. The search spread as far as the Little White House in
     Warm Springs. Sheriff Potts offered a $500 reward to anyone who brought in Turner's
     body.

May 27, 1948 - Newspapers report that State Revenue Officers E.C. Cook and C.E.
     Miller found 101 gallons of non-paid liquor within 75 yards of John Wallace's place
     near Durand. The officers said the liquor belonged to Wallace. John Bray was arrested
     as the operator of the still. *Very peculiar that this wasn't found on April 28th.

May 31, 1948 - Indictments

June 14, 1948 - Trial begins at 1pm.

June 18, 1948 - John Wallace is convicted of murder on Day Five. The Jury took
     seventy minutes to find him guilty. Scheduled for Execution July 30, 1948

June 24, 1948 - Filed for a new trial.

July 12, 1948 - Sixty four-year-old Hardy Collier dies from a heart attack.

Nov 15 1948 – Attorneys present their arguments before the Supreme Court

Jan 13 1949 - Supreme Court upholds the Death Sentence. Execution set for February 11

Feb 3 1949 – Governor Talmadge grants a 30-day stay of execution.

April 30, 1949 - Extraordinary motion for a new trial was filed.

August 24, 1950 - Turner's widow is awarded $7,500 damages against John Wallace
                    and Herring Sivell. She had sued for $74,280 against all four men.
                    Wallace in a cell at Fulton Towers in Atlanta about to be electrocuted
                    was expected to pay the wife of the man who had been stealing from
                    him. Ironic.

October 26, 1950 Unanimous decision of the Pardon and Parole Board in denying
     commutation of death sentence.

November 3, 1950 - Dies by the electric chair at Reidsville State Prison, Tattnall county.

Chapter One

What did John Wallace do?

John Wallace died in the electric chair on November 3, 1950. He was convicted of murder in Coweta County, Georgia on June 18, 1948 based on the following evidence.

Four eyewitnesses at the Sunset Tourist Camp state they saw John Wallace get out of a green Ford car with a shotgun in one hand and grab William, a.k.a. Wilson Turner with the other hand. Wallace then drug or pushed Turner back toward the car he had just vacated. The witnesses state that Turner had both his hands free and was putting up a heck of a fight. Once Wallace got him to the car, Turner reportedly was knocked in the head with the butt of the shotgun. The man then fell unconscious into the car. Three of the witnesses state they had never seen such brutality and in their opinion the young man was dead the instant he fell into the car.

Two out of the three witnesses proceed to say that Wallace appeared to be hitting Turner with his fist or with a short object while in the back seat although they could see nothing but the top of Wallace's hat once the men had gotten inside the car. Herring Sivell was driving the car and although he played no active part in the scuffle he had a pearl handled pistol in his hand and helped in putting Turner's feet into the car.

When asked by defense counsel why anyone would be hitting a dead man, the reply was along the lines of "for the brutality of it." The entire scene lasted anywhere from one to four minutes.

Interestingly, the State's expert, Dr. Herman Jones, toxicologist was called in and states that there was not enough blood in the car for the man to have had his head crushed in while in the vehicle.

It is reported in the court records by Revenue Agent Lucas that Turner had once ran from him, stopped suddenly and blacked out. He came to a few minutes later and returned to the house to face Lucas. He was pale and had a difficult time talking. When Turner had recovered sufficiently to explain what happened, he lifted his arm and Lucas saw where he had injected himself with a needle. In all likelihood the injection had occurred just moments before Lucas's arrival. Lucas did not know why Turner had done this to himself.

This testimony was given close to the end of the trial, just moments before the State closed the first time. It is unexplainable why the defense counsels did not follow up on this line of questioning. This information was not followed up on by either counsel. It is unclear as to whether Turner had a medical problem or if he was a drug user. Regardless of the reason why, obviously, it was not uncommon for Turner to pass out in a seemingly dead faint. I'm sure the Sunset Camp witnesses had never seen a man do this before either. It is certain that Revenuer Lucas, never had.

It is rational to presume that having spent the last few nights in jail that upon Turner's release one of the first things he would do is to inject himself with whatever it was he was taking.

It is also reported that Wallace took the body to Meriwether county, where he lived, and dumped the body in a well. He then became scared that the body would be found and decided to burn it. He preceded to get two of his helpers that lived on his farm to help him retrieve the body. They were either sharecroppers or hired hands, or perhaps they were a bit of both. In any event, Brooks and Gates state that they helped Wallace retrieve the body from the well and put it in an old moonshine still pit and burned it with a cord of fresh-cut pine wood and some gasoline. This occurred around midnight. They watched it burn for thirty minutes before leaving. When they came back the next morning all that was left were ashes. They cleaned out the pit, which held two full bags and part of a third bag and dumped it in a nearby creek.

The biggest problem with their story is that it is not possible to cremate a body to ashes over night, outdoors, with a cord of fresh-cut pine wood and gasoline. A little thing called common sense would tell a person that this is not possible otherwise, it is highly doubtful that there would be any murdered bodies ever found. The killer would simply burn them to ashes.

But just to be on the safe side, I contacted two cremation facilities and was told the possibility is "absolutely non existent. The fire could not stay hot enough, long enough to accomplish the cremation state." There will be more about this later in the book.

Yet the fact remains that John Wallace was convicted of murder in Coweta County on this evidence and sentenced to the electric chair. But the local law enforcement didn't stop there. They charged everybody even remotely connected to the events with murder. Brooks and Gates were among the list along with four others that were arrested and charged with the murder. These two men were later found not guilty and released based on their testimony at the Wallace trial. Very convenient for them, wasn't it?

The following 42 items were presented as State's evidence. All but nine were allowed by the Judge to be entered as evidence.

1. Photograph of William, a.k.a. Wilson Turner. Allowed in evidence.

2. Picture of the pit where it is claimed the body was cremated after the death. Allowed in evidence.

3. Cartridge box of ashes that holds bone fragments claimed to be the cremated remains of William, a.k.a., Wilson Turner. Allowed in evidence.

4. The package of ashes that Mr. Potts testified they got out of the creek or on the side of the creek? Allowed in evidence.

5. Mr. Henson, defense counsel, objects to the fifth item by stating: "I don't know what this is. It appears to be a box of trash and dirt, and so forth." By Mr. Goldberg (prosecutor for the State): That box contains -- Sheriff Potts testified he got it by the side of the pit. By The Court: I overrule the objection. The box is allowed in evidence.

    *Obviously the jury does not know what this box is suppose to represent nor was it attested to by anyone during the trial.

6. An axe used by Brooks and Gates in cutting poles. Allowed in evidence.

7. A knife belonging to Brooks, used in cutting twigs. Allowed in evidence.

8. Twigs - Brooks and Gates say the body was moved and covered up all day with twigs until they eventually took the body to the pit for cremation. Allowed in evidence.

9. Two gas cans that were taken from Wallace's house. Judge did not allow them as evidence since it was brought out that these cans could have been gotten from anybody's house in the county. They are a common item.

10. and 10-B. Photographs of a pit. Allowed in evidence.

11. and 12. Pictures of a well. Allowed in evidence.

13. A blood stained pole that had only scattered amounts of blood on it. The pole was not objected to. Allowed in evidence.

14. A hook that was claimed to be used in lifting the body from the well. Allowed in evidence.

15. Burned tobacco can Not objected to. Allowed in evidence.

   *Interesting to question just exactly how many tobacco cans does a man carry on their person at any given time?

16. Three sacks used in carrying ashes to the creek. Allowed in evidence.

17. A bucket. Allowed in evidence.

18. A stump. Judge did not allow.

19. Tree top. Allowed in evidence.

20. Shirt and pants belonging to Wallace. Allowed in evidence.

21. A rock. Allowed in evidence.

22. Bucket containing a small bucket. The contents of this bucket contains another bucket containing brain matter, along with a piece of wood. Allowed in evidence.

23. Another bucket filled with wood. Allowed in evidence.

24. Cigarette leaves (papers) found in the well with some writing on it. Mr. Henson objected to this as not having been shown to have been the

letter or writing of the deceased or of anybody else, no identification of it. Mr. Goldberg wanted to get with Ms. Turner to find out if the handwriting was that of her husband, William Turner. He took a few minutes and checked with her then came back and withdrew the item from evidence. *We would have to assume by this action that the writing was not that of her husband's. So who wrote it and who planted it there?

25. Photograph of defendant s scratches. Not objected to. Allowed in evidence.

26. Car door panel from black Ford. Not objected to. Allowed in evidence.

27. Car door panel from green Ford. Not objected to. Allowed in evidence.

28. Floor mat from black Ford. Allowed in evidence. The black Ford belonged to Mobley.

29. Floor mat from green Ford. Allowed in evidence. The green Ford belonged to Sivell.

30. Seat cover. Allowed in evidence.

31. Long pine pole. Allowed in evidence.

32. Pole admitted as test samples (meaning law enforcement cut) Allowed in evidence.

33. Another Pole admitted as test samples. Allowed in evidence.

34. Twigs admitted as test samples. Allowed in evidence

35. to 40 were plaster cast - Judge did not admit as they were not proven to be connected to the case.

41. Blackjack - Judge did not admit it because it was not found in any car that the defendant was allegedly beaten in.

42. Pistol that was not identified. Allowed in evidence.
*We are to suppose that this is the gun Sivell had in his hand while at the Sunset Tourist Camp although it was never used in any way.

Number 41 is a black jack. The Judge did not admit it as it was found in Mr. Mobley's car and not Mr. Sivell's. No blood was found on this blackjack but Steve Smith, one of the eyewitnesses, swears under oath that although he couldn't see it, he believed that Wallace was beating Turner (who he believed was already dead) with a small object. The State left the impression that it was with this blackjack.

Surprisingly Mr. Goldberg made the following offer when the Judge did not allow the blackjack to be used as evidence. "In the interest of this case, I would like to call your attention it may be the rug and floor mat of Mobley's car should not be admitted.

By Mr. Henson: We want that in.

By The Court: He didn't object and you offered it.

By Mr. Goldberg: Well, if he wants it in, all right.

The letter is held until Mrs. Turner identifies whether it is her husband's handwriting.

By Solicitor Wyatt: Give us a minute.

(A five minute recess is called)

After Recess

By The Court: Let's have order. Let the jury come back.

(Jury returns to the box)

All right now I understand you withdraw the letter. The letter is withdrawn, is that correct?

By Solicitor Wyatt: Yes, sir.

By The Court: All right, and that disposes of everything. Now, gentlemen of the jury. I have admitted certain twigs in evidence solely for the purpose of corroboration, if it does corroborate Robert Lee Gates and Albert Brooks in the case. You will consider it only for that purpose. All right, what else now, gentlemen, for the State?

By Solicitor Wyatt: That is all for the State. We rest.

12

By The Court: All right, what about the defendant, Gentlemen?

By Mr. Henson: I was conferring.

By The Court: The State rests.

By Mr. Huddleston: We would like for the Court to recess at this time in order to give us an opportunity to hold a conference, because we have a large number of witnesses here. We have to check with some witnesses, and if possible, we can save a good deal of time.

By The Court: I realize that. I think probably by recessing now if you will take this opportunity to confer with your witnesses so we won't have to be stopping along. I want to give you all the time you want and need nevertheless, or use all the time that you have. Gentlemen, I caution you as I have done before, with reference to discussing this case or permitting anyone to discuss it in your presence. Keep your minds open until the case is finally disposed of and submitted to you for consideration. You may go to your room.

(Recess until 9 am Thursday morning.)

Later on in the book you will be able to read about Thursday's testimony. Not one single witness was called by the defense. It is unclear as to why they were in such a rush to save time. A man's life was at stake, it would be natural to presume that they would take as much time as needed in order to see that justice was done. For whatever the reason, this defense counsel seemed to be in a hurry. It is highly likely that based on the evidence presented, the attorneys never believed that any jury would or could possibly find Wallace guilty. They underestimated their opponent.

A summation of the evidence that was used to convict John Wallace of murder is as follows.

Out of the thirty-three pieces left as evidence we have six photographs, one of the victim although we are not privy to when the photograph was taken. It was shown in the newspaper and it appears to be Turner at the age of twenty or thereabouts. He was between 24 and 26 when he was killed. There were two photos of the pit where the body was supposedly cremated. We know this is an impossibility. There were two photographs of the well where the body allegedly was thrown before cremation. A picture of John Wallace with scratches over his arms, hands, and legs and he claims the tablespoon of blood found on his shirt and pants that were in evidence came from these scratches. His story is quite plausible and makes much more sense than to believe he was beating a man until his head crushed in and did not get anymore blood on him than a tablespoon full.

Next we have six items that consist of poles and twigs in which it was stated that the law enforcement could easily have gotten several truck loads of these but chose not to do so. There was no evidence provided regarding these things other than the testimony of Brooks and Gates saying that they took the body out of the well early in the morning, covered it with twigs and brush and left it all day. Coming back for it later that night to place it in the pit for cremation. I find this to be a very unlikely story partially for the smell that would have to be coming from a decomposing body and the animals that wander throughout an open field. There would be absolutely nothing that would prevent them from dragging this body off or pulling it out into the open. This just seems to be an entirely absurd story to come up with. But Gates knife and Brooks axe were also entered in evidence to show that this is what they cut the twigs and poles with.

There is a small cartridge box that is attested to by Dr. Jones, as having small human bone fragments although he does not say whose bones they belong to, or how old the bones might be. He only knows that they are human.

Next we have a bucket of ashes and debris and two other sets of ashes that Dr. Jones attests as being a mixture of pine ash and red clay dirt. He does not attest to anything else. There was no human element in these ashes. The three sacks were attested to as having had this same pine ash and red clay mixture inside of them.

A rock and a bucket that contained brain matter was attested to as having been taken from the well. Dr. Jones attested that he could not confirm that it was human brain but that he believed it might be and he had ruled out the possibility of the brain matter belonging to a smaller animal. There was also a hook produced that Brooks and Gates claim they used to get the body from the well. It had no signs of blood on it and was a normal well hook that most every farm owner owned.

Two door panels, a seat cover and two mats obtained from Sivell's and Mobley's cars showed small traces of human blood. Dr. Jones could not determine whose blood it belonged to but did state that there was not enough blood on any of it to indicate someone's head had been crushed in while in either vehicle. He did not check for blood type as the State did not request it. So again, the little amount of blood there was could have belonged to anyone.

A pistol was presented in evidence which Sivell held in his hand while at the Sunset Tourist Camp but Wallace was never implicated as ever having used the pistol. I'm not sure why this was even allowed in as it had no bearing to Wallace and Mr. Sivell was not on trial. Wallace merely stated that he owned the pistol. The pistol was not fired nor was it used in any way, it was seen in Mr. Sivell's hand by one witness, that's all.

That brings us to the last item which is a Prince Albert tobacco can. Reportedly Sivell threw this can out into the weeds when he had the flat. How did it end up burned in the pit? This question was never addressed during Court but it does make one wonder just how many of these tobacco cans were we suppose to believe Turner was carrying on his person. It is highly unlikely that he would have had more than one. He may have kept a back up in his truck but not on his person.

That's the total of the physical evidence that was presented against John Wallace. None of it indicates murder. John Wallace gave a six and a half hour statement in his own defense. It has been written that his counsel was against it but they weren't. They were in full support of Wallace taking the stand. John acknowledges of his own free will that he did shoot Turner but that it was an accident. His words ring true and come straight from the heart.

But these good people of Coweta County turned a deaf ear to the truth, choosing instead to believe what their sheriff and the newspapers told them. We have to assume this because there is no way, looking at the evidence that anyone would be convicted of murder based on what was presented to the jury. There is more to this story, much more. Something else had to be going on here, something sinister and dark. Normal people would not find this man guilty on what was put before them but they did. The question is why?

On November 3, 1950, John Wallace was strapped into an electric chair at Reidsville State Prison in Tallnall County, Georgia and killed. He was convicted of murder in Coweta County, Georgia in 1948. The jury made up of twelve white men from that county had the option of acquitting him to which he would be turned free. If he was found guilty, he would either get the electric chair or the jury could ask for mercy, which would have gotten him life in prison.

Wallace was found guilty based on the evidence and testimony that I have just shared with you. More details will be forthcoming in this book. In essence, the State contended that John Wallace along with six of his cohorts and with the full cooperation of the Sheriff in Meriwether county did hunt down and murder William H, aka Wilson Turner.

The State contended that they did this in broad daylight, after a very dramatic chase scene that traveled from Meriwether to Coweta counties and that the man was killed in front of a public business with several witnesses around.

A book was written and a television movie made that starred Andy Griffith as John Wallace and Johnny Cash as Sheriff Potts. If you read my foreword then you already know my feelings regarding this book and the movie.

At any rate, the question never arose in court and was never addressed in the book or in the movie as to the illogical substance of this allegation. This, of course, became much more than an allegation, it became a death sentence for two men.

I'm referring to the fact that if John Wallace had the full cooperation of the local Sheriff, he did not need any cohorts. He wouldn't have needed anything. The Sheriff would have simply handed William Turner over to him in the dead of night with no witnesses around and John Wallace would have been free to do anything that he liked with him. If he wanted to murder Turner he could have done so in complete anonymity. No one would have ever known.

Testimony in the record from the assistant jailer acknowledged that she did not always record immediately every time a prisoner came in or left the jail. She waited until she was in the room with the books based on her memory. Regarding this particular prisoner she did not have sufficient time to record Turner being brought in or released. She states that she subsequently recorded it in the books but she had not done so at the time. Sheriff Potts suggested that Sheriff Collier was somehow a party to this oversight. Per the assistant jailer's testimony Sheriff Collier had nothing to do with it. This was her habit and she had no reason to treat Turner any differently.

In essence, there was absolutely no reason if Wallace had intended to murder Turner and if he had the full cooperation of the Sheriff then he could and I believe would, have done so in complete and utter silence.

This very simple fact was never brought out during the trial. It was never presented before the jury. At least it was not in any court records of the Coweta Superior Court that I was given access to. The contention of the State was not logical. The allegations had no substance yet the jury believed there was some type of conspiracy to murder Turner. That's a completely illogical conclusion and is not supported by any of the facts shown during the trial.

If John Wallace and Sheriff Collier from Meriwether had been in cahoots together and if the Sheriff knew John Wallace wanted to see Turner. He would have simply and quietly in the dead of night released Turner into Wallace's hands. The murder had it been intended could have and more than likely would have been committed much more quietly.

Therefore a person is left wondering how did this really all come about? What were the motives behind it? Why did the Coweta county Sheriff and his brother, the deputy go to so much trouble in their attempt to prove John Wallace had committed murder? Sheriff Potts even paid a Revenue Agent $500 out of his own personal fund. The record does not say exactly why this money was paid other than it was intended as a reward in the Wallace case. It makes a person look a little deeper into things. The newspapers tell us that Hancock was the one who discovered human bone fragments that the State alleged belonged to Turner. Potts states during court that he paid the $500 to Hancock.

The things I have discovered about this case have been disheartening. It has filled me with dismay for more than a night or two. Not at John Wallace, no that man was pushed beyond all known limits, Turner just would not leave him alone. He kept at him and at him and at him for over a year. Wallace went to the Georgia Revenue Authority asking for help to stop Turner from making moonshine on his land. He went to the police and/or Sheriff's office in several of the surrounding counties asking for help when Turner began stealing his cows. It is documented that Wallace went to the Georgia Bureau of Investigation asking for help. He even asked for help from the Solicitor-General Wyatt who later worked for the State in prosecuting him. But help was hard to come by. All of these law enforcement figures gave him very little. The Solicitor-General Wyatt even told Sheriff Collier to release Turner because in his opinion Meriwether county didn't have enough to prosecute him for stealing Wallace's cows.

My dismay comes from the things I've heard about concerning the corruption in the law authorities during this time frame and about the Georgia's Pardon and Parole Board. These stories have come to me from all over the place. Not via the cousins but from people who were born and raised in Georgia, graduated from college there and then left.

I'm sure we would all like to think of the world as being a perfect place and that life in the 1950s was like the television shows of the time. Mayberry USA and Father Knows Best but this was not reality. Reality was much harsher, much more brutal.

It's amazing how one little question can open up a whole can of worms. You receive information that you would really prefer not to know about. The only consolation in knowing these things is in knowing that as time progressed and women and African Americans gained equality that life and the way business was conducted has improved considerably. But for our purposes, we're traveling back in time now, to a time when things were less than prefect. Our judicial system is still less than perfect but things are much better than they were.

We're talking about a time when although women had gained the right to vote in the 1920s, Georgia did not see fit to give them the right to sit on a jury. In 1946 the U.S. Supreme Court made the following ruling in the Ballard V. the United States:

The systematic and intentional exclusion of women, like the exclusion of a racial group, or an economic or social class, deprives the jury system of the broad base it was designed by Congress to have in our democratic society. . . . The injury is not limited to the defendant -- there is injury to the jury system, to the law as an institution, to the community at large, and to the democratic ideal reflected in the processes of our courts.

The first woman to sit on a jury in Georgia occurred in White County on April 12, 1951, the bill was not signed into law until December 21, 1953 when Governor Gene Talmadge signs the Womens Juror Bill, but he stated he did so with misgivings. You read correctly. Governor Talmadge signed the Womens Juror Bill with misgivings. For many of us it is difficult to imagine a time when equality was not given to all human beings, but history records the facts and these events occurred during such a time.

The John Wallace story is really a most bizarre and unbelievable tale. A story where a self-proclaimed 'Oracle of the Ages' gets on the witness stand and testifies that she saw a cow being taken to Carroll County in a truck. That she later saw a dead man in a well with green flies around him. And she testifies that she did not see these things with her physical eyes but with an eye toward the stars. Amazingly she did not claim to have seen the fire that went sixty feet in the air but then again, no one else

18

seems to have noticed it either.

Obviously, this woman would appear to most of us as being a bit of a loony tunes. But I am assured that many of the town folk in the area really believed in this woman's powers. Evidently the twelve men sitting on the jury - twelve of the good old boys from Coweta - believed that this woman saw all these things in the stars and her testimony helped sentence a man to death.

I've been told on several occasions that this woman's testimony was a key factor in the case. The newspapers report that she "stole the show. Pardon me! The testimony of this woman was a key factor in the case? Unbelievable! A man's life is on the line and this woman "stole the show. That is so very hard to understand but it was the mentality of these people. Her testimony, if any of it were true, reads as though she instigated the entire killing. She states she told Wallace that he could find one of his stolen cows in Carroll County and a man named Turner took it. Wallace then in outrage threatened to kill Turner if he found out he was the one behind it and Miss Lancaster said, "Oh, don't do that. That would be murder. She then states she saw a dead man in a well being carried off on horseback. Then at the end of her testimony she threatens the defense counsel by stating she could see that he would have the same ending as Turner got.

Lancaster's testimony is quite laughable if it hadn't had such serious consequences. When she told counsel that he might get what Turner got, the court did nothing except release her from the stand. It was later reported that she was on the police's payroll. A woman with this mentality was on the police's payroll. I've heard of some far out things with our justice system but that bit of news takes the cake.

The local townspeople believed in this woman's powers and would have done most anything she suggested. I imagine that fact alone gave her quite a lucrative business with being a police informant. I'd like to share with you just a sample of the information I have received concerning this woman. "Daddy went to see the fortune teller Lancaster. He was fascinated with her. He said she could tell what money you had in your pockets even when you had it hid before you went down to her house. He respected Mahaley completely. He said she could cast spells on people, make their crops die, their kids get sick all kinds of stuff. She's buried at Caney Creek Baptist church, just inside Heard County. Her grave has been vandalized pretty bad."

Yes, I'd say right off hand, those people who believed that this woman could make their children sick or their crops die would be likely to do anything she suggested to them. That would give her a very lucrative business with being a police informant. The very idea makes a person queasy at their stomach.

This lady's father, as well as several others I've communicated with were grown men during the trial and went to see it every day. There were numerous times when they couldn't get in the door. And although they did not personally know John Wallace, they believed what the newspapers told them or at least what their local sheriff told them. They believed it all and accepted it as fact without question. And why shouldn't they? After all it was being printed in papers all across the South. In Missouri, Florida, Alabama and probably various other states that I don't know about. I have received comments like "if it's in the newspaper it must be true. Well, not necessarily folks, sometimes and especially before anyone gets condemned to death, you gotta dig a little deeper. Because the truth may not always be staring you in the face.

In all probability, Miss Lancaster never saw Wallace. He certainly doesn't mention her in his closing statement but he does state and it is known by the family that he did go all over the surrounding counties asking if anyone had seen any unaccountable cows show up in their neighborhoods. He went to several of his cousins houses that lived in neighboring counties and beyond inquiring into this so it is vaguely possible that in desperation he went to see this woman once. It is extremely doubtful that he would have gone back for a second visit.

It is much more likely that she got her information either from the police with whom she was on the payroll or from the local newspaper. She then decided she wanted a little more notoriety and joined the ranks of those who felt the need to testify against John Wallace. It has been reported that her "business took an upswing after the trial. It's anyone's guess as to whether this woman was ever actually contacted by John Wallace. I find it possible but extremely doubtful.

Which brings up another interesting point. The Coweta county sheriff offers a $500 reward to any man who can bring him evidence against John Wallace or maybe it was for information in locating Turner's body. What the reward was for, is not really made clear. What is clear beyond any doubt is that the good old boy sheriff of Coweta incited every man in that county with the offer of paying anyone that could prove John Wallace was guilty. These are the same people who later formed the jury at Wallace's trial. Talk about a man not getting a fair trial. There is no way in this world that Wallace could have a fair trial in that county. The sheriff had seen to that. Yet the trial was held in Coweta and it was sanctioned by

Judge Boykin over and over again.

It really doesn't take a rocket scientist to know that under these circumstances a fair trial for a man is not going to happen. According to the newspapers, the majority of men in that county were either hoping for the reward money or watching as a spectator but they all knew that the sheriff wanted the man to be found guilty and from all the accounts I've read and have heard from people, the people of Coweta worshiped their Sheriff. They thought that he could do no wrong. What he said was law and it was that way for some thirty-two years. It is said that Sheriff Potts never had a felony case go unsolved. Well, I can truly believe that. If the Wallace case is any example of his work then I can very well believe that he found someone guilty for every single crime that was committed during his thirty two-year reign. Regardless of what he had to do, someone was going to get convicted. It is sad to know that Coweta countians are proud of that fact.

One of the few occurrences in this tale, which is without a shadow of a doubt, is that Wallace finally got fed up with the justice system. He was fed up with Turner's harassment. He had put up with this young man's treatment for over a year. When he finally had the man off his property and as he hoped, out of his life, the man came back and started stealing from him. In Wallace's mind the only alternative left was to rough Turner up a bit in the hopes that he would finally stay out of his life. He also, hopefully would find out where his other twenty cows where in the process.

The intention to intimidate, to teach Turner a lesson with the hope that he would finally leave him alone is evident but not to murder. As one of the cousins told me. "Those boys wanted to teach a lying, thieving deserter a lesson but they never meant to kill him. Not those boys. They never meant for that to happen. Those boys were good old boys, the cream of the crop kind. They never meant to murder anybody.

The problem with this scenario is that from all accounts and purposes, no one at the time knew that Turner was a deserter. Had Wallace known this then it would have been a very simple matter to get Turner out of his life with one single phone call to the U. S. Army. They would either have picked Turner up and put him in prison or they may have put him in front of a firing squad and killed him like they did with Private Eddie Slovik on January 31, 1945. Regardless of what they did. The end result would have been that Turner was out of Wallace's life. He would have been removed from tormenting Wallace. Which is all John Wallace ever wanted.

It is interesting to note that William Turner's father stated that while his son was in the army he was an excellent marksman. He had won a marksmanship badge out of 3000 men. This is the same William, aka Wilson Turner who had threatened to kill John Wallace. This point was never probed into during the trial either. The Judge stopped the defense counsel from asking anymore questions regarding Turner's background. The Judge stopped Mr. Turner from divulging more along this line. Maybe it's just my own curiosity but I'd really like to know why Turner decided to desert. Had he killed someone? Was he having black out spells? What made him desert?

I've not looked into the Turner line but I have read that his father owned quite a bit a land himself and was a successful farmer and planter. His father admits that Turner stole his brother's draft card from a drawer inside their home. Why William Turner took the easy way and turned to a life of crime and became a deserter is anyone's guess. It's clear that he liked new vehicles and since his in-laws were part of the gang of cow thieves that were terrorizing the area, this may have seemed like easy money to the young man. I don't know anything about his wife's family except that they were part of the moonshine and the cow stealing. His wife was cross eyed and this probably created a great deal of sympathy for her. Especially when you read the newspapers who continuously report Josephine as young and pretty. The contrast between Mrs. Wallace and Mrs. Turner was pointed out over and over again and somehow that was even turned against John Wallace. Josephine and John had been married seventeen years. The fact that she was still young and pretty at the age of 36 is not a reason to convict someone of murder but the newspapers sure worked up that angle as if something was wrong with it.

After having looked at the case files and seeing the evidence that was presented to the jury, there's much more than a shadow of a doubt in my mind. I don't believe for a minute that John Wallace intended to murder anyone. Of all the material that I've read about John Wallace, not once has he ever been referred to as half witted. Quite the opposite, most people make him out to be an intelligent, ruthless S O B. The people who never knew him, that is. The people who believed the newspaper or believed what their sheriff told them.

Everything that John Wallace did in his personal life was twisted and turned into something evil. He went to church and gave of his time and money to his church. I have read that this was to "keep up appearances. I can only say that if a person claimed this about everyone who gave money to the church, then there would be no church additions, no food banks, no missionary trips. That's just an absurd statement to make. John gave money to the church because he was a Christian and that's what Christians do. Period. No evil intended.

It's been reported that Sheriff Potts stated that although Wallace lived a modest life, he was power hungry. It's a shame that no one ever asked Potts, "power in what way? John Wallace never ran for office, never wanted to. He never asked to be in the spot light. He was quite content to operate his land, run his own dairy business and have the comfort of his family and friends around him. That's all John Wallace ever wanted. He tended to his own affairs and did his best to stay out of the affairs of others. Right off hand, I would have to say that Wallace was not the one on a power trip. It seems to me that spending thirty two years as a sheriff and having your brother as your only deputy is being on some kind of power trip. Even the President and Governor are limited to two terms.

People wanting a sense of power run for office of some kind. A politician has a certain amount of power. A sheriff, a deputy, these people have a certain amount of power. A Judge has power. Political figures have power over people. Cattlemen, dairy farmers, planters, these are not people who have power over others. They may be a part of an association with like-minded people but there is no power there unless it's a lobby group sent to Washington. These people are the backbone of America and they are quite content, unless someone stirs them up, to live and love and get through life as peaceable as possible. But power? John Wallace didn't have any power except on his own land, running his own business and he never once wanted anything else. He looked up to people like Will Rogers and often said that he, too, had never met a man he didn't like. He may have outbid a man or two at an auction but he never did it out of malice. It was strictly business. But he knew there were a few people who resented that fact. He had influence over people to a certain degree because he was well respected in his community but he did not have power over others except pertaining to his own land.

One of the biggest factors in the murder case is the lack of blood found in the car or cars that Turner was supposedly transported in and believed to have died in one of them. The State's witness, Doctor Herman Jones states that if Turner's head had been crushed in, or knocked off as some implied, there would have been much more blood than the small samples that he found in the car. The car had been washed or cleaned but it was done so very haphazardly that the doctor was able to tell with his equipment the approximate quantity.

The man who cleaned the car said he just took a rag and scrubbed it. He also stated that it was a fresh puddle of blood that he saw. It was not, day old blood. His statement indicates that it was not Turner's blood. It couldn't have been if it was fresh. The newspapers and the jury seem to have completely ignored that fact. The papers only saw fit to mention that the man had seen blood in the car.

Dr. Jones was highly trained in the area and using his techniques stated that there was not enough blood in the car for Turner to have sustained the injuries earlier described unless there was some container for the blood to have gone in. No one reported seeing such a container and the doors were wide open so the witnesses reported. There was no blood found at the Sunset Tourist Camp.

These are photos of some of the foliage that could be found on the Wallace property. Figs, twigs, brush and sticks used as evidence.

Chapter Two

Who is the real John Wallace?

Sixty One years have passed since the insidious events of 1948 to 1950 happened. All the key players have long since passed away with God alone as their judge. Yet still the toxic poison spreads like a wildfire into the night over something that should have been put to rest long ago had justice been served properly.

People have a hard time forgetting an injustice. They have an even harder time forgiving it. I've been asked to tell the real John Wallace story and tell it I will. But then it needs to be placed in the annals of history and allow life to go on free of the bitterness and the outrage that has perpetrated his image for so long.

The sentiments of public opinion would not run as strongly as it does, for so many years after the event, had the truth been told from the beginning. Nothing will ever right the wrong that was done. The detrimental waste of human life cannot be recovered by the truth. But perhaps this will bring closure for a very barbaric and brutal time in Georgia's history.

In this day and age it's difficult for us to comprehend the events that were going on in Georgia in the late 1940s and early 1950s. You had the Good old boy network going strong, a fortune teller whom everyone swears had some kind of mystic power and biased newspaper reporting.

It's difficult to imagine that the John Wallace murder by electric chair is still causing high emotions between Coweta and Meriwether County. But the fact is that the conflict of that very dramatic day lives in the minds and hearts of the people in those two counties and they appear to be in a silent war with each other over those events. There is a huge difference of opinion for the people who actually knew Wallace and the people who only knew what they were told about Wallace.

John Wallace was a southern gentleman who was only trying to help a fellow man. He had no way of knowing the depth of lies, corruption, deceit and death that he would become entangled with by simply agreeing to help a young man and his pregnant wife.

It is true that John Wallace was a dairy farmer in Meriwether County, Georgia. He was a pretty big dairy farmer. He had, in his own statement, about 800 head of cows when he decided he would get into the pure bred business. He purchased some prize Guernsey Cows and was building quite a decent herd. But this was not the beginning of the trouble. Oh no, it went far deeper than that and for far longer.

From most accounts I've read, people love to give the impression that John Wallace had a split personality. Something akin to Dr. Jekyll and Mr. Hyde but I soon discovered that was only what people wanted us to believe. And some of them have even implied that this belief was based on his mother's statements. I seriously doubt that since Myrtie adored her only living son. It would be very doubtful that she would make any disparaging remarks about him unless they were made during his teenage years, long before he settled down and became a respectable citizen.

Most of us have experienced those growing teenage years from our own children and we may have made certain remarks that would have been better left unsaid. One certainly would not expect those words to come back and haunt one a decade later. Myrtie died in 1941. She had seen her son join her brothers in their moonshine operations and was very relieved when those days came to an end. I do not know that the things written about her comments regarding her son in his youth are not true but I do believe that if they are true then they have been taken out of context. They would have occurred during a time when John was not the level-headed business man that he became.

Since Myrtie did die in 1941 which was several years before the death of Turner, you'll have to pardon me if I'm a bit skeptical over any remarks that she supposedly made.

Allowing for the fact that everyone has a story and John Wallace went to the electric chair proclaiming that the death of Turner was an accident, I'm inclined to believe him. The facts just don't add up any other way.

One of the few certainties in life is that life is like an artichoke for all of us. You have to peel back the many layers before getting to the heart of a person. Any person, that's not just limited to John Wallace. We all have layers of who we are.

From most written accounts, John was a man with a split personality. But during my research, I've gotten to know quite a different John Wallace. Most people who actually knew him, say that he was a generous man. That he donated money for community causes and he fed the poor. And he did this for many, many years. He was known for his generosity and giving nature. He was jovial and caring. He gave local people jobs when the economy sagged. For all accounts and purposes he would have been considered a good-hearted man.

Even if not exactly a law-abiding one. Yes, he had spent time in prison for moonshining and I'm sure he had no desire to go back. That's why I'm reasonably sure that when he found out his young sharecropper, William Turner was making moonshine on his place, he told him very emphatically to stop. When John Wallace said stop, he meant STOP.

John Wallace was a man who was born in 1896 in Chambers County, Alabama. The Wallace's and his uncle Mozart Strickland owned property in the panhandle of Texas. It is said that his father was once a Texas Ranger. His father died a month after his eleventh birthday. His mother struggled for five years trying to make it on the farm in Chambers County. It was rough. It was too rough for her so when John was sixteen years old she moved back to her family in Meriwether.

From that point on, John Wallace was raised a Strickland. He was the only grandson of Ezekiel Lafayette Strickland. A man who had lived in Meriwether County most all of his life. Ah, a few short years spent in Coweta County and an even shorter time spent in Carroll, but old Ezekiel was a Meriwether man through and through.

But these were tough times to be living in. Ezekiel's oldest son, Mordaunt was shot down in his own cotton field in 1897. He was shot in the back by someone he had called friend. His death affected Ezekiel like nothing else ever could or ever would. He mourned for years over the loss of his first born son. It hardened him to a large extent. Something the Civil War had not been able to do, the death of his oldest son did.

Ezekiel taught his boys how to survive and he was darn well going to teach his grandson the same lesson. These boys didn't grow up mean. They grew up to defend their own. To take care of family. They were given a set of values that we ourselves try to instill upon our children. In other words, don't be a bully but don't take any crap off of a bully. According to the newspapers these were not the easiest of times. Guns were typically still packed by most men at sundown when they took a trip to town.

Along with other injuries, Ezekiel had sustained a severe wound to the head while in the Civil War. The wound always gave him trouble for the remainder of his life. He developed migraines. As a young man, he took to drinking the pain away. As the years rolled by, it became a way of life. As unintentional as it was, he was teaching his sons how to drink.

And ahh, those boys could drink. In 1916 the drinking caused Ezekiel to lose yet another son. This time it was his youngest one. The events that happened on that terrible day never left his mind. As hard as that was to take, he gave thanks that his son John had been spared . He never shed a tear until his baby girl, at the age of 36 lost her life. Then he wept. This tough, rough Strickland who never minced his words. He always said what he thought and meant what he said. A seventy nine year old, veteran of the civil war, put his face into the palms of his hands and he wept. He'd finally been broken. This time even the whiskey wouldn't cure him.

On May 14th 1920 he took the property he had planned to give his baby girl and sold it for $2000.00. He divided this money up and gave each of his four granddaughters $500.00 a piece. That translates into about $5440 in today's market. Jean Wallace was one of the granddaughters.

Mozart Strickland took care of his parents until they died in 1925. His parents died and are buried on the land they loved as is Mozart. Mozart was a lively fellow. He has some interesting stories of his own but that's not for this book. He did play a big part in John Wallace's life. Mozart loved his sister's children, very, very much and they adored him. But for the purposes of this book we have to get back to John's granddaddy.

Ezekiel made his will in 1912 and stated the following.
"Having given my daughter, Mrs. Myrtie Wallace, more than I am able to give my other children, I leave her my love and the hope that she may prosper in life.

Ezekiel had already given his daughter, Myrtie land in which to build on. Now all her son, John Wallace needed was some capital. He got this

28

capital by running moonshine. It was what he knew. He served two prison terms for moonshine. When he was released the last time, he gave his word that he would no longer make moonshine. And a Strickland never broke his word. He stood for what was his. He stood for what was right. He honored his words. He'd learnt something useful from his grandpapa.

So he used the money that he'd earned by planting cotton and yes, some even from the moonshine business and he bought cows. Soon his interest became consumed with the pure bred.

Hence the Kingdom was born. It always makes me smile a little when I read comments about his Kingdom, "Oh that man thought he was something else. He thought he controlled everything. He had the nerve to call Meriwether his Kingdom.

Well, no he didn't. He called his acres his Kingdom. Frankly, I haven't met a man yet who didn't consider himself to be king of his castle, or in other words, king of his home. John Wallace was of the same mind and he called his home and the land he owned, his Kingdom. He didn't have children so the land meant everything to him. If things had not gone so terribly wrong, he would have been buried on that land.

In any event, the Kingdom was formed and he bought and sold land quite often. The deed book shows us that he had quite a few land transactions. He was guilty of being a proud landowner. The road his property was on is called Wallace road. The road leading into his property is called Kingdom Lane. Many, many people have roads named after them. It's generally not a reason to put people to death over. But envy knows no boundaries.

John was a frugal man. He didn't believe in waste, he didn't believe in owing more than you had to. He didn't drive a fancy car. He didn't even have a phone. But the one thing that he had, was good credit and he meant to keep it that way. When you don't have a lot of cash, credit comes in handy for keeping a business growing and John Wallace was doing a right smart of business with his dairy farm but not enough where he could waste any money on what he considered to be frivolous wants.

Before I get to the dairy business, I'll inject a story about the big barbeques he would hold on his place. Now, his great granddaddy had fed both the Union and Confederate armies several times as they passed through Carroll County. Well, John Wallace was able to feed an army too although he never had to. He did, however, put on some barbeques. The story I'm about to tell occurred in 1946 or 1947 and was in celebration of his Uncle Mozart's birthday. And oh, what a day it was.

"Oh my, child, I can remember that day just like it was yesterday," she said with a twinkle in her eyes as she looked at me and winked. "But you know I'm near eighty years old and sometimes I can't remember these current days too good." She sighs and smiles, "but you don't want to hear about all that. You want to know about that John Wallace fellow. It just ain't true what they say about him. Why, he wasn't that way at all. He was a fine man, although I wouldn't say it too loud around these parts but he was. John Wallace was a fine man but he never minced his words. No sir. None of us Strickland's did. If we had something to say, we'd just say it. Freedom of speech and all that. Yes, we knew about that back then. But nowadays, I just keep my thoughts to myself."

She closed her eyes and traveled back in time. To a time where a party was going on. "It was a party, Old Mozart Strickland's birthday and the whole clan was there." She stirred herself and opened her eyes. Giving me a rather sharp look. "I'm talking about the Strickland clan. You know people say we're kind of clannish."

I reassured her from words that came from the heart. "Well, I haven't heard anything about the Strickland clan but if that's what people say, I believe I'd just tell them that we have good reason to be."

She smiled, "that's right. That's right, you're one of us."

"Yes ma'am, I am and very proud of the fact."

She leaned back and closed her eyes again. "We came from far and wide. My mother never would let my daddy leave our county but they let me come. My mother always kept daddy close to home. But they said I could come. My two Aunts brought me down with them. Oh, Lord child, you should have seen us that day. Why there was Strickland's as far as the eye could see. I don't know how many was there that day but there sure was a bunch of us. And me just fourteen years old. Why, I was all dressed up in a pretty black dress. I thought it'd make me look older, you know."

She sat up and laughed, "about the only thing that dress did was make me sweat like somebody was pouring water on me. Oh, my stars, it was hot that day. But nobody, no family ever had a better time than what we had that day. Everybody was happy and laughing. You know John Wallace didn't have much hair, did he? If I remember right, he was bald as an eagle on top. He didn't live in a fancy house either. I was expecting some gold chandeliers or something. Well, I don't know what I was expecting but my Aunts and I was very excited about going to the party and I just thought he'd live in a fancy house but he didn't. It was just as ordinary as it could be.

But I discovered it wasn't about that. It wasn't about how much you had or didn't have. It was all about the family and just being around each other. And food, oh there was plenty of food. That's what I remember most about that day was the food and the laughter.

The little children all loved John Wallace. The boys and girls alike. They'd gather round him and he'd tell some story and they'd roll around on the ground they'd laugh so hard. He sure was a nice man. There wasn't one cross word said that day by man nor child. There was just love. Strickland love for every man, woman and child that was there and there was some people I didn't know. Plenty of em. They weren't all family but the biggest part of em, I guess was.

People used to say that you could tell a lot about a man the way they treated children. John Wallace was as fine a man as ever was put on this earth. He did a lot of giving. A lot of giving, a lot of helping. It ain't right what happened to him. It just ain't right. My Aunts went to their graves knowing that he didn't murder that man. They just never could understand why people said he did."

She leaned over towards me while in her seat. "Now I've told you what you wanted to know. Now I'm going to ask you to do something for me."

I looked at her a little bewilderedly. "What can I do for you? I don't know anything about John Wallace. That's why I came to you, so you could tell me about him. I mean, I've read the book but that's all I've done. The book is not very flattering, I don't think you would want me to tell you what's in it about him."

Shrewd eyes sparkled at me. "You don't have to tell me what's in it. I know and I'm telling you it ain't true. Now, what I want you to do, is prove it ain't."

I shook my head. "I don't know that I can do that."

She smiled and leaned back. "Just get the facts, dear. The real facts. That's all I want you to do. The truth will take care of itself."

In 1947 a little company known as Coweta Dairies was formed. All Jersey milk and by products were being produced and it was growing extensively in size. On August 3, 1947, seven dairymen banned together and a co-op enterprise was formed. Coweta Dairies served six counties in the area, Coweta, Meriwether, Heard, Fayette, Carroll and South Fulton.

I'm sure John Wallace would have joined his cousin in making that an even bigger success, had he had the time, but he had his hands full with a man named William, aka Wilson Turner.

But I'm jumping ahead in the story and I wanted to tell you what I've discovered about the Wallace family. The question arises as to what kind of man John Wallace really was.

John and Josephine Wallace did not have any children. Josephine became ill during high school days in Florida and was sent to her Aunt Ida Belle's in Georgia, that's where she and John met. They fell in love. She was eighteen, he was thirty five. Her parents believed in the health benefits coming from the waters in White Sulphur and Warm Springs and sent her to Georgia for healing. She was not seriously ill but she was in a fragile state. She lived to be ninety two years old so how sick could she have been? Maybe the water gave her body what it needed and made it stronger. Shortly after their marriage she had a hysterectomy perhaps that was the cure. I don't know and I don't think it really matters except in our own curiosity. It is well known that her health both physically and mentally were always considered to be fragile.

The most apt description I've ever heard about Josephine is that she was always considered to be a bit of an eccentric. She was also a bit of a flirt. She was a free spirit. Her thoughts ran a little differently than most and as nice a person as she was, she was not understood by a lot of people who met her. She was in essence, a poet. She wrote poetry and songs long before she met John and she wrote them long after his death.

She is described by her family as being a wonderful, lovely lady who was constantly plagued with reporters. Reporters wanted to do an interview with her regarding the fiftieth anniversary date of John's death. She refused. She was the quintessential lady of her time. She never spoke ill of her husband. Her husband had helped her family the entire time of their marriage. He clothed them, fed them and provided anything else they needed. They took trips together. He was a prince of a man but he could and did get riled to anger upon occasion. They had disagreements as all married couples do. Their personal relationship was not open to discussion, not then and not fifty years after her husband's death. She did not want reporters hounding her.

During their marriage, with no children to fill her hours, time hung heavy on her hands. She wanted to work. John being raised from the old southern gentleman age, did not want his wife to work. This was a cause of some stress within their marriage. After John was taken prisoner, Josephine had a very difficult time finding work. Once the book "Murder in Coweta County came out she was shunned by people.

It is strange what we as a society do to our fellow man. Dear Josephine was tormented by absolute strangers, shunned by the people of her community because of her relationship with the man she loved. When the book was released she was upset at how her character had been written. Her brother was an attorney in Florida and she asked his advice on suing Ms. Barnes. She was told that it would be best to leave it alone, that it would only enhance the book. So nothing was done to correct the misconception that so many people believe, even to this day.

The fact is that Josephine was smart, pretty and had her full set of faculties right up until her death. She was not dim-witted or beaten into submission by her husband or her mother-in-law. These things were written about her strictly for dramatization of a book that the author wanted to sell. The statements were hurtful, mean and completely without merit.

Josephine wrote John letters almost every day while he was in prison. Some people say these letters were taunting but her family say they were not meant to be. John knew his wife. He knew how she thought and he did not find them offensive. Perhaps a few little digs were shot with an arrow straight and true. The struggle these two were facing were astronomical. John facing death and Josephine being prodded and probed at every turn; having to live in the aftermath with the knowledge that her husband would soon be dead and that there was nothing anyone could do. I can't imagine the pain and suffering these two people went through during those final hours but I can feel for them. Everyone's nerves would be edgy. They were bound to be.

I haven't read of any other man, during this time frame, being put to death for killing someone who was stealing from him. Whether intentional or not, people were just not given the maximum sentence for defending their own property. The sentence was harsh, brutal and completely unjustifiable. Yet the attorneys could not get a fair trial for him. There is something very odd about that.

John had a lot of time on his hands and he also wrote a lot of letters. I'm not in possession of any of these letters. I have no idea what they say. I am very curious about them. A man with the electric chair looming over his head, knowing that the man's death was an accident yet having no way of getting a fair hearing, could say a lot of things. It is to be expected that he would have high emotions about his situation.

Regarding John and Josephine's childless marriage, there is another side to the story. Grandpapa Ezekiel Strickland's line was not blessed by having a lot of descendants. Although he and Nancy had seven children of their own, they ended up having only four granddaughters and one grandson. As of this writing I know of only two great grandchildren. John's mother Myrtie was their oldest daughter. She had three children, only two survived to adulthood.

Not much is known about Myrtie other than her great love of horses. People say she could ride bareback and often did in her youth. Her great love in life was riding, feeling the wind against her face. That was her great love until she had children. Then they became the center point of her life. She doted on her daughter and son. They were the universe to her. But she never lost her love for riding. It just abated a little once her children were born. All the Stricklands, male and female, loved to ride. Some of them were great horse breeders. They cared for their horses as well as they cared for their land.

But something happened to Myrtie while she lived in Chambers County, Alabama. It may have been due to the death of her husband and/or the death of her little Louie. No one seems to know why but when Myrtie returned home around 1912 to her Strickland family, the light in her eyes had been extinguished. The young girl with big dreams of starting her own family had found despair instead. But she was very happy to be coming home. It didn't take her long to find out just how welcome they were.

Family lore has it that when she and John arrived back in Meriwether. She tentatively stepped one foot out of the buggy and before she could put it on the ground, old Ezekiel had lifted her out and had her wrapped in his arms. The only words recorded is found in an old torn letter written by one of John's uncles to his sister who had missed out on the festivities. The words out of Zeke's mouth were, "You've finally come home girl, right where you belong.

That's when mama Nan took over and made him put their daughter down so the women folk could go in the house and discuss personal business. This left John outside with his grandpapa and his uncles. Yes, the whole family had turned out. There was quite a party that day. But regrettably we don't have any more details about it. But it was quite a homecoming, that much we know for sure.

It was not uncommon to find John and Josephine riding their horses around early evening. One of their favorite pastimes to do together was to take their horses out for a leisurely ride and talk about the day's events. There is no doubt in my mind that they cared for each other. She and John were married for seventeen years at the time of the trial, yet the newspapers refer to her as his young, pretty wife as though it were a crime to be either young or pretty or be married to someone that was.

They married at his uncle Maynard's and her Aunt Ida Belle's hotel at White Sulphur Springs. This hotel was only open in the summer because they had no heat in it that's why it was a summer resort. The Strickland's had a house in town that they lived in. Because of their closing during the winter months the hotel was broken into and caught on fire around 1947-1948. It's interesting to note that the guest register books were stolen around this time. Some of those books have since shown back up and if

I'm not mistaken, the Harris County Historical Society has some of them.

John was in his thirties and had no intention of ever marrying. He, like some of his uncles was going to remain a bachelor all of his days. That's what he intended right up until the day he met Josephine.

He was operating a little hotdog and hamburger stand out by one of the gazebos on his Uncle Maynard Strickland's White Sulphur Springs property. Josephine had been sent to stay with her Aunt Ida Belle Strickland for reasons of her health. The love bug was in the air. She walked out into the open, their eyes met and bam, it was all over. It was love at first sight.

A wedding was planned just after Christmas but before the new year. One of the ladies remembers with fondness how she helped make the decorations. They made little sweet peas. It is reported with all modesty that the decorations were simply beautiful.

White Sulphur Springs Hotel

In any event, John and Josephine were joined in matrimony in December of 1931.

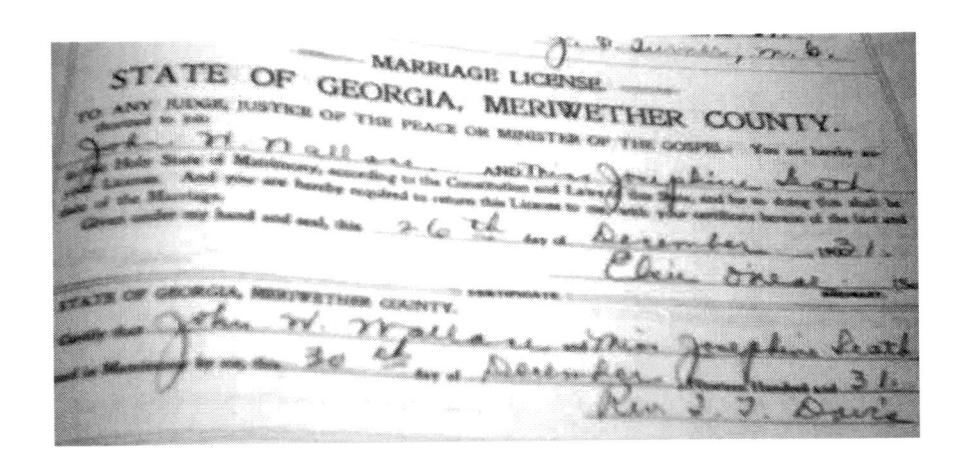

From 1931 to 1948, during those almost seventeen years of marriage, they were bound to have had some disagreements. It is said, that both of them were having affairs. I don't know if either one of them really did. I know that there is a little thing called divorce that was available to either one of them had they so desired that path and since neither one of them filed for a divorce, I'm going to assume that they still loved each other. At least they cared about each other enough to stay married. John had been friends with the Dunlap family for many years. They were like family to him. He had many long time friends and Josephine accepted them all with open arms. They took many road trips together and had many wonderful, happy times.

Josephine's father, an ex County Judge from Calhoun County, Florida, stood beside her and John through the whole ordeal of the trial. Her father was with her every terrible step along the way. Josephine had for some time been a bit of an eccentric. She was as sane as anyone but her mind was like a delicate flower. She was a free spirit and the poetry she wrote reflected these inner qualities that she possessed. A lot of people didn't understand her poetry but she had several pieces published. You can find some of her work at the Harris County Historical Society. I've read several of her pieces and find her thoughts to be charming and well constructed. She was a delightful, wonderful lady.

After John's death, she lived for a time with her great aunt Ida Belle Strickland or more accurately, I should say she lived on some of the property owned by Ida Belle. I haven't done any research into the Leath line and I'm not sure if Ida Belle was her aunt or great aunt. She was known to the family as Aunt Ida Belle. Josephine was called Tegie by the family.

In later years Josephine moved to LaGrange and was able to find work at Mansour's. The LaGrange Daily News reports "Financially strapped Mansour's clothing store went out of business Monday after 92 years on Lafayette Square in downtown LaGrange."

In her later years, she lived with a sister. She died in Troup County in 2005 and is buried at Union Baptist Church Cemetery. She died peaceably with her family at her side. Her obituary was not placed in the paper because of the morbid curiosity of the public and reporters. The family did not want her funeral to be a three ring circus nor did they wish to answer questions from a prying public. They wish only that her true character be cleared of the erroneous information that has been previously written about her. The misconception as to her personality and her state of mind, I hope, have now been put to rest.

Josephine was a wonderful, delightful lady that was both intelligent and charming. She was human and had human failings as we all do but there is nothing mysterious or dark about that. If she did not go to her husband's funeral it was because of the publicity and the never ending prying questions that it would entail and not because of any other reason. She visited with her husband the day before he was killed. Under the circumstances I should think that would be more than a lot of people could take. Her life was made miserable by the actions of her husband and a book titled, "Murder in Coweta County that was filled with half truths to downright lies. She and her husband both had hearts of gold but they were not prefect. Nor are any of the rest of us.

Everyone that I've spoken to that knew John Wallace (and I've spoken to quite a few of them) say he was a kind and generous man. He'd be the first one to lend a helping hand to anyone in need. He was a Mason and a Shriner. He gave much more than he ever took out of this life. And I've been assured by more than one that he'd never cheated anyone or harmed anybody up until this Turner episode. He was a happy, jolly person who never tried to be Lord over anyone. He tended to minding his own business and let others do the same. He was a good business man and a good friend to anyone who needed a helping hand. He'd drop anything that he was doing, regardless of how important, to give support to a neighbor.

At the same time, I've heard stories that his black tenants were afraid of him. I do not know what this knowledge is based on but the person who told me truly believed it and even said that as of fifteen years ago, the black people were terrified if they even heard the name John Wallace and believed that it wasn't possible to kill him, that somehow he or his spirit would get them.

Even though I am not a superstitious person and it is difficult for me to understand the beliefs of those who are, I do not discount their feelings in this matter. The lady that I spoke to, truly believed what she told me as if she had personal knowledge of this. She seemed to have personal knowledge of this. Although she was only three years old at the time and did not know the Wallace's personally, I will not disregard what she told me. She is in a position to have known some of the families of the black tenants that did live on Wallace's land. However, her statement puzzles me because it is so far removed from what I have been hearing from the old timers and is more in conjunction with local legend.

I will say that I have interviewed one black man who grew up on the Wallace farm and he did not share these feelings. He is currently residing in a nursing home but talked with clarity when remembering his time on the Wallace estate. He said that Wallace was a likable fellow, that he worked his hands hard but fairly. This gentleman was not afraid at the mention of his name.

Other people remember seeing some women sitting in the breezeway of the old house before it burned. They said the women were sitting, talking and laughing. They did not appear to have been misused in any way and never gave the impression that they were the entire time of their visit.

Yet, I am not a fan of the way Wallace talked about African Americans during his 1948 statement to the jury. I realize that this was a different time. A time when the black population and women had few rights in the deep south. In the rural southern states it was even more so but I do not believe that Wallace being raised a Strickland would have misused anyone. It just wasn't in his nature. His opinions were not any different from other males during this time. His views were wrong but they were merely a sign of the times.

May and Ted Turner, a black family who lived on the Mozart Strickland estate, stayed with Mozart all through his illness. In 1951 when Mozart died, they were with him, right up to the point when the family took him to the hospital. I do not believe they would have stayed if there had been any abuse or hard feelings. It is much more likely that the false horror stories have been told so much that perhaps people in the area have just accepted them as fact when it is quite the opposite. But this is only my opinion based on people I have interviewed that I know for a fact knew Wallace and so far I haven't met one person who had anything ugly to say about him. He, quite simply put, was not the man who he was perpetuated to be in the newspapers or by Sheriff Potts.

We know from Wallace's own words that he was thrifty and frugal because cash was hard to come by. He used credit as a means of doing business. Paying his creditors off as quickly as he could. He was a working man, trying to build a business, a dairy farm, and he was doing a pretty good job of it.

He was a man who was 100% American. He believed in our country, had fought for our country and had faith in our justice system to the bitter end. He believed in people and the goodness in them. Even though he had gotten fed up with the local authorities, he believed in the over all principles of our judicial system. He believed in the system right up until the day he died.

He'd never had any experience with corruption or greed or whatever it is that makes people in law enforcement do anything for a victory. If he had read about the Leo Frank, or Lena Baker cases, he was naive in thinking those were rare cases. But I think most Americans would hope that things like that don't occur too often within our judicial system.

Things have changed greatly in this time and age that we live in. We, as a people are not so thirsty for more blood. We've seen cases televised like O. J. Simpson and currently, Casey Anthony and regardless of our personal beliefs as outsiders looking in, the only important things are what is and is not presented in evidence to a jury. This is what the justice system in our great nation is suppose to be all about. Every person is presumed innocent until proven guilty.

The John Wallace case is a part of history now. He's already been judged and paid the ultimate price. Our opinions are not going to change any of that. Nothing will ever undo the wrong that was done.

Our justice system has already made major improvements insuring that defendants are treated fairly and that they are indeed presumed innocent until proven guilty through actual facts and evidence. I don't think it will serve any purpose, at least not in my eyes, to take his case before the

Georgia Board of Pardons and Parole again. If they couldn't look at his case between 1948 and 1950 when it would have done some good and know that something was amiss then I don't see a need for them to acknowledge it now.

This book is written for you. To let you know who John Wallace really was and to allow you to see the type trial that he was given. It makes no difference now, whether it was right or wrong. It happened, it's history but the lies and misconceptions that were told, needed to be corrected and I hope this book will accomplish that.

My ancestral roots are firmly planted in Georgia soil. I've always thought of Georgia as being a wonderful, nurturing place but now with the education scandal in the news and the discovery of these vial corruptions in Georgia law enforcement and political leaders, back in the day, it makes a person wonder how any of our ancestors survived.

The Leo Frank case is one of the saddest things in history that I have ever read about regarding injustice and the people who go to such extremes using the name of humanity as their excuse to commit the most notorious acts to their fellow man. To know that Judges and political leaders were at the front of it, is extremely disheartening.

Thank goodness, times have improved considerably and the last legal hanging occurred in 1923 and in 2001 Georgia decided that the electric chair was cruel and unusual punishment. Indeed it is an uncertain justice when we discover that the condemned person's trial was not all that it should be and that people were misled.

In Wallace's statement to the jury he gave us a small glimpse into his life's history and some of the mistakes he had made along the way. He defends his cohorts to the very end stating how they had nothing to do with Turner's death. He took full responsibility of the terrible accident that cost a man his life. He asked for mercy but his plea fell on deaf ears. In later days, he asked for a fair trial but that too, fell on deaf ears.

John's biggest failing, if you can call it that, was that he believed in the goodness of people too much. He believed that everyone was his friend. This was a mistake. Someone wanted John Wallace dead. They went to a lot of trouble to come up with the bones to ashes story to achieve that very purpose. John and his attorney's never saw it until it was too late. But the truth is that wives begged their husband's not to go to that court room in real fear that the Potts brothers would drum up some charge and arrest them to. Based on the way Wallace's arrest and trial was handled, it appears that they had good reason for believing these things.

The trial John Wallace received was a farce. There was no justice involved. The case was rushed through. A body was manufactured. It's a pretty safe bet to assume the defense counsel were shocked when a guilty verdict came back because there was absolutely no evidence to support that a murder had occurred.

Injustice is one of the saddest things in the world for a just society. Those men on that jury wanted to know that Wallace would be cooked alive. When they sentenced him to the electric chair they knew full well that his blood would boil and he would literally fry. It is beyond human understanding how any man, woman or child could ever be proud of that knowledge. The very thought sickens most of humanity.

Georgia's Supreme Court ruling, "We hold that death by electrocution, with its specter of excruciating pain and its certainty of cooked brains and blistered bodies, violates the prohibition against cruel and unusual punishment..." Justice Carol Hunstein wrote in the ruling. Thankfully, Georgia has abolished the use of the electric chair but at what cost? How many innocent people were put in that seat before it was deemed cruel and unusual?

There is a huge difference in murder or accidentally causing the death of someone. When our society becomes unable to distinguish the difference, that's when the devil takes control.

1900: Bethlehem, Chambers, Alabama
Thomas Wallace 36 Sept 1863 married 6 yrs AL AL AL
Myrtie Wallace 35 Dec 1864 GA GA GA
Joan Wallace 5 daughter Sept 1894 AL AL GA
John W Wallace 4 June 1895 AL AL GA
Henry Thomas 35 black servant 1864 married 5 years
Hattie Thomas 25 black servant 1874 1 ch 1 living
John W Thomas 3 black son 1896

John Wallace

Photo provided by a dear friend of the family

1910: Langdale, Shawmut and River View, Chambers, Alabama

Welsey Wallace (Mrytie) 44 female widow   3 ch 2 living GA GA GA
Jean Wallace 14
John W Wallace 13 AL AL GA

It is listed as Welsey Wallace on the census but should read Mrs. Welsey Wallace.

John Wallace

Photo provided by a dear friend of the family

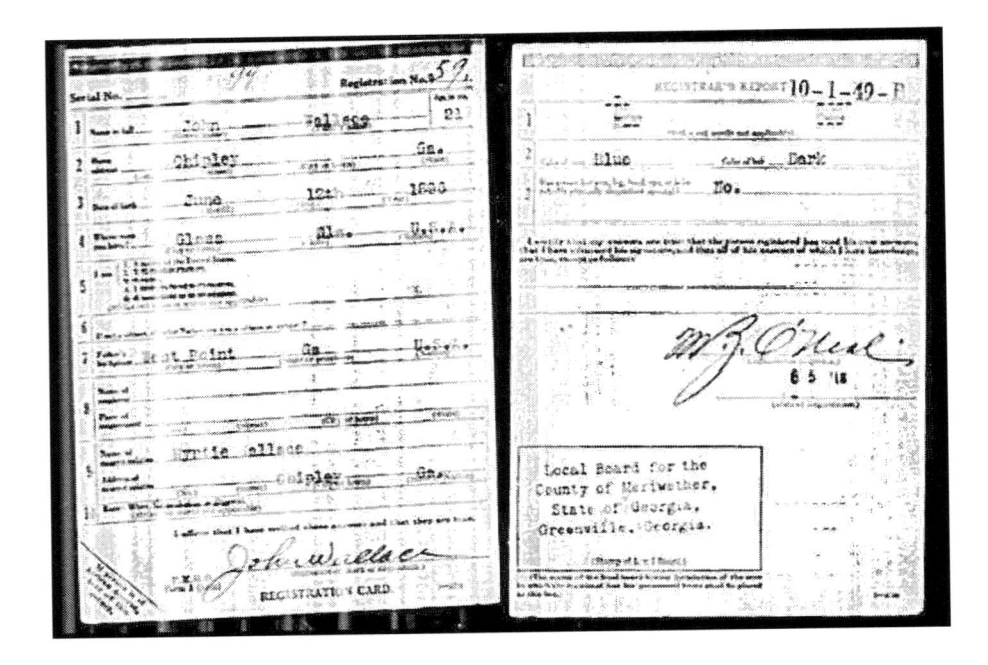

World War I Draft Registration Cards, 1917-1918

Name: John Wallace
County: Meriwether
State: Georgia
Birthplace: Alabama; United States of America
Birth Date: 12 Jun 1896
FHL Roll Number: 1558449

John Wallace age 21
home address: Chipley, Ga
date of birth June 12th 1896
where were you born? Glass, AL
Father ? West Point GA

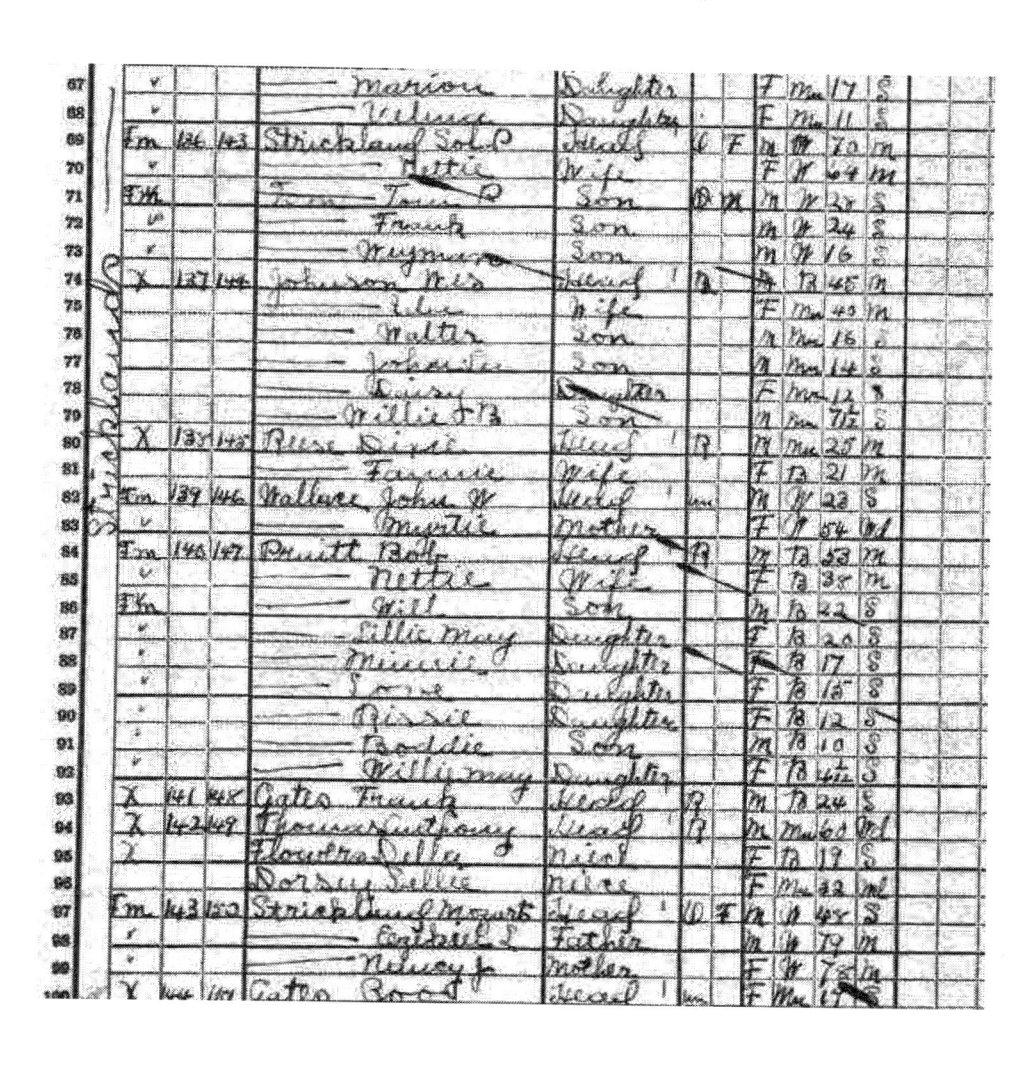

1920 Meriwether Co GA White Sulphur Springs

John W Wallace 23 single GA GA GA farmer general farm

Myrtie Wallace 54 widow GA GA GA

1930: South Bend, Fulton, Georgia Federal Prison taken on April 5th
The prisoner list showing Mozart and John - moonshining days

Mozart Strickland 60 GA GA GA single
John Wallace 33 GA AL AL single

John Wallace never ran for office. He never had any desire to. The spotlight of politics was not for him. He was a farmer. He loved the land just like his ancestors had. He planted his crops and raised his cattle. He was happy until one night in October or November of 1945 a young man with a pregnant wife showed up on his door asking for a job. Little did he know that this man and his activities would be his downfall. It was the beginning of the end for John Wallace.

John was by this time fifty years old. As the young 23 or 24 year old persisted, John wavered. He looked at the man and took compassion on him. John Wallace states he remembered what it was like starting out and how he could have used a helping hand in the process so he said yes and an agreement was formed. You can read all about that in Wallace's own statement but the gist of it is that a year had gone by before Wallace found out that Turner was making moonshine on his land. This was the one thing that he could not allow.

He, himself, with his past history would be the first person the authorities would blame if the still was located. So he went to Turner and explained why he could not operate a still on his property. Turner turned deaf ears to him.

Finally, in desperation Wallace called the Revenuers and reported the still. The Revenue agents eventually came out, located the still and Turner was fined.

Turner told Wallace, he promised he wouldn't make moonshine any more so Wallace paid part of the fine for him, got him out and allowed him back on his property. Within a few months, Turner was back at it again. This time, Wallace told him to get off his land. He hadn't kept his word. He had to go. Only Turner was in no hurry. He had a crop in the field and he was determined to make John Wallace as miserable as possible. You can read all about the crop in John's own words in his statement to the jury.

When that sharecropper William Turner alias Wilson Turner didn't listen to him. John Wallace told him to get off his land again. I think we can be reasonably assured that he meant GET OFF MY LAND.

Obviously, the sharecropper had no fear of John Wallace because after leaving Coweta County and moving to Carroll County, he came back to Wallace's farm and proceeded to steal three of his prize cows and possibly twenty others. The Carroll County police Chief attested to the fact that there had been an outbreak of cow stealing and that a gang was involved. Turner, of course, knew of John Wallace's herd and upon his arrival to Carroll County he became part of this gang.

I have not looked any deeper into the records to find out if anything was ever done about the cow stealing that was originating from Carroll County. The trial records make mention of a gang of cow stealing thieves and that William Turner was part of it. The Carroll County chief of police received a confession from Turner. They later found one of the cows and Turner's brother-in-law also confessed to being part of the cow thief gang. The second cow was located at the real Wilson Turner's farm. Then the third Guernsey cow turned up dead with its head cut off while the trial was going on so the people knew that Turner was a cow thief and not just stealing from Wallace but also from surrounding farmers in the area. Yet the authorities kept pushing the moonshine theory, something that had ended months earlier when Turner finally moved off Wallace's land. It's completely unexplainable. Even today many people think the stealing was something made up by Wallace. It wasn't. It really happened. It's part of the record.

Stealing the cows was enough to push John Wallace over the edge to the point where he wanted to teach the sharecropper a lesson. He wanted the man to leave him alone. He never meant to kill. Never had any intention of killing him but when he couldn't get any help from the authorities of the time, he felt he had no other choice. He could not allow the man to go on tormenting him. In that day and age, sitting back and doing nothing while a man was stealing you blind was not acceptable. Men took action to protect what belonged to them. All the men did. It was not limited to the Wallace's or the Strickland's or the Sivell's.

The lesson, as history shows, went too far. An accident happened and Turner was shot. The man did die and he died due to John Wallace's actions.

After only four and half days of a trial that was widely publicized making John out to be a wealthy dairyman and Turner a sickly, weak tenant farmer, twelve people sitting on a jury took seventy minutes to decide that the only right thing to do was to kill John Wallace. They sentenced him to the electric chair.

Part of their decision was based on the testimony of a known fruit cake, Mayhayley Lancaster, and a few charred bone fragments. Bone fragments that were identified as human. But they were not identified as belonging to the victim. There was additional testimony by eye witnesses who saw

John Wallace and his friend, Herring Sivell roughhouse Turner and they believed that they saw Wallace hit Turner over the head so hard that the gun discharged. The testimony of the State Witness, Dr. Herman Jones verifies that there was not enough blood in the alleged cars for it to have happened that way. But the jury didn't listen to this or didn't want to hear it.

In any event, Turner died and he died at the hands of Wallace. As unintentional as the killing was, a man was still dead. The fact that Turner died in Meriwether County didn't seem to matter to the jury either. Although it should have. The Coweta county jury just wanted to shed more blood.

When Wallace saw that Turner was dead, he went into shock. As I would think anyone would do that had just killed a man through a freak accident. I should imagine that gut instinct set in and once he had recovered sufficiently to function, his reaction would be to dispense with the body. If a well was nearby and John says it was, then the body more than likely went into the well. What happened to it after that is most anyone's guess but that's all it would be, is a guess. It most assuredly was not burned to ashes, outdoors with a cord of wood and some gas. Several cremation authorities have assured me that it would not be possible for the temperature to stay hot enough, long enough for a body to be burned to ashes in that situation.

Due to Wallace's fatigued state, both mentally and physically, he blacks out and doesn't remember what happened after that. I believe this would happen to most people who had killed a man with absolutely no intention of doing so.

Drunk drivers who cause a wreck that takes a life or the kids who text on their cell phones while driving can have the same results. I can well imagine that the event would be so traumatizing to their psyche that they would black out those events. It would be a hard thing to have to live with.

There are no real facts as to what happened to the body. John Wallace states that he blacked out and he did not remember that part of the ordeal. He did remember the gun accidently going off and when he turned back around William, aka Wilson Turner was dead. Then Mayhaley Lancaster alleges that he came to see her again. The fortune-teller thing may or may not have happened but it is her testimony that it did. She told him she saw it being carried away from the well on horseback. I find it very interesting that she never once said that she saw a fire. She admits that Hancock

51

went to see her, which he adamantly denies. One can't help but wonder which one of them was telling the truth since neither one of them were on the high truth telling list.

Lancaster alleges that she knows more than what she is going to tell the jury. She even admits that there are still some things that have not been discovered. But no one at the jury seems to care. The prosecutor got her to say what he needed her to say and the defense counsel, although he tried, was unable to get anything else out of her and eventually, the judge stated to move on.

I'm not sure if Wallace actually went to her, it's highly doubtful that he did. Lancaster stated that they had never seen each other before his first visit to her inquiring about his cattle. It is extremely unlikely that she had any mystic powers. She was very shrewd in manipulation and made a living feeding off the fears of others and the people in that area, during that time did believe in her powers. The question arises, what was she implying that she knew that no one else did? I wonder if it had something to do with her saying Hancock had been to see her.

It was stated at the trial that Wallace along with two of his black farm hands retrieved the body from the well and took it to an old moonshine pit and burned it, then threw the remains into a nearby creek. The two black men also testified at the trial as to the part they played in the proceedings. The key point here is that they were also charged with the murder and were whisked away from everyone to a nearby county until the trial.

They told Wallace's attorneys later, much later, that they were threatened with bodily harm if they didn't go along with this story about the cremation. It is not known whose idea the cremation story originally belonged to. Since Potts paid Hancock to find Turner's body, I'm guessing it was Hancock's idea, but Potts had to be the one to insure that Gates and Brooks would go along with the story. I don't see how it could be Hancock because it was Potts that removed Gates and Brooks from the scene.

The attorneys don't say exactly what Brooks and Gates told them when they filed their affidavit for a new trial. Since Wallace could not refute their statements, we are left to this day not knowing what really happened to that body. It could not have happened the way it was alleged. But obviously a jury was convinced beyond any shadow of a doubt that it did happen. They believed it happened exactly as their sheriff had told them it did.

No fire, burning in the open air, can stay hot enough, long enough to turn a man's bones to ashes. We have all heard of house fires and forest fires, people will be found inside burnt to death but not in ashes. In order to cremate a body the temperature range is 1600 degrees to 1800 degrees Fahrenheit and takes around three hours. Paper burns at 451 degrees, wood burns at a slightly higher temperature with sticky pine trees maybe exceeding 600 degrees. Add some gasoline on top of that and it may be possible to bring the temperature up high enough but certainly not lasting for an extended period of time like two to three hours of intense, extremely intense heat.

There were no witnesses called at the trial to confirm the possibility of something like a cremation even being able to occur. I have no doubt that house fires occurred back then. I've read about a few of them. Common sense should have told the jury that it was impossible to make a man's body turn to ash simply by burning it overnight. Then again, a book was written, a movie made and not one person seemed to wonder about the likelihood of a cremation being possible. Or they didn't care about the truth. It made good reading; it made a good movie. That was all that was cared about.

It is also difficult to imagine that a fire raging 50 or 60 feet high is not going to attract some attention or the smell of a man's flesh cooking like that. I would imagine if these things occurred in actuality it would be bound to cause someone in the vicinity to notice.

Actually the court record concentrates more about on what happened to the body after the death than it does on the death itself. It's quite probable that the sensational way in which the body was claimed to have been treated after death outraged the good old boys that formed the jury. It certainly outraged the public at large. This may have been the deciding element that caused Wallace's conviction without mercy. Something amiss was certainly going on here because what was presented to the jury did not establish murder so there had to be other reasons why they convicted him.

Frankly, this entire story is shaky from beginning to end, because supposedly, Wallace had the Meriwether sheriff in his hip pocket. If this was the case, and if John Wallace was the cold-hearted murderer people were making him out to be then he would not have freaked out. He wouldn't have cared less when Turner turned up dead. He would have simply told the sheriff of the accident and had the body taken to the morgue for a proper funeral.

There are just so many elements in this case that causes one to wonder how anyone, during any time period, could have believed the outrageous things that were told about the killing and the disposal of the body. It wasn't just the jury and the townspeople but the newspapers were eating it up and feeding it to the people on a weekly basis.

The newspapers were encouraging the misconception that Wallace was a wealthy plantation owner and Turner a poor tenant farmer. One of the papers writes that Mayhaley Lancaster stole the show with her testimony. She states that she and Wallace had never met before that night and Wallace doesn't even mention her at all in his six and half hour statement to the jury . So the truth behind that little tale is anyone's guess. But since she was being paid from both ends, from her client and also as a police informant, I don't put much stock in what she says. There were things going on in that part of Georgia that was simply mind-boggling.

You've got Mayhayley Lancaster out of Heard County, working both sides of the fence. John Wallace out of Meriwether calling every law enforcement agency he could think of, for over a year, to peaceably get rid of Turner for him. And then there's Lamar Potts wanting to make a name for himself out of Coweta County. I cannot figure out what the Potts brother's problem was. It may be due to a simple embarrassment because Sheriff Potts had jumped the gun and arrested everyone for murder so early in the investigation. Seven murder warrants for one murder. There's no way that would happen in this day and age and I would guess that it didn't happen very often in that day and age.

As more and more information was discovered I believe that Potts realized that all these people had not committed murder. He had to save face somehow and the best way to do that would be to go for a conviction with Wallace and try to scare everyone else into taking a life sentence with early parole if they would agree to certain things.

This is what happened but I'm strictly guessing as to his motives. But a man in that position wouldn't want egg on his face so this is most likely the reason. Of course there are various other elements that played a hand in it, too. This was a very tough time in Georgia history.

On March 5, 1945 Lena Baker, an African American woman was executed for killing her white employer. He had been keeping her a prisoner and using her as a sex slave. She killed him in her escape. It took many years but her family was able to eventually get the Georgia Board of Pardons and Paroles to acknowledge their error by granting a pardon saying that she should have been tried for manslaughter and not murder. I believe this happened in 2005.

The forties was not a good time in Georgia history in regards to justice. These men who governed and were picked as jurors appeared to be more interested in who killed who instead of the justice of it. It's very tragic. But the fact that at no time was murder proven during the trial didn't seem to matter to these men of the jury. They based their decision strictly on what their sheriff wanted.

Pott's being a man who knew everyone in his county. I've read somewhere that the people considered that to be one of his greatest assets. He knew the bad apples from the good apples. I'm sorry but this is too similar to the Jim Jones massacre and others like it where people just blindly follow one person and put them on a pedestal as though they were some kind of God. It's very disturbing to think that a jury could be made up of men that followed this type of blind leadership. The travesty of justice that occurred for John Wallace is more disturbing than anything else could ever be.

In the John Wallace case one man, Sheriff Collier, had already suffered and died because of the strain of these allegations. The accusations that after years of service to his community he was now being branded a consort to murder charges was too much for his frail heart.

A sixty-four-year-old Sheriff with a bad heart was indicted on charges as an accessory to the murder of William, aka Wilson Turner. Over and over again, it is shown that he was not guilty of any such crime.

Sheriff Potts stated that the Meriwether sheriff wasn't giving him any help in the investigation. I'm sure he's referring to the man hunt he had instigated to cover Wallace's property. The one where he offered $500 to the man who could find Turner's body. Sheriff Collier was not physically able to help in a man hunt and although he knew John Wallace was a man of his word, his weak health is the only reason that he did not help in that manhunt.

Collier died while performing his job. He did not shirk any of the responsibility that was entrusted to him but he was limited physically in just how much he could do. This man was in his sixteenth year as Sheriff of Meriwether. It was his last year to serve. His health had gotten bad. The new Meriwether Sheriff who would be taking office in January was a 32-year-old war veteran. I wonder if the people of Coweta also believed that John Wallace had the new, soon to be, sheriff in his hip pocket too.

The allegations made against Sheriff Collier were completely fictional. He had done nothing wrong. Wallace said in his statement that he had dinner with the Sheriff. During this time in Georgia they called lunch, dinner and Wallace had arrived at the jail just around lunch time and discovered the Sheriff about to finish his dinner. The Sheriff offered him some. Wallace ate a small amount and during their discussion he found out that the Sheriff had already released Turner from the jail a short time earlier.

Wallace left and seeing Turner at a nearby gas station the infamous chase scene happened. Sheriff Collier did nothing wrong. He never told one lie. I don't know where the allegations came from that Collier had the gas drained from Turner's truck. It was certainly not brought up during the Wallace trial. Jack, was a trusted prisoner who was told by the assistant jailer to bring the truck around. He was on the stand and never said one word about draining any gas. So this was either made up by the story teller or Jack was encouraged to say this after Sheriff Potts got a hold of him.

Even though the newspapers reported that Sheriff Collier did not have any children, that is not a reason to tarnish his reputation. His life mattered. His self respect, his self worth, his community service mattered and to have his name banded about on such frivolous charges is a shame. An awful, awful shame. It's a disgrace to Georgia and its history to know that the people were so gullible that they would believe the worse of people just because they were told to.

This entire sordid business has gone from bad to worse. The more I've uncovered, the more shocked I've become. The fact that no one, not a single person seems to have been interested in the truth or in justice. That not any one of them had the common sense to question such obvious discrepancies in the "so called facts.

No, it certainly wouldn't do for anyone to believe that the murder didn't happen in Coweta County. If that happened then the jury would acquit and Sheriff Potts would be embarrassed.

The testimonies of Strickland, Mobley and Sivell were never heard at the trial. It is also reported in the newspapers that they did not make a statement when they pled guilty. They gave no testimony and made no statement so where is all this other junk coming from? All the he said, she said, stuff? They didn't make a statement and they did not give any testimony. That's all there is. They were told to plead the fifth and not testify on Wallace's behalf and they would be able to live and get a shorter sentence. Naturally, that's what they did.

John Wallace was put to death in 1950. It was done legally by our justice system. It was an accident that was called a murder by the Coweta county sheriff. Hence the book, Murder in Coweta County published in 1976 and a movie in 1983 was made from it. Everyone involved had a reason for exaggerating the events and for making John Wallace out to be a cold-hearted son of a gun.

His entire life story tells us that he wasn't. But every good, noble action that he did during his life has been twisted and turned into something with evil intentions. Small-minded people can come up with the most outlandish ways to justify something that is just not justifiable. The trial was a farce, that's as plain as a clear day.

It is undoubtedly true that Wallace got pushed beyond his limits with Turner. He may or may not have been encouraged by the fortune teller. There is not one person alive that knows whether he went to see that woman or not. It is evident that from the time Solicitor General Wyatt told Sheriff Collier to turn Turner loose, that Meriwether did not have enough to prosecute him even though the Carroll county chief of police has stated that he got a full confession from him, from that point things went spiraling out of control for Wallace. There was no where left for him to turn except to himself. He hadn't received any cooperation from the authorities and he wasn't about to sit back and watch Turner steal from him, day after day.

John Wallace was not a man who went around killing people. Nor did he ever have any intention of killing anyone. He was kind, considerate and, I'm told, would give the shirt off his back if it would help someone. He was a man who helped his community, and his church. He fed the hungry and he gave employment to the needy. He was a normal southern gentleman. He wasn't mean to his wife nor did he treat her in any way with disrespect. I don't know if there is any truth in the alleged affairs that they were both gossiped about having. Nor do I think that it should have had any bearing on the outcome of his trial. Josephine most assuredly would not have left the memorial plaque by his tombstone that she left for him had she been mistreated in any way. It reads:

"I kept the pleasant memory   Just rest in peace

In later years, his wife, Josephine went to work at Mansours in LaGrange. She always wanted to work but this was a time in history when southern men wanted their wives to stay at home, for the most part. In her case, when you don't have children to care for, time weighed heavy on her hands and she wanted to get out and about. Working was one way that she could do this so she had the desire to work. I am not implying that all her time was idle, it certainly wasn't. She helped her husband by delivering dairy products to Columbus on a daily basis, amongst a mountain of other things that needed to be done. Unfortunately, it took John going to prison for him to agree to her working outside of the home. Because of the situation, jobs were not easy for her to find.

I'm told that Josephine was a wonderful lady who had health problems. She wrote poetry which does not mean that she turned inward. It's usually a sign that a person has a free spirit and a love of the universe. It is certainly nothing to be ashamed of.

Based on what I can determine, John Wallace was convicted, in part, because he came from an old established family and owned a lot of land. This somehow infuriated Sheriff Potts and based on the newspaper reporting done at the time, I'd have to say, the people at large. It angered the Coweta people to the extent that they could not or would not accept that the killing of Turner was an accident. Nor would they accept that it could not have happened in Coweta County.

Of course, what was claimed to have been done with Turner's body after he died was shocking to the community and was based on an entirely false premise but that action unto itself did not warrant a death sentence to be imposed.

There is something more to this story. Something behind his conviction that we are not privy to. I am told that in the movie, somewhere close to the end, that John tells Sheriff Potts that he killed four people in his life and all of them had it coming. And then the Sheriff shakes his head and walks away. The average person would know this was put in there for dramatization. John Wallace did not say that and if by some weird circumstance that he had, any detective in their right mind would have whipped out a notepad right then and there and said, "I want names and what you did with the bodies. Law enforcement would not have walked away from a statement like that. It didn't happen. John Wallace had never killed a man before and was extremely distraught over having killed Turner. Any stories about him having killed anyone is just that, stories to go along with the myth. There aren't any facts to support such statements.

The facts that came out in the trial leave us with a feeling of frustration both at the prosecutor and the defense counsel. Questions that should have been asked were, quite notably, not asked.

1. Bone fragments were discovered on a bank that had been freshly cleaned out in Meriwether County. The small bone chips were confirmed by Dr. Herman Jones to be human. But no one asked the question as to how old the bones were. This is an important factor considering the old Indian tribal grounds that were once on that land and the size of the pit plays an important role as well. You will discover these dimensions later on. It was not uncommon for people to discover all matter of things when digging out these pits.

2. Low quantities of human blood were found in both cars and on the clothes that were discovered in Wallace's house. Wallace had scratches on both his hands and legs. Sheriff Potts admits to taking photographs of these. The photographs were not included in the court records that I saw but it is evident that the small amount of blood on those particular clothes were Wallace's and not Turner's although no proof was offered either way.

3. Another factor is that no one bothered to inquire as to what clothes they were wearing. Is it possible that the eye witnesses didn't remember and hence the question was never asked by the prosecutor? If so, that still doesn't explain why the defense did not ask these, so-called eye witnesses, this question.

4. The blood type was not checked. The prosecutor specifically did not ask that the blood type be checked. The blood on the clothes and in the cars could have belonged to any of them. Defense counsel did ask if it was possible for a man to have his head crushed in and not have any more blood than what was found in the car and Dr. Jones answered, "If he was laid flat on there with nothing protecting him, that is nothing protecting the floor mat or any other part, there should have been more blood than I found.

5. The witnesses only remembered the fight. It took approximately two to four minutes. Then Steve Smith changes his story from the one he gave at the commitment hearing and now states he saw Wallace hitting Turner with an object while in the backseat. Another witness states all you could see was the top of Wallace's hat once he got in the foot of the car. Wow, which one do you believe? Steve Smith tells the news reporters that his business increased considerable with his story telling of the events. And it appears that the more times he told the story, the bigger it got.

6. Then there is the little matter of the Prince Albert can. Was it found thrown out at the side of the road where Sivell had his flat tire? Or was it found burned in the pit? Surely no one, especially in this time frame, would have thought that Turner had two cans on his person. That would be a bit much for even the broadest minded thinker.

The only thing in the records that was not offered as evidence was the one that Sivell threw out of his car after he had the flat tire or is it the same can?

Chapter Three

Georgia's Good Old Boys

Our story begins with the good old boys of Coweta County and the Good Old Boys of Meriwether County who weren't seeing eye to eye in the late 1940s. I have no idea what caused the conflict but it existed very strongly. I have a hunch and I've been given a few reasons that others believe was at the root of the conflict but they do not know this to be the case.

They seem to feel that Sheriff Potts believed that John Wallace was still in the moonshine business and he wanted his cut in allowing moonshine to be run through his county. John Wallace had not run moonshine in a number of years so naturally if this was propositioned to him, he would have refused. These events occurred during an era when the Good Old Boys reigned supreme.

We are all familiar with the Good Old Boy network, or "Good Ol' Boys. Whichever way you want to call it, we all know what it is. We know it existed. I think once the equality of women was accepted in the nation that it busted up a lot of the Good old boy network. But in the not so distant past, the group existed and not just in the South. Groups of the good old boys could be found in every state. This was during a time when women and African Americans had little to no rights.

The Good Old Boy's were not evil men. They mainly consisted of men in business or power positions who thought they knew best and took it upon themselves to see that their will was done. They did a lot of good, fine things for their community, their town, their county but they could also do a lot of damage.

Regrettably, in my opinion, the Good Old Boy network is still running strong within our justice system. You hear about it every day on the news. There is always some case where detectives and lawyers are wheeling and dealing with human life, in their opinion they know what's best for the community at large. They know which criminals to set free and which ones need to pay the price. They know which ones to make an example of. They feel no need to abide by the law because to them they are the law. To that philosophy, I can only say bullocky.

That's unhealthy thinking, regardless of who's doing it. The Good Old Boy network should not exist anywhere. Justice is justice, the law is the law and the only person who is God is God himself. The rest of us are just human beings who should not be putting people to death unless there is extreme just cause.

It is with certainty that the law should not be allowed to coerce people or threaten them into saying what they want them to say. That is not justice and they shouldn't be allowed to get away with it. Yet every day we hear or see police brutality. The power of the position appears to go to their heads after a while and they get out of control.

We, as a nation have the best judicial system in the world but it is flawed by human behavior. Our courts seem to be filled with men who cannot handle the power that is entrusted to them. Not all men are like this but a lot of men are. Some of them are Judges, others are District Attorneys who influence the police to do things that should not be done. These people have allowed the power of their position to consume them. They have gotten to the point where they feel that they no longer have to abide by the laws of the State because they are the law.

I've spoken to a few attorneys and I'm told that the court system is a business. It has to make money just like any other business. And that a local attorney would be a fool to take on a corrupt Judge, a Judge that he, the attorney, must go before on a daily basis to either win or lose his cases. It's sad but it's just the way it is. Our justice system has flaws and it was even more so back in the 40's and 50's. Things have improved considerably since those very ruthless times but if you sit in a courtroom and listen to the proceedings a few times, you will see that it is still very much a problem.

John Wallace was just a man, not the monster that he's made out to be. He did not have a Dr. Jekyll and Mr. Hyde personality. He was simply one of the good ole boys from Meriwether County who repeatedly asked William Turner aka Wilson Turner to stop running moonshine on his land. John had good reason to make that request. He'd already served two terms in prison for moonshine, now he was a married man and a relatively successful dairy farmer and he had no desire to go back to prison. He was building a business that he was quite proud of and he had been trying to live his old reputation down. I believe he said he'd been trying to do that for twelve or thirteen years.

I know what you're probably thinking. You're probably remembering that Joseph Kennedy the father to our late President John F. Kennedy did some moonshine running himself. Only he took that money put it in the stock market and made a fortune with it.

John Wallace was not so quick thinking. He took the money he had made and put it in the dairy farming business. The question in your mind may arise. "Running moonshine, you mean they actually put people in prison for that? Yes, they did. It was against the law. The government wasn't getting their share of the pie.

In the case of Revenue agent Eliza Hancock, they even killed a few men doing it. I have to wonder just how many men he did murder or kill in the so-called name of justice. In 1932 he, along with four other men, put four bullet holes in John M. Strickland, John Wallace's uncle.

According to a local newspaper the five men claimed thirty shots were fired with sixty-one-year-old John Strickland having fired the first shot. The agents were hiding under cover watching Strickland's moonshine still when they saw him and another person walking down the road toward the still. Hancock shouted out and Strickland, standing out in the open road, having nothing but a rifle with him, fired. Naturally, these five agents opened fire with their revolvers. They gunned him down putting four bullets in him, then they ran to Hamilton and called the local sheriff to tell him what they had done. The sheriff reassured them it was safe to come back, since they were agents of the law, no charges were ever filed against them. Four bullet holes! After studying the Wallace case it really makes a person wonder as to the truth. Let's just think about this for a moment. A man on his own land carrying a rifle against five men hiding in the bushes with revolvers. Oh yes, Hancock and his crew were certainly brave, brave men to go against an old man in that fashion or were they the worse sort of murderers? Men with a badge.

It seems hard for us to digest that the government went to such extremes over whiskey. In this day and age we can buy any kind of liquor we want in most any steak house in the country but before 1978 it was illegal.

Now you can actually make enough for your own consumption but the minute you try to sell it, it becomes illegal. It does not however, get anyone the death sentence.

Prohibition existed from 1920 to 1933 which prohibited the sale, manufacture, and transportation of alcohol. Prohibition didn't go over very well during the Great Depression and people started making their own. By the end of 1933 the laws were changed but still prohibited the manufacture of distilled spirits without a license. Distilled spirits are such things as brandy, rum, whisky etc. Beer and wine do not fall under this list and people were allowed to make enough of these for their own consumption.

Men drank the stuff so there was plenty of demand for it. I've read about moonshine ever since I started researching my family lines. It seems most all of my varying lines was either making it or hunting the stills to bust them up. Moonshine was everywhere and it was these male members of the community who was drinking the stuff.

A terrible thing occurs when a guilty person gets off free from a crime but an even greater tragedy happens when the punishment does not fit the crime. When the laws of the State are twisted and turned to the point where the truth is unrecognizable. When the prosecuting team seeks the maximum penalty and the police department uses coercion and threats to get others that are key witnesses for the defense to make incorrect statements or convinces them that unless they want the same thing that is going to happen to Wallace, to happen to them, they will not testify. I think that most men would say what they were told to say if threatened with the electric chair. Or plead guilty to anything that would allow them to live. And I can't say that I blame them.

The electric chair is a chair that was known to fry a person's brains. I am told that the body is strapped into the chair. Their head and right leg are shaved so that a saltwater or saline solution can be applied to the area that is connected to the electrodes. An electric current surges through the body. Their muscles contract to a state of rigidness. If the procedure has worked properly the heart and lungs stop. Some medical professionals say your blood boils. The flesh is seared. The person is literally cooked alive.

Twelve white men from Coweta County, Georgia formed a jury and were convinced that four intelligent, upstanding members of the Meriwether County community, along with the help of the Meriwether county Sheriff conspired to commit murder in broad daylight.

They judged that John Wallace beyond any reasonable doubt deliberately killed William, aka Wilson Turner in Coweta county. The people of Coweta county wanted John Wallace dead. They got their desire, two years later.

Another great tragedy of this prosecution was that Sheriff Collier of Meriwether was also indicted by these men of the justice system. The very men who knew that the Meriwether Sheriff of more than fifteen years had developed a bad heart and was in a fragile state of health. They ruthlessly tarnished his name with this indictment. He died on July 12, 1948 having never gotten the chance to prove his innocence.

One of the absolute great things about this country of ours is that one is presumed to be innocent until proven guilty. What happened in Coweta County that made them disregard that great and powerful belief in mankind?

I'll tell you what I think really happened. William H. aka Wilson Turner was a young man with a family that John Wallace had taken into his fold, wanting nothing more than to give a young man a helping hand. To give him a good start in life by allowing him to be a sharecropper on his land. He gave him a house and acres to plant.

Instead of being thankful this young man wanted more. A lot more and he wanted it quickly. He began running moonshine to make some fast bucks. John Wallace having already served two prison terms for moonshine and having given his word when he got out that his moonshine days were over became extremely worried that the Revenue agents would think he was involved. He told Turner that he couldn't make moonshine on his property. Turner ignored him.

This young man began harassing and tormenting Wallace. This type of treatment went on for over a year. He defied Wallace at every turn. Wallace asked every local law enforcement agency that he could think of for help. He got very little. The court trial shows that the revenue agents admitted that Wallace asked them for help about Turner and his moonshine making.

The Revenuers did not put Turner in prison for making moonshine, instead he was given a fine. According to Turner's father, his son was a marksman in the US Army. William, aka Wilson Turner had threatened to kill Wallace for asking him to move off his land. These threats were ignored during the trial as though they were not relevant. It is difficult to understand why the defense counsel did not pursue this line by calling witnesses that had heard the threats.

In any event, the very next time Turner went in front of a judge, the judge suggested he leave town as soon as he harvested his current crop that was in the field. Turner finally left and Wallace thought he was free.

But no, Turner came back and back and back. Before Wallace knew it, he had twenty head of cows missing and three more of his pure bred Guernsey's gone. He'd used those Guernseys as collateral at the local bank. He couldn't afford to have too many of those come up missing. He'd be bankrupt and that in the forties was one of the worse things that could happen to a man.

Wallace being what he was, a gentleman from the South, it never occurring to him to think evil of any man, originally assumed that maybe his cattle had wandered off but when he and his hired man found evidence of tire tracks where a truck had pulled up to the gate and found evidence that the cows had been tied there before loading then he did what any man would have done.

He called and visited every local law enforcement agency within roughly a hundred-mile radius asking for help in finding his cows. At that time he only knew that two had been stolen for sure but now he was wondering about the other missing cows.

The Chief of Police in Carroll County Georgia came to the rescue and located one of them and arrested Turner for cow stealing. The Chief of Police states that Turner confessed to him that he was part of a gang of cow thieves who had been stealing for months. Turner stated that he was afraid this gang might kill him if he were ever caught by the law.

The Meriwether County Sheriff drives up and escorts the prisoner back to the county where the cows were stolen, Meriwether. But a surprise awaits that they weren't expecting. The Solicitor General Wyatt decides they don't have enough evidence in Meriwether County and tells the Sheriff to turn the man loose.

Wallace couldn't believe his ears. Turn Turner loose! Wallace did what so many in this time frame did when they couldn't get help through legal channels. He called on his friends and the good old boys of Meriwether were going to teach this boy a lesson. Then, maybe then, Turner would leave him alone. But that lesson went too far. There was a car chase and a scuffle that lasted about two to three minutes in the neighboring county of Coweta.

The people in that sleepy little camp ground had never seen a man being treated roughly before and thrown into a car. At first they thought it was the police but then they realized maybe it wasn't. They called their sheriff, Sheriff Lamar Potts of Coweta County.

Within three days Sheriff Potts had issued seven murder warrants along with a conspiracy warrant on the long-standing Sheriff from Meriwether county, Sheriff Charles Hardy Collier who had developed a bad heart over the years. Sheriff Collier never lived to see his court date.

Seven murder warrants for one alleged murder in which the witnesses said there were only two men involved in the roughhousing that occurred at the Sunset tourist camp. At first the witnesses claimed Turner was unconscious but the story soon changed, these same witnesses later decided the man was dead before he left the camp ground. Hence, murder in Coweta county.

The problem was the Coweta sheriff didn't have a body. In Georgia, during that time, if there wasn't a body it meant murder charges could not be filed. Correction, I guess they could be filed but they would not be prosecuted on.

There were several kidnaping warrants issued as well or so it is mentioned in the court records. The kidnaping warrants were never acted upon. They are not located in the files. I assume those charges were dropped.

Sheriff Potts had gotten in too deep, too fast. He'd be humiliated if there hadn't been a murder. No sir, there had to be a murder and it had to have happened in Coweta or he'd never live it down.

Sheriff Potts had two major stumbling blocks. There was no body and no blood. Not enough blood was found in either vehicle to indicate that Turner had received an injury sufficient to kill him in Coweta county.

The body could be manufactured. Just get some old human bone chips. Those moonshine boys had dug up many bones from the various wars as they dug those trenches for the moonshine. All it would take was a few bone fragments that could be verified as human. Presto, they would have the corpus delicti.

The vehicles had already been sent to Fulton County for testing. When the test results came back, there wasn't enough blood found in either vehicle to warrant the belief that a man had his head crushed in while in one of them. The green Ford, in particular. What now? This was all going to look bad. Those seven murder warrants kept flashing in his mind. Seven, seven, seven! And then it dawned on someone. They only needed one to actually get convicted. If the others could be scared into keeping silent with the threat of the electric chair looming over them, then a conviction for Wallace would do. In order to get a conviction, they had to make the jury believe a murder had happened in Coweta county or been the result of an injury received while in Coweta county.

This is exactly what I think happened. A man was sentenced to the electric chair because someone didn't want to be embarrassed by admitting they'd made a serious error in judgment.

On the other hand, I have heard of a more sinister reason. It seems the good Sheriff of Coweta was in the moonshine business himself. He owned several shot houses. Shot houses that people were known to come up missing from time to time. He and his crew would take the dogs out hunting in the swamps. Albert Brooks stated that the Sheriff had cruel and unusual ways of getting people to do what he wanted. These are comments made to me by Coweta county people whose grandfather's worked for him in the moonshine business. Yet, some of them will also tell you that although they believe these things are true, he was still the best sheriff Coweta county ever had. Comments like these seem strange to me and leaves me pondering over what the truth really is. I don't know what the man was really like but I do know that odd, peculiar things occurred during the Wallace trial that was not on the up and up.

John Wallace admits to being so shocked over the shooting of Turner that he didn't remember what happened to the body. He couldn't dispute the testimony given by Gates and Brooks but if any of their testimony was true, even they stated that Wallace didn't know where the body was. They had to look for it. All night and on up into the morning.

Wallace's attorney claimed Gates and Brooks had been coerced into giving perjured testimony. After Wallace's death, Albert Brooks stated that "John Wallace was the finest man I ever knew.

John Wallace has already been judged and paid the ultimate price for it.

There's nothing we can do to rewrite history. His death happened surrounded by the arms of an electric chair. But the facts still matter to some people and they want the truth about John Wallace told. I want the truth told too and I firmly believe this is it.

As far as Sivell, Mobley and Strickland go, those men didn't do anything. This is according to Wallace's own statement and the trial records do not indicate that they had any hand in what they refer to as the murder. They were only guilty by association. Being in the wrong place at the wrong time. They didn't have anything to do with the accidental shooting of William Turner. They should have received no more than Gates and Brooks got. Gates and Brooks were found not guilty.

Sivell, Mobley and Strickland received life sentences with parole in five years as long as they agreed not to testify on Wallace's behalf. Five wasted years that they lost with their families and loved ones.

Margaret Barnes had quite a fanciful imagination. Murder in Coweta County was written in half truths and most of it was complete fabrication. She would have been an excellent writer for some of the smut magazines you see in the supermarkets today. This type of reporting appears to be right up her alley. I'm not sure how she got away with calling it a true story. Perhaps she thought that no one would actually read the court records of the case.

The trash she wrote about Tom Strickland and his arrest was just that, trash. Someone sent me an article from the Heritage of Meriwether County book. In it, we find the truth. I'm not listing all of it here but Mr. Bass was an honest, law-abiding man. His word meant everything to him.

William Coleman Bass was born in 1916. William's public service work was serving his county several years as deputy sheriff and he was serving in this capacity at the time of the John Wallace (Turner) murder. He represented Meriwether County and assisted the GBI and Coweta county officials in the arrest of Tom Strickland, a principal in the murder. William was later enraged by the account of this arrest as it was depicted in the book and movie "Murder in Coweta County." He stated many times the portrayal was just the opposite of what happened that night as Mr. Strickland offered absolutely no resistance and was a perfect gentleman during his arrest.

Meriwether a beautiful county with a beautiful name. A place with rich soil and home to some of the wealthiest people in the State. A lovely place where old established families worked hard and thrived throughout many generations.

To imply that John Wallace was ruler over Meriwether is absurd. He did not have the Sheriff in his hip pocket. John Wallace was not the only man in Meriwether to own a large amount of land. He was by no means the single distributor of moonshine. Once he got out of the moonshine business, he concentrated his efforts on dairy farming. He was not the only dairy farmer in Meriwether. The entire notion that he owned the county is ridiculous. Other families were just as prominent, if not more so. It does those families a grave injustice to imply that the entire town was controlled by one man. It is not sensible and it is not believable.

Current day photos of the court houses

Meriwether County court house

Coweta County Courthouse

Coweta County Courthouse, Newnan, GA 2011/02/18

Chapter Four

What went wrong in the Court?

Corruption, greed, or a personal vendetta against John Wallace and Sheriff Hardy Collier, I don't know which one it was. I don't know what caused it. It could have been as simple a matter as jealousy. But it was something. Something so strong inside that it made good men take the law into their own hands with little regard for anything or anyone else.

Why would the Solicitor General Wyatt tell Sheriff Collier to turn Turner loose after Turner had been caught red handed with a stolen cow in Carroll County? Something was amiss here.

It's all there in the public records for anyone to see. Deals were made in exchange for certain testimony and/or lack of testimony. Every single person that could testify on behalf of John Wallace was indicted on the charge of murder and later advised by counsel not to testify. We know that as the trial progressed, all three and a half days of it, that testimonies mysteriously changed. That defendants were taken out of their cell in the middle of the night. These are strange and peculiar law enforcement techniques. We are left to wonder why this was done. Were these men convinced to not testify on Wallace's behalf in exchange for a plea deal? That's exactly what appears to have happened.

All these things happened under the cover of darkness and shadowed from the public. Which leaves one to assume that the events happened just like John Wallace said they happened. So now one is left wondering why did Potts or any of the Coweta law enforcement go to so much trouble to exaggerate a case to the degree that's involved here?

The 14th amendment forbids States from denying any person "life, liberty or property, without due process of law" or to "deny to any person within its jurisdiction the equal protection of the laws.

Due process prohibits state and local governments from depriving persons of life, liberty, or property without certain steps being taken to ensure fairness.

The following was located online that explains what went wrong in the John Wallace case better than I can. It reads in part as follows:

A writ of habeas corpus, Habeas corpus. Before Judge Moore.
Fulton Superior Court. October 3, 1949.

WALLACE v. FOSTER, Sheriff, 206 Ga. 561. 561, 57 S.E.2.d 920 (1950)

John Wallace was convicted on an indictment charging that he murdered Wilson Turner. The judgment overruling his motion for new trial was affirmed by this court. Wallace v. State, 204 Ga. 676 (51 S. E. 2d, 395).

The judgment denying his extraordinary motion for new trial was likewise affirmed by this court. Wallace v. State, 205 Ga. 751 (55 S. E. 2d, 145).

After a hearing, his petition for a writ of habeas corpus was denied, and he was remanded to the custody of the Sheriff of Fulton County. The exception is to that judgment.

His petition for writ of habeas corpus (omitting the formal parts) in substance alleged:

The defendant's conviction of the murder of Wilson Turner resulted from the perjured testimony of Albert Brooks and Robert Gates, who were induced by Lamar Potts, Sheriff of Coweta County, to testify that they had been forced by the defendant to take the body of Wilson Turner and destroy it by cremation.

Such testimony was wholly false, but was controlling in the case and brought about the defendant's conviction.

After the alleged commission of the crime, Potts spirited these prisoners from the jurisdiction of the court to a place of imprisonment unknown to the defendant or his counsel, and refused to permit communication with them.

Neither the defendant nor his counsel was permitted to see either Gates or Brooks until they were placed upon the witness stand during the defendant's trial. Thus this officer illegally and wrongfully limited the defendant's opportunity to develop his case factually, which was a denial of substantial constitutional rights guaranteed by the Federal

Constitution, and particularly the 14th Amendment thereof.

Potts and other officers, unknown to the defendant, induced Gates and Brooks to waive their constitutional immunity from giving testimony which might tend to incriminate them. These officers forced and induced the witnesses to give perjured testimony, by threatening physical violence to their persons and by promises of immunity to prosecution, stating to them, in substance, that if they would give such testimony, they would be released, and if they refused, they would be tried and electrocuted.

The procurement of this testimony in the manner aforesaid was violative of the defendant's rights under the Federal Constitution, and particularly under the 14th Amendment.

Tom Strickland, Herring Sivell, and Henry Mobley were jointly indicted with the defendant, and they knew, and were willing to testify, that Wilson Turner was alive, well, and uninjured in Meriwether County several hours after the State contended that he had been murdered in Coweta County.

There was no evidence to the contrary, and such testimony would have entitled the defendant to an acquittal. Potts and other officers wrongfully induced his codefendants to claim constitutional immunity, the inducement being that they would receive punishment less than the maximum.

Within 48 hours after the defendant's conviction, his codefendants were given life sentences without trial. (They were all released after serving seven years.) The suppression of testimony favorable to the defendant's defense, in the manner set forth, constituted a violation of his rights under the Federal Constitution, and particularly under the 14th Amendment thereof.

Potts, as Sheriff of Coweta County, assumed the role of prosecutor against the defendant, and thereby became disqualified to function as an officer of the court. Potts made a contribution of $500 from his personal funds as a reward for evidence against the defendant. While acting in the prosecution of the case, Potts assumed to summon grand jurors, before whom he appeared to procure an indictment, and to summon traverse jurors, before whom the defendant was brought to trial. Potts otherwise functioned as an officer of the court, being unable to act free of bias and prejudice and unable to accord the defendant fair and impartial treatment, because of personal interest in the outcome of the case.

Immediately after the homicide of Wilson Turner became known, two cosmopolitan newspapers published in Georgia's capital city, having general circulation in Coweta County, where the defendant's trial was had, began an attack on the defendant by news stories, editorials, magazine articles, and radio broadcasts.

These articles went far beyond objective reporting, in that they falsely held the defendant out to be a "wealthy farmer," and Wilson Turner to be an innocent, unoffending "tenant farmer." Week after week this publicity covered the area from which prospective jurors were to be drawn, falsely parading the defendant before the people generally as arrogant, mean, and steeped in the crime of being "wealthy"; at the same time hurrying (burying?) the public records of Wilson Turner, as a cow thief and deserter from the United States Army in time of war, with the encomiums of innocence.

These newspapers inflamed public opinion against the defendant and effectively convicted him in the great court of public opinion long before his trial, without giving him a chance to be heard in his own defense.

A fair and impartial trial, such as is guaranteed by the Federal Constitution, was impossible. The withering blast of publicity by the publication of "letters from the people" has been continuous. The publicity campaign became intense, by editorials and by "letters from the people," when the defendant's case was presented to the State Board of Pardons and Paroles.

This publicity robbed the defendant of a fair and unbiased consideration of his case by the Board of Pardons and Paroles, and the inflammatory matter robbed him of a fair trial, and was a denial of his constitutional right to a fair and impartial trial under the Federal Constitution, and particularly the 14th Amendment thereof. The publication of the inflammatory material violated his rights as a citizen of the United States, as guaranteed by the 6th Amendment to the Constitution of the United States.

John Wallace's attorneys were: Charles A. Wofford, G. A. Huddleston, and Harris, Henson, Spence & Gower, for plaintiff.

Judgment affirmed. All the Justices concur.
FEBRUARY 13, 1950. REHEARING DENIED MARCH 15, 1950.

~~~~~~~~~~~~~~~~~~~~~

The Coweta County Superior Court record shows the following indictments:

Sheriff Hardy Collier gets charged

In the name and behalf of the citizens of Georgia, charge and accuse C. H. Collier with the offense of accessory before the fact to Murder.

For that the said John Wallace and Herring Sivell on the 20th day of April in the year 1948, in the county aforesaid then and there, unlawfully wilfully, feloniously and with malice aforethought did kill and murder William H. Turner, alias Wilson Turner, by striking and beating him, the said William H. Turner, alias Wilson Turner, with a pump shotgun, a more definite description of said pump shotgun cannot be alleged because a more definite description thereof is to the Grand Jury unknown, and by beating and striking the said William H. Turner, alias, Wilson Turner, with a certain blunt instrument to the Grand Jury unknown and thereby inflicting a mortal wound and wounds upon him from which wound and wounds the said William H. Turner, alias Wilson Turner, then and there died.

The said C. H. Collier being absent at the time of the commission of the crime aforesaid in the manner and form aforesaid by said John Wallace and Herring Sivell, did yet then and there unlawfully, feloniously, wilfully and with malice aforethought procure, counsel and command the said John Wallace and Herring Sivell to commit the crime of murder, as aforesaid and the jurors aforesaid upon their oaths aforesaid, do say that C. H. Collier, being absent at the time of the commission of said crime of murder did then and there unlawfully, feloniously, wilfully and with malice aforethought, procure, counsel and command said John Wallace and Herring Sivell to commit the said crime in manner and form aforesaid.

Recorded this 31st day of May 1948 by Wallace Gray, Clerk Superior County, Coweta county, Georgia.

At age seventy-eight Mozart Strickland gets charged.

In the name and behalf of the citizens of Georgia, charge and accuse Mozart Strickland with the offense of Murder for that the said Mozart Strickland on the 20th day of April, in the year 1948, in the county aforesaid then and there, unlawfully wilfully, feloniously and with malice aforethought did kill and murder William H. Turner, alias Wilson Turner, by striking and beating him the said William H. Turner, alias Wilson Turner, with a pump shotgun, a more definite description of said pump shotgun cannot be alleged because a more definite description thereof is to the Grand Jury unknown, and by beating and striking the said William H. Turner, alias Wilson Turner, with a certain blunt instrument to the Grand Jury unknown, thereby inflicting a mortal wound and wounds upon the said William H. Turner, alias Wilson Turner, from which mortal wound and wounds the said William H. Turner, alias Wilson Turner, and there died. Contrary to the laws of said State, the good order, peace and dignity thereof.

Superior Court. Coweta county March adjourned Term, 1948.
Luther M. Wyatt, Solicitor-General

The defendant waives copy of Bill of Indictment, list of witness sworn before the Grand Jury, and arraignment, and pleads not guilty.
(No date filled in)
Luther M. Wyatt, Solicitor-General

Witnesses for the State:
Ted Turner and Mary Turner

State of Georgia, Coweta county
I, Wallace Gray, clerk of the Superior Court in and for the County of Coweta, do hereby certify that the foregoing page contains a correct and accurate copy of the True bill in the case of the State vs Mozart Strickland charged with the offense of Murder.

Given under my hand seal of office, at office, this 31st day of May 1948
Wallace Gray, Clerk Superior Court, Coweta county, Georgia
Recorded this 31st day of May 1948 Wallace Gray, Clerk

Robert Lee Gates and Albert Brooks, alias Boy Brooks

The same exact charges are brought against Robert Lee Gates and Albert Brooks, alias Boy Brooks for Murder on the same day. They plead not guilty.

Witness for the State: A. L. Potts

John Wallace, Herring Sivell, Tom Strickland and Henry Mobley

Count One

In the name and behalf of the citizens of Georgia, charge and accuse John Wallace, Herring Sivell, Tom Strickland and Henry Mobley with the offense of Murder for that the said John Wallace, Herring Sivell, Tom Strickland and Henry Mobley on the 20th day of April, in the year 1948, in the county aforesaid then and there, unlawfully, wilfully, feloniously and with malice aforethought did kill and murder William H. Turner, alias Wilson Turner, by striking and beating him, the said William H. Turner, alias Wilson Turner, with a pump shotgun, a more definite description of said pump shotgun cannot be alleged because a more definite description thereof is to the Grand Jury unknown, and by beating and striking him, the said William H. Turner, alias Wilson Turner, with a certain blunt instrument to the Grand Jury unknown, and thereby inflicting a mortal wound and wounds upon him, from which said wounds and wounds the said William H. Turner, alias Wilson Turner, then and there died, contrary to the laws of said State, the good order, peace and dignity thereof.

Count Two

And the jurors aforesaid in the name and behalf of the Citizens of Georgia do further charge and accuse Tom Strickland and Henry Mobley with the offense of accessory before the fact to murder for that the said Tom Strickland and Henry Mobley being absent at the time of the commission of the crime aforesaid in the manner and form aforesaid by said John Wallace and Herring Sivell, did yet then and there unlawfully, feloniously, wilfully and with malice aforethought, procure, counsel and command the said John Wallace and Herring Sivell to commit the crime of murder, as aforesaid, and the jurors aforesaid, upon their oaths aforesaid, do say that Tom Strickland and Henry Mobley being absent at the time of the commission of said crime of murder, did then and there unlawfully, feloniously, wilfully and with malice aforethought, procure, counsel and command the said John Wallace and Herring Sivell to commit the said crime in the manner and form aforesaid, contrary to the laws of said State, the good order, peace and dignity thereof.

Superior Court. Coweta county March adjourned Term, 1948.
Luther M. Wyatt, Solicitor-General

The defendants waives copy of Bill of Indictment, list of witness sworn before the Grand Jury, and arraignment, and pleads not guilty.
(No date filled in)
Luther M. Wyatt, Solicitor-General

Witnesses for the State:
Mrs. Julia Turner
Steve Smith
Mrs. Meryl Hannah
Ted Turner
Mary Turner
Broughton Myhand
A. L. Potts

Coweta Superior Court   March Adjourned Term, 1948

The State vs. John Wallace, Herring Sivell, Tom Strickland and Henry Mobley MURDER

Tom Strickland and Henry Mobley accessory before the fact to murder

True bill J. Roy Brown foreman
Mrs. Julia Turner Prosecutor
Luther M. Wyatt Solicitor General

State of Georgia, Coweta county
I, Wallace Gray, clerk of the Superior Court in and for the County of Coweta, do hereby certify that the foregoing page contains a correct and accurate copy of the True bill in the case of the State vs John Wallace, Herring Sivell, Tom Strickland and Henry Mobley - Murder - Tom Strickland and Henry Mobley - Accessory before the fact to murder - Charges with the offense of (nothing written in).

Given under my and seal of office, at office, this 31st day of May, 1948
Wallace Gray, Clerk Superior Court, Coweta county, Georgia

Coweta county grand jury room

Plaque for the Creek Indian Chief, William McIntosh

Current view of the Coweta county court room

Chapter Five

The Commitment Hearing

There are so many mysteries about this case. So much that isn't logical. It goes way beyond a shadow of a doubt. The fact that twelve men of a jury brought back a verdict of guilty in less than seventy minutes leaves one wondering why? How? What did they know that was not brought out in the trial? Or the more reasonable assumption would be it was because they had already made up their minds before they ever took the jury seat. Wallace's attorneys had three affidavits stating this is exactly what happened with one juror by the name of Homer Lassetter. The State proceeded to produce six affidavits stating Homer was a good person and would never have prejudged anyone.

Looking at the case from a layman's point of view, and I think most juries are made up of everyday average citizens, there is doubt. There is major doubt and many, many holes in the charges that just don't add up. I don't believe for a moment that a conspiracy to murder was ever anyone's intention. These people where the backbone of their communities. They were intelligent, hard-working citizens.   They never conspired to murder anyone. If John Wallace had wanted to murder Turner he had many opportunities to do just that.

I've never looked into Sheriff Collier's history but I know he'd been a Sheriff for a long, long time and it's evident that someone in Coweta wanted him out of the way. If there were any truth in Collier and Wallace working together then the Sheriff would have readily opened the jail door and handed Turner to Wallace at, let's say, three in the morning. At least some time in the dead of night where there was guaranteed to be no witnesses and no chase. There would just be Turner and Wallace. And that ladies and gentlemen didn't happen.

This premise would be much more reasonable to believe than the fallacy of a big conspiracy with none of the men having enough brains to figure out that maybe they should do this thing at night. None of these men were stupid. Each and every one of them was strong, solid members of the community.

Therefore the normal person would have to presume that this was all poppycock and that there was no conspiracy.

No one is going to plan to kill someone in broad daylight if they have the local sheriff in their hip pocket. It simply would not be necessary.

There are approximately 1156 pages to this court case. Although I have read all the pages, I certainly am not going to put everything word for word here. I have done my best to hit on the important factors in the case but the following is by no means a word for word account of the proceedings. Many of the papers have been marked through or had things written in on them.

Turner died on April 20th, 1948.

The following statements were taken during the investigation:

Associated parties for the defense.
G. A. Huddleston AD
Henson Spence Harris AD
E. K. Whatley AD

Statement of Hugh C. Martin, operator of Greenville Service Station, Greenville, Georgia, made to Agent Woody Wilson of the Georgia Bureau of Investigation on April 24th, 1948.

"I saw John Wallace sitting in car with Sheriff Collier around 12:00 noon, maybe a little before. This was last Tuesday, April 20th. I put 3 - 9/10th gallons of gas in Sheriff's car. I charged it on book. I greased the Sheriff's car and changed oil in it that morning, this was between 9 and 10 am. signed H. C. Martin

---

Newnan, GA April 25th, 1948

My name is Archie M. Hodges and I live at 515 Lee Street in LaGrange, GA.

On Sunday night, April 18th, 1948, I was being held in the County jail at Carrollton, Ga about 10 PM this night a city policeman brought a white man, Wilson Turner, to the jail and locked him up.

I have known Wilson Turner for about 3 or 4 years. They locked Wilson Turner in the bull pen and I was on the run around. I talked to Wilson Turner about what charge they locked him up on and he said it was something about a cow, but that he didn't know anything about any cow, and that the only meanness he had ever done was make liquor.
About 1 a.m. April 19th I heard someone knocking on the jail door and calling Mr. King, the jailer. In a few minutes three men, the chief of Carrollton police, a man I later found out to be Mr. John Wallace and another man I do not know, came up to the bull pen where Wilson Turner was locked up.

I heard all the conversation between Wilson Turner and the above mentioned men. The men, mainly Mr. Wallace and the chief, were questioning Wilson Turner about some cows, especially one particular cow. They wanted Turner to tell what he knew about the cow, but Turner denied knowing anything about a cow.

Mr. Wallace told Turner that he was going to be carried back to Meriwether County to stand trial about the cow, and Turner was asking not to be carried back to Meriwether County.

Turner said to Mr. Wallace, "You know I don't know anything about this cow and you know you have threatened to kill me and that is the reason you want to take me to Meriwether; so you can kill me."

85

The three men left Turner and went back downstairs but before they got out the front door Wilson Turner told the run a round boy to tell Wallace and the chief to come back up stairs.

They, the Chief and Wallace came back to where Turner was and Turner asked for the keys to his truck. Mr. Wallace told Turner that he thought he was calling him back to tell him about the cow and that if he didn't he didn't want to hear anything he had to say. The chief told Turner that he was keeping the truck keys. Turner then told Wallace that if he didn't have him turned loose that he was going to tell the law the next morning about that big still he had.

About 3 or 3:30 a.m. on April 19th a man who I heard say he was the sheriff of Meriwether County came to the jail and Wilson Turner was waked up by me and Jr. Thompson, the run around boy and Turner was carried downstairs.
Signed Archie Hodges (his mark)

Witness:
A. L. Potts
J. H. Potts
J. C. Otwell

Statement of James L. Baker, Jr, Greenville, Meriwether County, GA made to Agents James P. Hillin and Woody Wilson of the GA Bureau of Investigation, at the Greenville Cafe, on April 29th, 1948.

I, James L. Baker, Jr., state that on Tuesday, April 20th, between 9 and 11 a.m., I saw Henry Mobley and Herring Sivell. Henry Mobley parked his car, a black 47 or 48 Ford across from my place, in front of the Court House and sat in the car for about five or ten minutes. Henry Mobley's car was parked headed towards Newnan, GA.

Henry Mobley came in the cafe and drank half of a Coca-Cola. I, asked him what he was doing up here and he just laughed and sat the coca-cola down and walked out. Mr. Mobley went back to his car and sat down. I don't know how long he sat there. While he was sitting in the car Herring Sivell came up and talked to him (Mobley) for about three or five minutes. Herring Sivell's car, a green two door five passenger 47 or 48 Ford was parked between where the newspaper is printed and the Standard Oil Filling Station, headed towards Cafe.

Herring Sivell left Mobley's car and went and got in his car. I looked out the window as people started coming in for dinner and did not see Mobley's car. Sivell's car drove off first, I don't know which way he went. There was someone sitting in the back seat of Sivell's car – I could not identify him. I noticed their actions were a little unusual and them being from my hometown was why I kept watching them out the window. I thought it was unusual for Mobley just to sit in his car for that long if he had any business to attend to he could not do so in his car.

I know Wilson Turner and he did not come in our place that morning, Tuesday, April 20th, nor did I see him in town. Mobley and Sivell just seemed to disappear into thin air after that. I did not see Sivell or Mobley anymore that day.

I know John Wallace, but I don't remember seeing him that day. Today right after dinner, around 1 or 1:30 p.m., Cecil Perkerson came in the front door and walked back to the kitchen where I was drinking a cup of coffee and motioned for me to come and follow him. He and I went out front door to corner of our Cafe where Cecil Perkerson said, "Do you know Herring Sivell is my Brother-in-law?"

I said, "Yes. Cecil then said for me to keep it to myself about seeing Sivell and Mobley in town that day. Cecil also stated that if I talked it around that the G. B. I. and F.B.I. would be in here pestering me and we don't want them around here.

Cecil said, "If I was you, I wouldn't talk for Sivell is my brother-in-law." That if he was me he would keep it to myself.
Signed James L. Baker, Jr.
Witnesses:
Woodey Wilson
J. P. Hillin

***** The following info was just kind of placed in the record. No report of where the info came from.

Jonnie Smith was killed in Sivells house about 9 or 10 years ago. Claimed Wyman Langford killed him (Game Warden) accidentally shot him with a Pistol. Mrs. Jonnie Smith married Harmon Sivell shortly after that.

Statement of Jake Howard, a prisoner at the Meriwether County Jail, made to Agent Woodey Wilson of the GA Bureau of Investigation on April 27th, 1948.

I, Jake Howard, state that Mrs. Mathews told me to back the new green Ford truck, looked like a 48 out from behind the jail. This was between 11:30 a.m. and noon. As soon as the truck was backed out, I left to see if noon mail had come in. I got back about 12:30 and the truck was gone. I did not see the Sheriff when I got back. Sheriffs' car was gone. I did not see Sheriff nor Mr. Wallace around dinnertime.

signed Jake Howard

****

Statement of Mrs. Beulah Baker, proprietor of Greenville Cafe, Greenville, GA made to Agent James P. Hillin of the Bureau of Investigation on Thursday, April 29, 1948 at 2:40 p.m..

Last Tuesday morning a week ago, April 20, 1948, the date of the crime, I was in my place of business taking care of my duties, when a Negro girl, Willie Joe Copeland, who works for me told me to look across the street, in the front of the Court house, at Mr. Henry Mobley sitting in a new black Ford Car. I looked out my front window and saw Mobley in the new black Ford car parked with the right side of the car parked up beside the wall around the court house. This car was heading North.

This was between 9 and 11 a.m.. I would estimate it was about 10am. I know it was Mobley because I've known him for about 20 years. I went to school with him. A few minutes after I saw him under the steering wheel of the new black Ford he came into my cafe and drank a coke. He drank about half of his coke and left and went back and got into the new black Ford car, and continued to sit there. I looked out the window around noon and he was gone.

While he was in the Cafe I asked him what he was doing up here and he laughed and said "nothing. About the same time I first saw Mobley in the black Ford I also saw Herring Sivell parked in a green Ford car on the South side of the Standard Filling Station which is across the street from my Cafe. There was a man sitting in the back seat of Sivell's car, but I could not see who he was. There was another man standing beside the green car talking to Sivell who was behind the steering wheel. This man had his back to me and I could not see who he was.

The green car pulled off a good while before the black one did. I am sure it was Herring Sivell because I went to school with him also. I've known him for over 20 years. The reason I noticed them was because I used to live in Chipley where they live. I did not see these cars anymore after they left. When I served dinner, they were gone.

I have made this statement to the best of my knowledge.

signed Beulah Baker
****

Statement of Willie Joe Copeland, made at the Greenville Cafe, Greenville, GA. made to Agent J. P. Hillin of the bureau of Investigation, on April 29, 1948 at 3:30pm

On Tuesday, April 20, 1948 between 9 and 10am. I saw Mr. Henry Mobley in his car which was parked beside the Court House. I also saw Mr. Herring Sivell in a green car parked across the street from the Court House. Mr. Mobley was in a new black Ford car. I also saw him, Mr. Mobley, come in the cafe where I work and drink a coca cola. I heard Mrs. Baker ask him what he was doing here and he laughed and walked on out the door. He left the cafe and went back to the black car. In a little while I saw Mr. Sivell and Mr. Mobley talking to one another. I went on back in the kitchen and didn't see them anymore. I have made this statement to the best of my knowledge.
Signed Willie Joe Copeland

April 30, 1948

My name is Albert Brooks and I live on Mr. Wallace's place in Meriwether County. On Tuesday of last week in the morning sometime, about nine or ten. I saw Mr. Henry Mobley at Mr. Wallace's. He was in his car. I also saw Mr. Tom Strickland come by in his truck and stopped at the house. He went on up the road. I also saw Mr. Herring Sivell. I didn't see any of them leave.

About two o'clock Mr. Sivell came back in his car. He had a flat tire in the back of his car. When I went to get the flat tire out, I saw two guns in there. One was a double barrel, the other a short barrel pump gun with a leather strap on it. Mr. Sivell took both guns out and told me to get them in the house. A tool house that's all he said. I put the guns there and haven't seen them since. I fixed his tire-- or carried it to town for him and had it fixed. I went in Mister Wallace's car. That's all I know about anything that might have happened on that day. This statement is made freely and voluntarily with no fear of threat of harm.
Albert Brooks his mark
A. L. Potts
Earl H. Lucas
Hugh Paul
J P Hillin

Greenville, Ga May 13, 1948 5:30 p.m. Thursday

Statement of Mr. Frank Pickerson, (address M. W. 49), made to Agent James P. Hillin of the G. B. I Georgia Bureau of Investigation

I saw John Wallace, who I have known for several years, walking across the street to the square on Tuesday, the day of the killing, sometime that morning. I also saw him again that afternoon between 3 and 4 p.m., walk up to Sheriff Collier who was sitting in front of Hill Brothers Store and start talking and they then walked off together. They walked north on the sidewalk. I couldn't say where they went because I wasn't paying much attention to them.
signed Frank Pickerson
****

Greenville, GA May 13, 1948 6:20 p.m. Thursday

Statement of Mr. L. F. Garrett, chief of Police, Greenville GA made to Investigator James P. Hillin of the GBI

On the day of the killing of Wilson Turner, which I think was the 20th of April, I saw and spoke to John Wallace, who I have known for over 20 years, on the street in Greenville. I just spoke the time of day to him. I think I saw him sitting in a car near the library or city hall just off the square. When I spoke to him it was about 11:30 a.m.. When I think I saw him in the car it was right about noon. I have not seen him since that day.

I left town for a little while with John Atkinson, owner of the Builders Supply Co., to go and pick a location to tap a sewer for his new home. I told him I did not know the correct location to tap it but Mr. Collier did, because he was Chief here for many years before he became Sheriff. We came back and run across Sheriff Collier walking from the jail right at the intersection of the street leading south from the jail to the square. This was 12:45 p.m. because I was late for lunch and looked at my watch.

I got out of Mr. Atkinson's car and Sheriff Collier got into the car with Mr. Atkinson. They drove off and I went on home to dinner. I did not see Sheriff Collier anymore that date.
Signed L. F. Garrett
****

Carrollton, GA May 14, 1948 12:30 p.m. Friday

Statement of Mr. E. R. Threadgill, Chief of Police, Carrollton, GA

made to Agents James P. Hillin and James McDuffie of the GBI.

On Monday morning, April 12, 1948 I received a long distance phone call from Chipley, GA. I'm pretty certain the man that called me was John Wallace. This party informed me that he had, or Wallace had, some cows, two registered Guernsey cows, stolen during the night. He described the cows to me and asked me to be on the lookout for them. He also asked me if I knew anyone up here named Wilson Turner that was driving a taxi. I told him I did not know of a person by that name that drove a taxi, but I did hear of a Wilson Turner that was working with a fellow named Millard Rigsby. I told him I would check up on this party. I checked and found a cow answering this description and got a register number off a tag that was on its ear. I then called the County Agent at LaGrange to ascertain who this cow belonged to, but she was unable to give me ths information.

Later I called the Sheriff at Hamilton, Ga, and asked him if he knew John Wallace and he said he did. I gave him the register number and told him to check with Wallace regarding this number and he stated he would. This was on Wednesday evening, April 14, 1948.

I didn't hear anymore from them until around midnight when Mr. Wallace, Myhand and another party came to my office and all of us went out near the city limits and looked at the cow and Wallace and Myhand identified the cow as his, Wallace's property.

Wallace agreed to do anything I wanted to do to help catch the thief. I said to leave the cow and we would try and catch the party that stole it. He said that he would help me watch for the thief; he said he would watch for the rest of the night with me.

Around 3am I left and went home and Wallace remained. Wallace was in my office the next morning, Thursday, April 15, 1948 when I came to work. He told me he would be back that night. Myhand and this other party went back when Wallace and I started to watch the cow. He came back Thursday night, and told me not to leave him out there by himself again, as he might have to hurt one of them or get hurt.

Wallace stayed in my office, while Smith and I watched the cow. Carnet came with Wallace on this night. About midnight Smith and I came back to town and told one of the policemen to take turn about with Wallace and Carnet to watch the cow. Wallace also came again Friday night to watch the cow and again Saturday night.

He told me his wife came with him and drove him. He was in a 1947 Chevrolet. I didn't see him anymore until Sunday night, to which he told an officer he would be back about 8:30 p.m., but he ran a little late. Pike and I was watching for Wallace Sunday night but when he didn't show up on time, we eased down to take a look at the cow and run into Turner. We found the cow missing.

When we got to our car and started back to where we saw Turner's truck he was starting up. We arrested Turner after he tried to get away. I didn't know Turner and I asked him what his name was and he told me Wilson Turner and he said "get me away from here or they will kill me."

I asked him who would kill him and he didn't say. I told him the cow was what I wanted and that no one would kill him. He pointed across the field and said "the cow is going across the field now and a man driving her." I put him in my car and told Pike to get the truck out of the street. He kept insisting to get away from there and also get his truck away. Turner told me that if I made Pike hide the truck he would talk. Pike did this and Turner wouldn't say anything. I then told Pike to get the truck and I would take Turner to town, I drove about 200 yards and he told me if I made Pike take the truck to town he would take me some place and show me something.

I kept him with me for about two hours and he did quite a bit of talking and when I brought him back to town he jumped out of the car and got away from me, this was around 11pm. We caught him in just a few minutes and I told three policemen in the presence of Wallace, who drove up, to take Turner and place him in the County Jail. I told them he had already talked and not to bother him.

We drove to the city hall and Wallace, Sivell and I got in Turner's truck and drove to where the man was to meet him with the cow. We looked for the cow, but didn't find her. We got back in the truck and drove a short distance and run into Millard Rigsby in his car with his wife and Mrs. Turner.

When Rigsby saw us he asked where Wilson was and I told him, Wilson was in jail. I told him to get out of the car and I would talk to him. I asked him where the cow was and he said he did not know anything about them, he was very scared. I did not put him in jail, but told him to come to my office the next morning.

We looked for the cow, but when we didn't find it we, Wallace, Sivell and I, went to the county jail and talked to Turner and at the time he told me he hadn't told me anything. He said he wanted to talk to Mr. John.

Wilson said, "Mr. John you know we used to make liquor." I told Wilson we were not interested in the liquor business, we were hunting for the cows. Wallace then told him he wasn't interested in whiskey, he wanted his cows. We left him at this point and went down stairs and as we started to leave someone called and said Turner wanted to talk to Mr. Wallace. Wallace went back to talk to Wilson and wasn't gone but just a minute and came back down. I asked him what he said and Wallace told me that Wilson wanted him to relay a message to his wife. After some conversation with Wallace, he called the Sheriff, Hardy Collier, at Greenville and told him to get a warrant and come and get Wilson Turner.

This is what he told me. I did not hear Wallace talk to the Sheriff over the phone. I guess it was about 3:30 a.m.. when Wallace called me at my home and told me Sheriff Collier was here to get Turner. I asked him over the phone if the Sheriff had a warrant and Wallace said "I reckon he has, I told him to get one."

Wallace asked me if I had the key to the truck and I did. I told him if the Sheriff had a warrant for him, Turner, and the truck to tell a policeman to come to my house and get the keys, which one of them did. I believe two policemen went to the jail and turned Turner and the truck over to them.

On Monday about 11 a.m. Wallace and the Sheriff came back and the Sheriff, Wallace, Officer Pike and I went and found the cow tied to a tree. I turned the cow over to them and Carnet picked up the cow in a truck about 2pm. While we were around the cow, where it was found, Sheriff Collier said "I don't believe we can convict Turner in Meriwether County."

I told him I could convict him here on what evidence I had. I also told him that any jury in this county would convict Turner. Sheriff Collier said we would probably have to try Turner in Carroll County.

On Tuesday Sheriff Kilgore contacted me about 1:15 p.m. and asked me what kind of a truck I caught Turner in and I told him a green Ford pickup without any license and he told me Sheriff Potts of Newnan, had called him and told me about a man being beaten up in a truck answering this description.

A little later I called Sheriff Collier at Greenville, but did not get in touch with him. On this same day, Tuesday, April 20, 1948 a little after 5 o'clock Sheriff Collier and Wallace came to my office and Collier told me that he had talked to the Solicitor General and the Solicitor said that he didn't believe they had enough evidence in Meriwether County to convict Turner and that he turned him loose and we can try him in Carroll County.

He asked me when the Grand Jury met here and I told him in October and he said he would come up and help prosecute him. Wallace didn't have much to say other than to thank me for my assistance in recovering his cow. He asked me to look out for his other cow as he was busy farming.

Collier left the office and while he was gone I told Wallace what Sheriff Kilgore had asked me about the green truck Turner was in, that they had found it wrecked or something had happened to it. I asked him to send me the rope that was on the cow and Wallace said he would mail it to me.

They left and Collier said if they didn't see me before October they would see me then.

I have made this statement and same is true and correct to the best of my knowledge.
signed E. R. Threadgill

****

Moreland, Ga May 14, 1948   5:30 p.m. Friday

Statement of Miss Geneva Yeager, made to Special Investigator James P. Hillin fo the Bureau of Investigation at the Sunset Tourist Restaurant on above date.

I am employed at the Sunset Tourist Restaurant. I was on duty on Tuesday, April 20, 1948 at about 12:30 p.m. when I saw a green 1948 model Ford pickup truck stop on the North side of the building and a white man jump out of it and ran around to the front of the building towards the front door.

Just about this time I saw a green Ford car stop on the North side of the building and two men jump out. I saw one of the men, the heavy set, with a short barrel shotgun. These two men run down the man that got out of the green Ford truck and they grabbed him and while they were dragging him back to the green Ford car, the heavy set man hit the man on the head with the shotgun.

Before this man was hit with the shotgun, he was screaming for help. After he was hit on the head with the shotgun, the man never uttered another sound. I think the man was killed by the severe blow from the shotgun, which discharged when the blow was struck.

They put him in the back of the car, on the floor and the heavy set man got into the back with him. The other man drove the green Ford off south on 41 Highway. I have not seen any of them since.

Miss Yeager could you positively identify the two men that were in the green Ford car?
"Yes sir, I could."

I have made this statement free and voluntary and same is true and correct to the best of my knowledge.
Miss Geneva Yeager
****

Subpoena Mr. Wilson
May 14, 1948
Moreland GA 5:45 p.m.

Mr. C. W. Wilson, Moreland GA

Mr. Wilson will testify that at approximately 12:30 p.m. on April 20th, 1948 that he was at his home located about 60 feet from the Sunset Tourist Court when he heard a gunshot.

Mr. Wilson said he ran out of the house and saw John Wallace and Herring Sivell dragging a man toward a car. They pushed him in the car on the back floor board and John Wallace got on top of him and had him by the neck and was hitting him.

Mr. Wilson can't say whether Wallace had any thing in his hand or not. Mr. Wilson will testify that Wilson Turner was unconscious or dead when Herring Sivell drove off.

****

Statement made by A. L. Whitmire, Chipley, GA to J. H. Potts, Marvin   May 18, 1948

Last fall, not long before Wilson Turner left Chipley and about the time he got the gray Ford, Wilson came to Whitmire's place of business to get some work done on the car. Wilson Turner told Whitmire that he was going to have to move, and that he hated to leave as he had made good crops both years he had been down there, but if he did not leave he was afraid John Wallace would kill him.

Commitment Hearing

of John Wallace and Herring Sivell, charged with murder, held in Newnan, Georgia, on April 27th, 1948, before justices W. S. Carswell and J. O. Brown.

Appearances of Counsel:

For the Defendants: Gus Huddleston, and John Watley (I think this should read E. K. Whatley, Jr) both are from Greenville, Georgia

For the State: Luther Wyatt, Sol General LaGrange, Georgia and Meyer Goldberg Newnan, Georgia

By Justice Carswell: proceed

By Mr. Wyatt: Your Honor, Mr. Goldberg has been employed to assist in the prosecution of the cases, and has talked to all the witnesses, and for that reason he will examine the witnesses.

By Mr. Goldberg: If the Court please, we would like to proceed, if there is no objection, jointly against these two defendants on two warrants, one against each, sworn out by the widow of the dead man; one, the State against John Wallace, charged with murder, and the other against Herring Sivell, charged with murder.

By Mr. Huddleston: You have some other warrants?

By Mr. Goldberg: We will not proceed on the other warrants. We will just proceed on the murder warrant.

By Mr. Huddleston: Wait a minute before we proceed. Wait a minute. I want to discuss this with my client, because as I understand it, they have warrants for kidnaping and assault with intent to murder, and I don't think we want to make the case of perpetual motion of going from one warrant to the other. I don't know that is their idea, and I am not accusing them of it. It occurred to me if they have a multiplicity of warrants we would certainly like to clear the entire matter up while we are at it.

By Mr. Goldberg: If your Honor please, first there were warrants issued against both of these two men at the inception of this case; one charging assault with intent to murder, the other against both of them charging kidnaping. The State now elects to proceed on the murder warrant, and I don't think there is any doubt about our right to do that.

By Justice Carswell: All right, proceed.

By Mr. Huddleston: I would like to invoke the rule and ask that the witnesses be excluded from the courtroom.

By Mr. Goldberg: We will do that. Let's get all witnesses first.
  (All witnesses are sworn and retire from the room.)

Mrs. Julia Louise Turner, having been first duly sworn, testifies as follows:

Direct Examination

By Mr. Goldberg: You are Mrs. W. H. Turner?

a. Yes, sir

q. When is the last time you saw your husband?

a. I would say the sun was about thirty minutes high when he left the past Sunday a week ago.

q. April 18th

a. I don't know what day of the month it was, this past Sunday a week ago. (She identified the photo of her husband.)

q. Who is your husband?

a. His name is William H. Turner

q. Has your husband ever been referred to as Wilson Turner?

a. Yes sir everybody that knew him. I didn't know his real name was William H. Turner. His sister told me. I knew him as Wilson.

q. Do you know Mr. John Wallace?

a. Yes sir, we moved on his place this past August was two years ago.

q. You and your husband lived on his place until when?

a. I don't know the exact date and all. It was around the last of November, something along in there.

q. This past year?

a. 1947, yes sir

q. Then you moved off and went to Carroll County?

a. No sir, we went to Franklin when we moved.

q. Do you know Herring Sivell?

a. I know his face but I would not know his name.

q. Why did you and husband leave Mr. Wallace?

a. Well, he and Mr. Wallace had some trouble over twenty gallons of whiskey. My husband wanted to gather his crop, and he sold part out of the corn crib and part of it was in the field on the ground and part of it was still in the stall. Just to get off of his place. All I know is just what Wilson told me.

By Mr. Huddleston: I object to all of it if that is all she knows.

By Justice Carswell: Cut that out

By Justice Brown: Yes, cut that out.

By Mr. Goldberg: q. Did you ever talk to Mr. Wallace?

a. Yes, sir

q. Did you ever have any conversation with him about the trouble between your husband and him?

a. No, sir, not about that, but he did before they had this other trouble. He come over to the house one night, that was before we moved over there on his other place a good bit from his house, and he told me that night Wilson–Wilson was gone and I didn't know where he was gone -- then he asked me where he had gone, and I told him I didn't know. He said well Wilson should have known better than to have got O. C. Hattaway to move a liquor still for him to the other place, and he said the reason he wanted us to move he could not afford for Wilson to be handling liquor and sugar almost in his back door, because if they caught him he would go to the pen, and he was not going back to the pen and said he could not afford for it to be in the paper and get them.

q. In any subsequent conversation that you had with Mr. Wallace or that you heard Mr. Wallace have with Wilson did he ever make any effort to get Wilson to stay on there at his place when Wilson was going to move?

a. Yes sir, I heard that on Sunday evening after they had this here dispute on Saturday. He called Wilson over when we were down at the pond, and we were talking to Cap, Mr. Wallace's uncle, and Mr. Wallace come up and stopped in the "A" model, and he asked Mr. Wilson to go up and fix his stove, it was tore up. Wilson didn't want to go. He was afraid he would have trouble if he got in the man's car, and he didn't want to go. He told Mr. Strickland, that is Cap's, (Wallace's) uncle, he told him he didn't want to go, and he said if he would go up and fix it he would see there would not be any trouble. --so we went on up there then and he fixed the stove, and then we started to leave and after he fixed the stove and we started to leave Mr. Wallace called him off and they went on the porch and talked a good bit, and when Wilson started back to get in the car Mr. Wallace asked him about not moving. He wanted him to stay on, and Wilson told him he was going to move. That happened along in August and we left there -- that was about the last of August or the first of November, and we left there -- I mean the last of August or first of September, and we left about the last of November as soon as we could gather the corn, and then we didn't get it all gathered.

q. Do you know that your husband was put under arrest by officials in Carroll County and then transferred to Meriwether County?

a. Yes, sir. I can tell you what the chief of police in Carroll county told me.

q. Do you know why he was arrested?

a. Yes sir, cow stealing from Mr. Wallace

Cross Examination by Mr. Huddleston

q. Were the cows stolen in Meriwether County?

a. I don't know that he got these cows. They said they were stolen in Meriwether County.

q. You were talking about moving a still. Who is O. C. Hataway?

a. A man that lives in Chipley.

q. And Wilson got him to move a still near Mr. Wallace's house over on the other place you moved to?

a. The still was quite a distance from Mr. Wallace's house. It was half way between Mr. Wallace's house and where Robert Lee Gates lives.

q. Mr. Wallace told you he couldn't afford to have whiskey made on his place?

a. He didn't say about having it made on his place. He said he couldn't afford them handling it at his house, because he was not going back to the penitentiary anymore.

q. Mr. Wallace was trying to protect himself?

a. Yes, but he was in fifty-fifty with it.

q. And he always counseled with you and Wilson about getting in trouble about whiskey and tried to keep him out of trouble?

a. Yes sir

q. Mr. Wallace was very kind to you people while on his place?

a. Yes sir in a way and in a way he was not

q. When you moved down there were numerous warrants out for your husband in Carroll County?

a. Yes sir

q. And Mr. Wallace went over there and interceded perhaps with Mr. Wyatt over here and the authorities, and got his case settled.

a. He had to go to trial for it. Mr. Wallace didn't get it settled.

q. He didn't go to jail?

a. He did. He stayed a week in jail

q. But he didn't go to the pen?

a. Mr. Wallace didn't completely get him out

q. He didn't? He had a lawyer?

a. He had a fine. He didn't have a lawyer. He had a fine and he paid the fine.

q. Now you are talking about in Carroll county or down in Meriwether?

a. I am talking about the one that was in Carrollton

q. The one in Carrollton, and he also paid a fine in Meriwether?

a. Wilson paid the fine. Yes, he did.

The witness is excused.

S.A. Smith having been first duly sworn, testified as follows:

Direct Examination

By Mr. Goldberg: he asked name, where he lives, for how long and where he works etc.

He replies. Steve Smith, live at Moreland in Coweta county all my life, I run a place called Sunset Tourist Court.

q. Mr. Smith, on last Tuesday did you have occasion to see an event that transpired there where a man was beaten up and killed?

a. Yes, sir.

By Mr. Huddleston: Now if your Honor please, let him tell what happened, not answer the question that is seeking a conclusion, "where a man was beaten up and killed.   That is seeking a conclusion. This evidence is being taken down and will be transcribed. It might be circumstances will arise whereby it will be read in the Superior Court at the trial, and I ask that the question seeking a conclusion like that where a man was beaten up and killed -- let him tell what he saw, the condition of

101

the man if he knows, and those things --but not answer a question like that, which is definitely a conclusion of the witness.

By Mr. Goldberg: In all murder trials you have to show a man was killed or is dead, and we propose to do that.

By Mr. Huddleston: There are other methods of showing other than asking a direct question seeking a conclusion of that kind and my brother knows it.

By Mr. Goldberg; I think the question is a proper question.

By Justice Carswell Just go ahead.

By Mr. Goldberg continuing: What was the first thing you noticed? Was that in Coweta County?

a. Yes, sir

q. What time of the day was that, Mr. Smith?

a. About 12:20, 12:25, or 12:30

q. That is Tuesday, April 20th?

a. Yes, sir

By Justice Carswell: q. at night or in the day?

a. Daytime

By Mr. Goldberg: q. Daytime. Now tell the Court what you first saw, how your attention was attracted, and then go on and tell exactly what you saw from then on.

a. Well, there was a '48 pick up truck, a '48 Ford pick up truck run up to my window, and a boy jumped out hollering for help, and a man run after him and grabbed him just as he reached my door, the front door, and he had a sawed off shotgun, a pump shotgun, and grabbed him and commenced beating him and the boy hollered for help, and he hollered until he could not holler, and he drug him to the car, and this other fellow --

q. First, there were two men?

a. That is right, two men.

q. That grabbed this man whom they were beating?

a. That is right.

q. Would you recognize those men?

a. Yes, sir. I know both of them. I had seen them somewhere, some cattle sale or another. I told the sheriff I had seen their faces. I didn't know who they were.

q. You had seen them at cattle sales somewhere. Now go ahead Mr. Smith and tell the court exactly what you saw after they grabbed this man.

a. Well, this fellow drug him around to the car, beating him all the time, (indicating Mr. Wallace) and the boy hollering for help, and he got to the car, this fellow opened the door (indicating Sivell) over here, and the boy --

q. Do you know their names?

a. No, sir, I don't know their names

q. Well, let's call this gentleman, Mr. Wallace.

a. All right

q. And that (is) Mr. Sivell. Now call them by name.

a. John *(Note: first names were never mentioned above) forced him up there, Mr. Wallace did, to the car, with his shotgun beating him, and the boy put up an awful fight and hollering for help all the time. he placed himself against the car, and they would not put him in, and he hauled off with the shotgun and come across his head and hit him as hard as he could hit him, and the gun went off in the air, and the boy fell in the car and he didn't make a noise, and they doubled him in with his feet --

q. Who doubled him in with his feet?

a. Both of them had a hold of him doubling him in the car, put him in the foot of the car, not on the seat, and I said to one "why don't you handcuff the man?" He said, "we don't need to handcuff him. He said "we need him for murder.

103

q. Do you remember which one told you that?

a. Mr. -- the one here.

q. Mr. Sivell?

a. Yes, sir. He went and got in the car, and I said "what will you do with the truck, and he said he would come and get it, and they started to drive away. I thought I would see what county they were from. I thought they were officers using the gun, and I looked at the tag and the car, and I noticed the tag number, and the car.

q. Did you see the car in which they drove up to your place?

a. Yes, sir.

q. What sort of car?

a. '47 green two door Ford. I didn't get all the license number as I went across the house -- I run through the house and got it on the other side. A metal strip coming down through the number, I could not see it.
it had a rim around it and a little metal stripping come across the car. it covered up a "3"

q. In other words, the license plate was set in a frame?

a. Yes sir and it had a home made trailer hitch on the back of the car. I saw the car again the other day when the sheriff came up in it.

q. Describe the severity of the assault that was made on this man.

a. He hit him as hard as he could draw back with his gun across his head, and he hit him so hard the gun went off. They didn't mean for it to go off, but it went off.

q. It went off from the vibration of the blow?

a. Yes, sir.

Testimony of Mrs. Merl Hannah having been first duly sworn, testified as follows:

Direct Examination by Mr. Goldberg:

q. What is your name?

a. Mrs. Merl Hannah or Mrs. Otis Hannah from Newnan,

q. What is your relation to the Sunset Inn?

a. At the time it happened I was at the home of my mother right across the highway.

q. Tell us what you saw.

a. I would say approximately 12:20 or 12:30 I was standing beside the road, and the green pick up truck was followed by a green Ford, and both coming at highspeed, and sped into Sunset, the truck in front and it made the turn in and at the time it stopped this man jumped out and ran under the shelter.

(Note: She identified the picture of Turner as having been the man who jumped out of the truck.)

Well, this man jumped from the pick up truck and as he did he ran under the shelter, was trying to go in the door, however he missed the front door, and this man -- this heavy set man-- Wallace jumped out with a gun. These two men (Wallace and Sivell) jumped out of the car.

At the time they jumped out I was thinking it was someone stopped over for dinner to go, when this man jumped out with the gun. In the excitement I screamed "don't kill him.

This man shouted "hush. He deliberately told me to hush.

q. You made a motion with your hands. Is that your motion?

a. That is his motion

q. He did that at the time he told you to hush?

a. That is right, and then by then they had run and caught the man at the door. He never got in the building, and then they began to beat him and kick him, and bringing him back to the car. The car door was open.

q. Did he resist being brought to the car?

a. Yes

q. Did he say anything?

a. He shouted: "don't let them kill me" and they began to beat him. This man Wallace, the one that told me to hush. He hit him across the head with the barrel of the shotgun. He didn't shout or holler for help after they struck him. It was hard enough to kill anybody with the force. Wallace was slumped over turned in the foot of the car looked like he was still beating him. You could just barely see the top of his hat.

q. In your opinion, was he dead or alive when they drove away?

a. To the best of my knowledge, I would say that he was dead. That is my opinion.

Cross Examination
By Mr. Huddleston:

q. Would you think in your opinion it would be necessary to hold a dead man down?

a. No, I don't think in my opinion it would be necessary, but I think they just were so brutal he wanted to be sure he was dead.

q. You were rather outraged by the brutality of it?

a. That is right

q. And you are willing to testify to these things very positively because it was such a brutal proposition; that is the reason?

a. That is right

q. And you never had seen either one of these men before had you?

a. No

q. And all in the space of three or four minutes, did you get the tag number too?

a. No, in the excitement I didn't get the tag number. The men is what attracted me, especially the one with the gun.

q. And you watched them very closely as they were fighting?

a. They were scuffling with Turner

Q. Did Mr. Sivell get out scuffling?

a. This man Wallace got out first on the right-hand side of the car.

q. All right. Did Mr. Sivell then get out?

a. He got out

q. Did Mr. Sivell get in the scuffle?

a. Yes, he was holding the man on the opposite side. They were on either side.

q. What did Sivell have? Did he have a shotgun? Was he beating him?

a. No, he didn't have a shotgun

q. He had a big pistol?

a. I understand he had a pistol

q. He had a great big pistol?

a. I don't know that it was very big. He had a pistol.

q. How big was it?

a. Just an ordinary pistol

q. Just an ordinary pistol? What caliber was it?

a. I don't know. I know the shotgun was beating him.

q. It was a long barreled shotgun?

a. Well, it was big enough at that time, and I thought it was that.

q. Was it that long?

a. No, it was not that long.

q. How long was it?

a. I don't know how long it was. I could not tell you. I don't know. I still say it was long a plenty.

q. Did any of these officers talk to you?

a. Well, naturally Sheriff Potts and the lawyer asked me about it. They didn't show me the picture of Turner, it is the first time I saw it. His picture was in "The Atlanta Journal"

q. You saw it in the Atlanta Journal?

a. The same picture. The same pose, I would say so.

q. You also saw these fellow's pictures in the Atlanta Journal?

a. Yes

q. You looked at them pretty close

a. I sure did

q. And said that is the men

a. Absolutely

q. And you fixed their pictures right in your mind didn't you?

a. I had already had them pictured in my mind.

q. How long was that shot gun?

a. I don't know. It was long enough to hold it by the handle and strike a man with the barrel. I would say it was a shot gun and not a rifle. It was one that will go off when you strike a man on the head.

q. Which side of the car did they put him in?

a. On the right hand side

q. The right hand side, that was opposite from you?

a. Opposite the steering wheel. No, that was on the side I was standing

q. When they came up?

a. They came from toward Greenville. They turned in the left side of the station, would have thrown the car on the right

q. They turned around

a. Turned in

q. They headed back toward Meriwether county?

a. After they turned around they went back toward it with him

q. Circled around the Sunset Tourist Camp

a. They circled around. They stopped on the front side first

q. Which side was you on when they circled around?

a. Right hand side

q. How did you manage to stay on the right hand side when -

a. Well, I was standing opposite on the road, and the car come up, and the door over here opposite the driver's side would have still had the right hand side of the car to me.

q. Let this be the highway and the tourist camp over here and you standing here?

a. I was standing directly in front of it.

q. And this man told you to shut up?

a. He did

q. Did it make you mad?

a. It did, decidedly, it excited me.

q. They were, you guess, about bumper to bumper?

a. Bumper to bumper.

q. The pickup stopped, and then the Ford drove up along side of it?

a Pulled to the side of it.

She states Turner was about five or five and half feet, about the same height as Wallace and Sivell but not as heavy. Then decides she doesn't really know how tall they were.

Testimony of E. H. Lucas

Direct Examination by Mr. Goldberg

Earl H. Lucas is an investigator for the alcohol tax unit U.S. Treasury Department. They investigate violations of the internal revenue laws pertaining to alcohol tax violations. He has lived in Newnan for about six years.

q. Do you know John Wallace?

a. Yes for about five months. I have known Mr. Sivell for just a few days.

q. Do you know Mr. Turner?

a. Yes I met him about the time I met Mr. Wallace.

witness is excused

Testimony of J. A. Potts

Direct examination by Mr. Goldberg

q. Mr. Potts, what is your business?

a. Deputy Sheriff of Coweta county.

q. What did you find when you investigated the homes of Mr. Sivell and Mr. Wallace?

By Mr. Huddleston: If Your Honor please, if he found any articles or other evidence of any kind; I think those things would be the highest and best evidence rather than his testimony. He can say that he found certain things, and then I think it would be best to have those articles rather than his testimony.

By Mr. Goldberg: I have only asked if he found them. I am going to go further than that, not alone that he found them, but I will ask what he found on them and I will account for their presence to the court, where they are at the present time.

By Mr. Huddleston: I don't think that is sufficient.

By Mr. Goldberg: I think it is.

By Justice Carswell: We will rule that out.

By Mr. Goldberg: if it is being ruled out, in other words, I can't show what they found at the home.

By Justice Carswell: Ask what he found.

q. What did you find and take custody of?

a. At Mr. Wallace's house I believe it was a shirt. I don't know where it is to my own knowledge. It was brought to the sheriff's office.

q. You don't know where it is or why it is not here now?

a. Not to my own knowledge, no sir.

q. What did you find at Mr. Sivell's house?

a. I found a shirt, a pair of trousers, that is all. In Mr. Wallace's house, several shirts, trousers, shoes, hats. I think I brought back a pair of trousers, two pairs of trousers, one shirt, and a hat. One of the shirts had --

By Mr. Huddleston: I object to what one of the shirts had on it or what it might have been. The shirt is the highest and best evidence.

By Justice Brown: I think the shirt should appear.

By Mr. Goldberg: I want to say this to you in all fairness. Of course you are an investigating court. I want to make the statement to you. Of course the articles of clothing were in such a condition they have been sent to Mr. Jones.

By Mr. Huddleston: I object to his testifying,

By Mr. Goldberg: I am making it --

By Mr. Huddleston: I object to dooms day.

By Goldberg: There is nothing going to be hid from the court. The shirts and pants were sent to the State Chemist for analysis for blood stains, and that is why they are not here, and the people in this county and state have a right to know that and they are going to know from me.

By Mr. Huddleston: I move to rule that statement entirely out of evidence.

Bu Justice Brown: All right. Prove it.

By Mr. Goldberg: q. You don't know what was on them?

a. No

q. You don't know what became of the shirts, to your own knowledge?

a. No

the witness is excused

Sheriff Lamar Potts

q. Sheriff, these articles of clothing about which your brother testified, were they delivered to you?

a. Yes sir

q. What has become of those clothes?

a. I sent them to Dr. Herman Jones, the toxicologist of Fulton County.

q. The toxicologist of the State of Georgia?

a. Yes sir

q. Why were they sent to Dr. Jones?

By Mr. Huddleston: I object to that. The shirt would be the highest and best evidence.

By Mr. Goldberg: Your Honor, what is your ruling? I asked why it was sent. Of course I think it is obvious.

By Mr. Huddleston: I think the answer is obvious.

By Mr. Goldberg: I think the court is entitled to know why they were sent.

By Justice Carswell: I rule it out.

By Mr. Goldberg. q. Have they been returned to you?

a. No sir, they have not.

q. Sheriff, when was the first time you knew about this affair?

a. 12:35 Tuesday, April 20th

q. The report was made to you about some occurrence down there at Sunset Inn. In your own words tell as to your activity or what you did.

a. The call came from Steve Smith at Moreland, who operates the Sunset Tourist Camp. I drove down there immediately. Some of the State Troopers went with me, I believe Mr. Malone. I know he went and I don't remember who else went. We went down there and Steve related to me what has been told here about the truck and the automobile and the men coming up in his yard and the subsequent beating and driving off with the man.

By Mr. Huddleston: I don't like to interrupt the Sheriff. He is a good witness and a fair witness. I object to what was told him. I don't object up to the point where they told him what occurred. From there on I object to what was told him by the people. That is hearsay evidence, and of course is not admissible. What he did of course is admissible.

By Justice Brown: I should think they had a right to tell him what occurred.

By Mr. Huddleston: They have a right to tell him, but he did not have a right to testify in court what they tell him. The men were not present, and have no way to defend themselves.

By Mr. Goldberg:
q. Did you get the information from Steve Wallace? He testified in the court room.

a. Steve Smith?

q. I mean Steve Smith.

a. Yes, sir

q. You got that information?

a. Yes, sir

q. What did you do in pursuance of that information?

a. The first thing we did was try to establish ownership of the truck. It was sitting there, didn't have any tag on it. We ran in difficulty finding out who owned it. We had to go to the factory and have the motor number traced. It was some three or four hours before we could find out who the truck was sold to.

q. Who did you finally find the truck belong to?

a. Sold to the LaGrange Motor Company from the factory.

By Mr. Huddleston: I hate to interpose objection, but that is hearsay evidence he is giving now.

By Mr. Goldberg: q. Who did you discover the truck belonged to?

a. Wilson Turner

q. Now after you made that discovery, what did you do, Sheriff?

a. Well, before we made that discovery, I think that is the first call we made. We made the call from the Sunset at Steve's phone. They were in doubt there as to the reason for this. He said these men said this man was wanted for murder.

By Mr. Huddleston: I object to what they said. This is all hearsay.

By Mr. Goldberg: I want to make this observation. Of course you gentlemen know that this is an inquisitorial hearing, and you are charged with only one duty under the law at arriving at a decision as to whether there is probable cause to hold this man for murder, and while it is well to observe all of the niceties of the rules of law, this Court neither convicts anybody of any offense, but you are to use whatever means you have at your hand to discover all the facts, whether these men should be held for the charge, and I say there is no appeal from your decision, and you are interested in getting all the facts of what happened. My suggestion is that you go into it fully. It is inadmissible in a trial before a jury. It will be excluded, but you are merely a court of inquiry.

By Mr. Huddleston: I will agree with him on all that, but I won't agree with him on the fact you should go into hearsay. I don't know what the Sheriff is going to tell, but he is telling what somebody told him, what they said, and it is being transcribed, and as I said in the beginning, it is perfectly possible that somewhere along the line the Court may order part of this record read to the jury. They might try this case, therefore, I don't think any inquiry by this court or any investigation would justify the court in admitting hearsay evidence to go in this record.

By Justice Brown: I think you are right in part, but yet on the other hand, the Sheriff has to have information when he goes out.

By Mr. Huddleston: I grant that is true if he says he got the information. I am not objecting to getting information. I have no objection to him saying he found out it was Turner's car, although there are other records and better records he might get to that, but at the same time, he was going on what they told him at the tourist camp.

By Mr. Goldberg: q. Just tell what happened.

a. Well, we went on the basis -- Gus, I am not going to say about what they said.

By Mr. Huddleston: I realize you are a fair witness.

a. On the basis of what I was told. I made several phone calls. The first call was Sheriff Collier at Greenville to inquire if he had any knowledge of any escaped prisoner from the public works camp or the jail or some prisoner he was seeking, if he had any officers chasing a man up the highway. I described the truck to him and told him what I had heard happened. He said he didn't know anything about it. Well --

q. Did you describe the truck to Sheriff Collier and tell what sort of pick up truck it was?

a. Yes, sir, I did.

q. Did you give him the license number?

a. There was no license on him.

q. But you described the pickup truck found at this station to Sheriff Collier?

a. Yes, sir, he was the first person I called because they told me the truck come from toward Greenville.

q. Did he deny he knew anything about that truck?

a. I would not express it that way. He said, "I don't know anything about it. I don't know anything about anything that could have happened.   I called Columbus.

q. Before you go in that, did you also describe to Sheriff Collier the sort - had you a description of the car?

a. Yes, sir

q. Of the Ford?

a. Yes, sir.

q. And you described and told him what sort of Ford it was?

a. Yes, sir

q. What was his response to that?

a. All he told me was that he didn't have any knowledge. Didn't know anything about it, that is right. I called Columbus and called the Columbus Sheriff's office. I called Carrollton. I made several calls. I won't say who else. Nobody knew anything about it. Then we continued into our investigation to find out whose truck it was, and there was some several hours before we didn't know whose it was. In the meantime, I sent some officers down into -- on down the road toward Luthersville, and it was Friday morning before I saw John Wallace or Herring Sivell either.

They were brought in by Mr. Huddleston Friday morning about ten o'clock.

q. Well, did you ask for their apprehension by the Sheriff of Meriwether County?

a. Yes sir

q. When did you ask that he apprehend them?

a. On Tuesday night. He told me this: he said "I will see that they are brought up there, and then they didn't come, and I called him again. He said, "I will vouch for John Wallace. I said "I don't want any vouching, I want John Wallace." He said I will have Mr. Huddleston call, and Gus called, and he said he would bring them, and he didn't bring them. He brought them the next day. Now that is what happened.

By Mr. Huddleston: I didn't promise you but once and that was Friday morning.

a. I think you told me twice. Anyway, they were not brought until Friday morning.

By Mr. Goldberg: q. When they came in here, what did they come in?

a. Well, I told Mr. Huddleston and I told Sheriff Collier that we had seen - -some of the officers had seen Herring Sivell's automobile, and that we wanted that car brought and I wanted Herring Sivell brought, and I wanted Mr. John Wallace brought, and I told Mr. Huddleston that, and they came in Sivell's car.

q. This same car?

a. The four of them.

q. Did you find any weapon in Sivell's car?

a. Yes sir, a Smith and Wesson, 44 caliber nickle plated, imitation pearl handle. It was in the glove compartment. It is currently in Atlanta, with Dr. Jones. I asked Sivell about it and he told me two different things. First he said it was his. Then he said he guessed it was Sheriff Collier's. Said he didn't know whose it was definitely.

q. Did you ask Mr. Wallace about it?

a. Yes sir. He said it was his.

q. Have you talked to Mr. Wallace about an accusation which he made against Wilson Turner about stealing some cows?

a. Oh yes. I have talked to John several times about it.

q. Well, what did Mr. Wallace say about having had him in custody over in Carroll County?

a. Mr. Wallace lost some cattle, expensive cattle, registered Cattle, I don't know how many but I think he said three, at different times probably. It seems that one of the cows was located in somebody's lot or pasture over in either Carrollton or close to Carrollton-- I don't know- in Carrollton probably, and of course Mr. Wallace had been interested in recovering his cattle, and he spent a considerable amount of time over there at night watching this lot where the cow was.

q. This is his story to you, what he has done?

a. Yes sir. He told me that, and it is borne out. This is right, and then of course they could not stay there all the time, and during two times they were there the cow disappeared. In other words, they were there say today and the cow was there; they went back tonight, if I understand it, and the cow was gone. Anyway, whoever had the cow got it out between the watching. And they enlisted aid of the Chief of Police over there, and for some reason-- I don't know what -- they arrested this Turner. Mr. Wallace was over there, and Mr. Sivell was over there, and when they arrested him and locked him up in jail in Carrollton, then they notified Sheriff Collier to come for him, and the Sheriff went over there that night. It was Sunday night. And they carried Turner back to Greenville. Mr. Wallace and them told me that. That is as far as I know about it. They said the truck was carried back. Mr. Sivell's car is also in Atlanta with Dr. Jones laboratory. Mr. Sivell said he had the car washed that morning when he brought it in.

No questions by Mr. Huddleston

The witness was excused.

A ten minute recess was given

By Mr. Huddleston: May it please Your Honor, in order to shorten this case, I will let these defendants make an unsworn statement. I will let Mr. Wallace take the stand and make his statement first, whatever he wants to say.

John Wallace makes an unsworn statement as follows.

By Mr. Huddleston: Mr. Wallace, I will not ask you any questions. I am not going to examine you. You make whatever statement you see fit to the two Justices.

By Mr. Wallace; Gentlemen, I don't know anything about this charge that has been made on me. I didn't see Mr. Turner on that day. I have not seen him since. I have never offered any harm toward Wilson Turner in my life, nothing but counsel trying to keep him out of trouble.

By Mr. Huddleston: If that is all you want to say, come down.

By Mr. Wallace: That is all.

(Note that in his statement to the jury. He stated that he was in jail for ten days before his mind could accept the fact that Turner was dead and he had killed him.)

~~~~~~~~~~~~~~~~~~~~~~~~~~~

Herring Sivell a defendant, makes an unsworn statement as follows:

By Mr. Sivell: Gentlemen, I know nothing about what I am charged of. I am absolutely conscientious. I am not guilty of what I am charged of.

By Mr. Huddleston: Come down. That is all we have to offer, Your Honor.

~~~~~~~~~~~~~~~~~~~~~~~~~~~

Mr. Earl Lucas recalled for further examination, testified as follows:

Direct Examination

By Mr. Goldberg: q. Mr. Lucas, at any conversation that you ever had with Mr. John Wallace, did he ever at any time threaten the life of Wilson Turner?

119

a. Yes, sir, he talked about killing him.

By Mr. Huddleston: I object to leading the witness. I think it would best ought to let him state whatever conversation he might have had, but not to suggest to him the answer. I don't think it is right.

By Mr. Goldberg: q. If he did, tell what he said.

a. Well, he said he had thought about killing the boy on several occasions, and cited one instance there that he had made up his mind to go through with it and could not do it because his wife -- it was in the presence of his wife and baby.

q. How recent was that?

a. You mean the conversation?

q. Yes, the conversation when he conveyed this.

a. It was made on October 22nd last year.

q. October 22nd of last year when he was with you.

Cross Examination

By Mr. Huddleston: q. Mr. Lucas, who was present?

a. Mr. Bedenbaugh

q. Was that the same day you came by my office?

a. It was.

q. Was not I present at the time?

a. No sir.

q. I was not present at the time he told you that?

a. No sir.

q. Didn't he tell you in that connection that Mr. Turner had been gunning for him?

a. He did, yes sir.

q. And that he overtook him down there, as Mrs. Turner related a few minutes ago, talking to Mr. Strickland?

a. He didn't go in these details on this occasion. He did the other day.

q. He told Mr. Turner he wanted to see him, and he come up to the house and fixed his electric stove, and they settled the differences then and there?

a. At the time he didn't, but the other day I talked to him again and he did mention about the electric stove then.

q. And on that occasion he reported to you and tried to get your aid, or did give you information where you could raid stills that belonged to Wilson Turner, because of the probability it might get him in trouble making whiskey.

a. Yes, sir. That was his complaint, yes, sir

Re direct examination

By Mr. Goldberg - q. Mr. Lucas, I would like for you to tell the court about the stills Mr. Wallace talked to you about and said they were Wilson Turner's. I would like for you to tell the court whether you had those stills under observation and knew about the location at the time the complaints were made on Mr. Turner.

a. No, sir, I didn't have the still located. I was called from Atlanta down there on October 22nd, had orders to go down there and see Mr. Huddleston, and Mr. Huddleston in turn carried me to John Wallace's house. We were around there about four or five o'clock in the afternoon, all night and way up until the next day. This distillery we destroyed was several miles from his house. Mr. Wallace gave the location. I heard it was there somewhere, but I could not find it. I had been looking for it some time.

By Mr. Huddleston: q. He actually gave you the first information?

a. He gave me the exact location. In fact he went with me to it.

q. And showed it to you?

a. Yes, sir.

The State closes

By Justice Brown: Mr. Huddleston, do you want to argue it?

By Mr. Huddleston: I have one thing I want to call your attention to. They have not produced the corpus delicti. They have not shown the man is dead. You can't hold them for murder if you don't produce the dead man's body.

By Justice Carswell: We the Justices find the evidence is sufficient to hold Mr. Wallace and Mr. Sivell over to the Grand Jury for investigation without bond. W. S. Carswell and J. O. Brown, J. P.

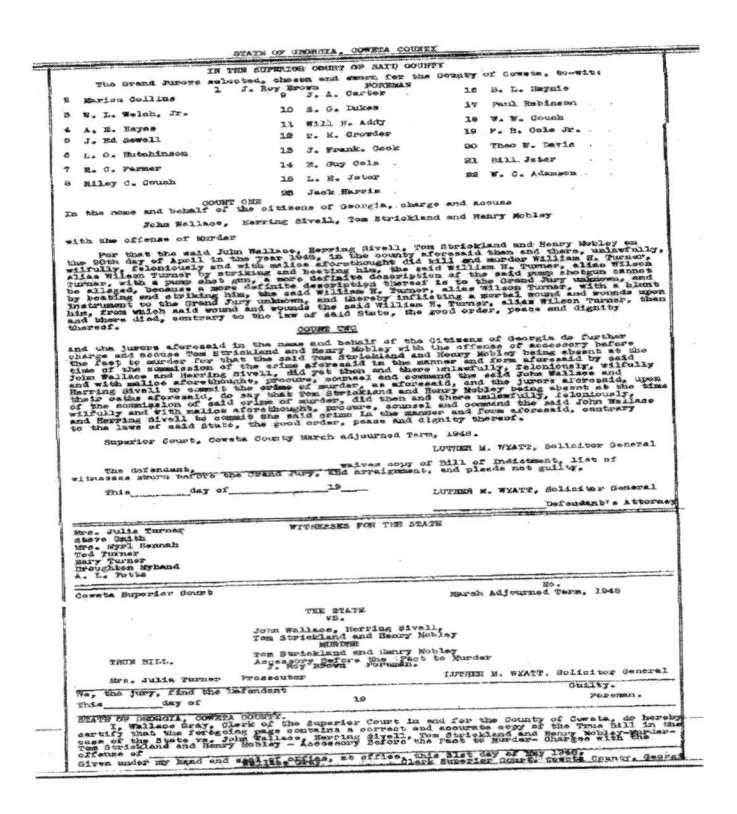

Chapter Six

Newspaper reporting of events

The newspaper carried the stories in varying representation far and wide. All of them seemed to insist that Turner was a tenant farmer. I'm guessing they had their own reasons for not calling him what he really was.

Harris County Journal – April 29, 1948
Where is Turner? Alive or Dead?

Four are Under Arrest as Search Continues –   Bulletin
At the hour of going to press the search for Wilson Turner's body was continuing. Up to that time the search had been fruitless.

New leads were being followed by the Coweta sheriff's office today, but nothing has developed from them up to this hour.

A fifth arrest was made in the case today – Tom Strickland, Meriwether county farmer, a first cousin of John Wallace.

NEWNAN, Ga. – The mystery of the disappearance of young Wilson Turner deepens. Was he murdered? If so, where is his body?
Coweta County Sheriff A. L. Potts says Turner was beaten to death by two dairymen who chased him into a tourist court last week. The sheriff has filed murder charges against the dairymen and two other persons. However, unless Turner's body is found, or it can be proven that he is dead, the murder charge won't stick in Georgia. Witnesses say he was unconscious when the two dairymen took him away in an automobile following the beating.

A day-long search of thickets, lakes and old wells in adjacent Meriwether County yesterday produced no evidence of a body. Today, Potts shook his head and said, "Somebody's going to have to talk."

One of the spots searched yesterday was a bauxite pit near the Little White House at Warm Springs where President Roosevelt died. The pit holds 30 feet of water. Grappling hooks were used.

A state trooper said it would be almost impossible to drag the 40-acre lake on the 2,000-acre plantation of John Wallace, one of the accused men. The lake flows over what was a wooded swamp, and before water was let in, trees were cut down. Now the trees form a mat upon which grappling hoods catch.

Accused with Wallace are three of his close friends, Herring Sivell, Henry Mobley and Broughton Myhand. Witnesses testified at a justice of the peace hearing that Wallace smashed Turner's head with a shotgun butt, and that he and Sivell drove off with the prostrate man. Mobley and Myhand are accused of being in an automobile which also was chasing Turner.

Turner, a young tenant farmer had just been released from jail in Meriwether county for lack of evidence in a cattle theft case.

(Jim Furniss in The Atlanta Constitution)
DURAND, Ga. – A group of 200 farmers, former neighbors of 26-year-old Wilson Turner, Wednesday joined police officials in an all-day search for Turner's body on the 2,000-acre sun-baked farm of John Wallace. Wallace is being held with three others in Coweta county charged with chasing Turner into the Sunset Tourist Court south of Newnan last Tuesday, and murdering him in full sight of a number of the court's lunch-hour customers.

From 9:15 a.m. until well into the afternoon, groups of men who knew Turner when he lived on the Wallace farm last year met at Mrs. Clyde Byrd's general store here and filtered into the network of dusty roads traversing Wallace's huge dairy farm.

"We saw some buzzards sitting on a house over to White Sulphur Creek, but it was nothing," one grizzled farmer reported to Coweta Sheriff A.L. Potts' makeshift headquarters at Mrs. Byrd's store.

"Drug the Wynn's Quarry Lake over near Warm Springs," another group announced. "Didn't catch nothing but stumps."

Still other groups of men in overalls combed the one-story house where Turner lived before moving to Carrollton, checked in abandoned wells, kicked through sawdust piles and scrambled through briar patches around streams.

The missing man's 72-year-old father, John H. Turner, rode over from Lovejoy with his nephews, Robert and Solomon Turner, hunting for his youngest son.

Bent from injuries received Christmas, when a mule stepped on him, the gray-headed old man watched a line of men filter through woods below the white one-story tenant house in which Wallace's pretty young wife had been living with her husband after their large house had burned.

A large number of men also reported back to Turner's father the news they had been unable to find a trace of his boy in the swamp adjoining the large artificial lake below the Wallace barns and outbuildings.

Mrs. Wallace, meanwhile silently watched the proceedings from a distance from a window refusing to comment on events which brought men from all neighboring counties to her husband's domain. The uninvited visitors, however, commented on seeing that a "For Sale" sign had been placed the day before on a partially completed restaurant building built by Wallace and his wife.

In Greenville, nine miles north, white-haired Sheriff C.H. Collier said heart trouble prevented his taking part in the vast search organized by Sheriff Potts of neighboring Coweta county.

Wallace was a man of his word, Collier said, describing events preceding Turner's beating allegedly at the hands of Wallace and Herring Sivell. Collier said he saw Wallace about noon in Greenville the day

125

eyewitnesses saw Turner beaten 21 miles away and about a half hour later. "It's a lie what they say about anyone waiting outside the jail here to catch Turner when I turned him loose the day he was beaten," Collier said vehemently.

Collier explained that Turner had been arrested at Carrollton the previous Sunday on information from Wallace in the theft of one of Wallace's cows. Turner was released the morning after Wallace agreed he did not have sufficient evidence against his former tenant to bring suit. Collier also said he and Wallace had dinner together the day of Turner's supposed death.

Meanwhile two additional men were in the Coweta county jail on a warrant sworn out by Sheriff Potts charging they had joined in the chase after Turner. They were arrested Tuesday night at their homes at Chipley. They were identified as Henry Mobley and Broughton Myhand.

The Newnan Times-Herald April 29, 1948
WALLACE AND SIVELL HELD WITHOUT BOND

Photo 1 - W. S. Carswell, Justice of the Peace, at the extreme left of the photo, listens to the testimony of Mrs. Turner, wife of the missing man, who is pointing at Wallace and Sivell during questioning. Mr. Brown, of the County Police Department, is directly behind Mrs. Turner. Wallace and Sivell are charged with the murder and kidnaping of William Turner.

Photo 2 - Steve Smith, operator of the Sunset tourist Camp, which was the scene of the assault on William Turner. Smith positively identified Sivell and Wallace for the state, in the preliminary trial at the Newnan Court House last Tuesday morning.

Photo 3 - William Turner, alias Wilson Turner, who was last seen Tuesday afternoon, just after noon, at the Sunset Tourist Camp, where he was reportedly assaulted by two men, thrown into the rear of a green two door Ford, and carried away in a southward direction on Highway 41, presumably heading toward Greenville. $500 reward for information leading to his recovery.

Photo 4 - Questioned in Farmer's death - Herring Sivell (right), prominent dairyman, is questioned in Newnan, Ga, jail Saturday by J. P. Hillen (left), agent of the Georgia Bureau of Investigation, in connection with the beating to death of a Carroll County tenant farmer. Sheriff A. L. Potts of Coweta County said that a bloody shirt was discovered at Sivell's home in Chipley, GA., and that Sivell had not explained the stains on the shirt.

The sheriff said a stained shirt had also been found at the Meriwether County home of John Wallace, another dairyman. Both Wallace and Sivell are charged with kidnaping and murder in the death of the tenant farmer, Wilson Turner. (AP Photo)

Steve Smith Identifies Assailants of Carroll County Farmer

John Wallace, Meriwether County, and Herring Sivell, Harris County are presently guests in the Coweta county jail as Sheriff Potts, his aides and Newnan repeatedly made the headlines of the metropolitan papers and of the press association wires.

Held without bond by order of the justices in the preliminary trial, the principals, in the mystery are the only men in this or neighboring counties who are sitting still, as the search for the missing man, William Turner, goes on.

Estimates of from 200 to 500 were reported describing the posse which made a search of something over ten square miles yesterday. Many were mere spectators and many more were well intentioned volunteers tremendously interested in seeing a great crime and mystery cleared up. Sheriff Potts said absolutely nothing was found.

Equipped with drag equipment, an old boxite mine site was searched and many wells and haunted houses were combed. The main group met and separated into searching groups. All headed by somebody well acquainted with the local terrain.

Tuesday, April 20th, a Ford pickup truck raced into the Sunset Tourist Camp and a man leaped from it, shouting. "Help, don't let them kill me!" A green Ford tudor (two door) pulled alongside it, and two men intercepted the path of the former as he attempted to reach the inside of the camp. Thus began the murder mystery and disappearance that has obsessed the State.

All three men were positively identified by many witnesses, three of whom testified at the preliminary trial. The victim, identified as Turner, was dragged and beaten to the door of the Ford. The other two, said to be John Wallace and Herring Sivell, attempted to force him into the car. he balked at the door. Wallace reportedly hit him with a shotgun after taking a full swing.

That climaxed the action, according to the testimony given Tuesday morning. Turner never again made a noise or a move that was attested in court or elsewhere. He was tucked into the car and Wallace climbed into the rear on top of him. Sivell drove off.

Steve Smith, owner of the tourist camp, had run out and advised the men to handcuff Turner, rather than to manhandle him. They said he was a tough hombre, wanted for murder, and they were "taking him back."

Smith assumed they were officers, but became suspicious when they struck Turner on the head with the shotgun and took down the license number of the car.

He testified that he got the first section on one side of the building, and the second section on the other. The plate was unusual, in that it was separated in the center by a diagonal strip. It has been positively identified as the one on Sivell's car. The car headed south on highway 41, presumably toward Greenville, and that was the last seen or heard of William Turner.

Turner had been arrested in Carroll Count on charges of stealing Wallace's cattle. He had been taken into Meriwether County and held in custody by Sheriff Collier. There were no records to show that a warrant had been sworn out or that Turner had been held there, other than the testimony of Collier, who claims to have held Turner since the preceding Sunday.

Wallace and Turner were no strangers -- Turner had been in the employ of Wallace and lived on his place. Last November they had a falling out over said Mrs. Turner in court, "20 gallons of Whiskey."

Turner was so anxious to leave the place that he sold his crop of corn, took his wife and baby and left Meriwether County at a loss in investment. He had supposedly not been back until the Sheriff of Meriwether called upon him for the cattle theft charge. He was released for lack of evidence and way laid en route to his home.

The action occurred at 12:30 Tuesday afternoon. Sheriff Potts followed the telephoned lead he got from Sunset tourist Camp and immediately identified the truck of Turner, which was still at the court.

From there he was able to follow the clues to John Wallace and Sivell. He called for them to be sent to Coweta and Meriwether's Sheriff promised he would send them. The following day they had not been delivered, nor confined in Meriwether, and Potts spoke to their lawyer. Sheriff Collier said he would vouch for the two men. Said Potts, "I don't want any vouching. I want Wallace and Sivell." It wasn't until Friday that he got them.

Sivell's car had been completely washed and cleaned, said Sivell. It was sent to Atlanta to the office of the south's foremost toxicologist. The car is believed to have hidden evidence of the violence committed at Sunset.

Potts complained of lack of cooperation from the county of Meriwether and Atlanta sent him four Georgia Bureau men to aid in the investigation. Going to the homes of these two men, they found clothing that was bloodstained. This too was sent to Atlanta, and was not revealed at the preliminary trial.

The preliminary trial was a bit of drama which was played to a full house. Both Sivell and Wallace made pleas of not guilty in their formal statements. Wallace said he never meant to harm a hair of Turner's head. In rebuttal for this, prosecutor Goldberg called an internal revenue officer, E. H. Lucas, to the stand. Lucas said that Wallace had told him he would have killed Turner on several occasions.

Steve Smith, proprietor of the Sunset Court, testified also against Wallace and Sivell. Said Smith afterward, "I hope Wallace and Sivell get more justice than they showed Turner."

Admittedly a terrible thing, Smith could not understand why the assault having taken place at his court affected business as it did. He said he couldn't keep enough food in the kitchen. Hundreds came by and evidently ordered food and drink, just to sit there and talk the crime over with him.

Gus Huddleston, Greenville lawyer for the defense, was cross examining Mrs. Merle Hannah. Goldberg having established the assault with the shotgun, and the fact that Mrs. Hannah witnessed it, Huddleston wanted to know how long the gun was. She said it was long enough. He persisted, and she admitted, it was long enough to hold by one end and hit with the other.

The attorney went on to something else, and suddenly popped the question to her again. Said Mrs. Hannah, "the gun is the same length now as it was the first time you asked me."

Goldberg, in questioning Steve Smith, established the fact that the shotgun went off when the blow was struck on the head of Turner. Said Goldberg, "the blow was so great that the vibration caused the gun to go off."

Huddleston, for the defense, objected. Said he, it is not fair, nor wholly accurate to say that it went off because of vibration. Goldberg obliged. Said he, "It's all right with me if you want to say he pulled the trigger and shot the gun on purpose." The gallery laughed freely and loudly.

Every press service, and all the major means of communications have been at the service of Sheriff Potts in encouraging the public to take not only an interest but an active part in finding either Turner or some clues which will lead to his discovery.

It is the one keynote of his appeal as Sheriff of Coweta County: "encourage everyone to be on the lookout for signs or clues of some kind." A $500 reward still stand, along with the assurance that any information given will be kept in the strictest confidence.

The Manchester Mercury – April 29, 1948
Body of Tenant Farmer Sought Near Durand
Meriwether Man, 3 Chipley Men Held on Murder Charge

Whereabouts of the body of Wilson Turner, 26-year-old former Meriwether county tenant farmer, was the big question as a group of 200 farmers and former neighbors joined Coweta County Sheriff A.L. Potts in an all-day search Wednesday on the huge farm of John Wallace, Durand dairyman.

Wallace is being held in Newnan along with Herring Sivell and two other Chipley men, charged with chasing Turner into the Sunset Tourist Court south of Newnan Tuesday of last week and murdering him in full sight of a number of the court's lunch-hour customers.

Since the breaking of the story last Thursday it has been a matter of state-wide shock because of the brutality of the alleged handling of Turner.

Speculation was high in this county that the "corpus delicti," necessary for prosecution of the men on murder charges, would never be found. It was pointed out that successful prosecution could, however, be pushed on assault with intent to murder charges and that heavy prison sentences could be meted.

Turner was said to have been accosted by Wallace and Sivell following his release from Meriwether county jail after Wallace had agreed that he did not have sufficient evidence to bring suit against his former tenant for the alleged stealing of a cow.

Eyewitnesses said Wallace and Sivell caught up with Turner in Coweta county between Moreland and Newnan and that agonized cries by Turner accompanied his clubbing with a shotgun butt.

In a hearing Tuesday in Newnan Wallace and Sivell were bound over to Superior Court without bond.

The Newnan Times-Herald May 6, 1948

Photo with caption: Where Charred Bones Were Found Buried in Swamp - Sheriff A. L. Potts of Coweta County stands in a pit in a swamp on a Meriwether County farm where he says the charred remains of tenant farmer Wilson Turner were unearthed. The sheriff said the body had been burned with wood and gasoline. Turner disappeared more than two weeks ago after two men beat him savagely, threw him into an automobile and hurried way from a tourist court near Newnan. Held in connection with the case are seven men, including John Wallace, prominent Meriwether County dairyman, for whom Turner formerly worked. (AP Photo).

{Photo with Caption: Remains of Turner, Says Sheriff. -- Coweta County Sheriff A. L. Potts displays charred fragments which he says are the remains of Wilson Turner, tenant farmer, who was spirited away from a tourist camp near Newnan more than two weeks ago by two men who beat him brutally. Sheriff Potts said the remains were dug up in a swamp on a Meriwether county farm. John Wallace, dairyman and former employer of Turner, and six other men are held in connection with Turner's disappearance.

Kidnap-Murder Mystery solved by Lamar Potts and Assistants

The murder-kidnapping of William Turner was cracked by Sheriff A. Lamar Potts, his deputies and aides and residents of Coweta breathed a sigh of relief and contentment for the first time since this case opened some two weeks ago.

The signed confession of Myhand, the testimony of the colored men who were witnesses to the brutal burning, and instrumental in arranging the affair, seemed to clinch the case to the satisfaction of local law enforcement officers.

Although the information in Myhand's confession was not released, it was implied that although having no direct connection with the kidnap-killing. Myhand was quite well versed on the plans as they were made and carried out by Wallace and his group.

Identification of the charred remains of Turner is rumored to have been made by means of a package of cigarette papers on which was scribbled a note to Turner's uncle; requesting bond for his cattle dealings. The note had been written on the inside leaves, and was found in the well from which the body was taken to be burned.

A part of the confession that was given and then retracted by Sivell was again verified just yesterday when a party looked through the house in which Turner had previously lived. The testimony; when Sivell's automobile had a puncture and the body was transferred from his car to another. Sivell testified that he could walk to the spot and find a can of tobacco which he had thrown into the bushes. This he did. The tobacco was Prince Albert.

Today, while walking through the house once occupied by William Turner, several packages of Prince Albert were lying around. Mused Deputy Sheriff J. H. Potts, "I see he was still smoking P.A." It has been suggested that irregardless of the outcome of the murder trial, John Wallace is in deep enough with the Alcohol Tax boys from both State and Federal Divisions, to be in very hot water.

Some criticism was made today by Defense Attorney Gus Huddleston regarding an editorial which appeared in the Atlanta morning paper. He said it appeared to be calling for a decision of public sentiment long before the trial; which was, in his estimation, a bit premature.

....

Photo with caption: Trailer - Elzie J. Hancock (above), state revenue agent from Columbus is credited by Sheriff A. L. Potts of Coweta County with following dim footprints of men and a horse that led to discovery of Wilson Turner's burned body buried in a swamp on a Meriwether county farm. John Wallace, prominent Meriwether County dairyman for whom Turner formerly worked and six other men have been arrested in connection with the case.

The Manchester Mercury – May 27, 1948
Still Found Near John Wallace Place

State Revenue Officers E.C. Cook and C.E. Miller found 101 gallons of non-paid liquor Wednesday at a still operated within 75 yards of John Wallace's place near Durand. The officers said the liquor belonged to Wallace, one of the principals arrested in the sensational Wilson Turner murder case. John Bray was arrested as the operator of the still.

Herald - Journal Jun 1, 1948   Jury to Consider Death of

Farmer   (This one goes so far as to describe Turner as a weak and sickly man.)

Newnan, Ga - A grand jury is scheduled Monday to consider charges that four influential Meriwether county men beat to death William Turner, a tenant farmer, after a cross-country chase.

Held by Coweta County Sheriff A. Lamar Potts on charges of murdering Turner, described as a "weak, sickly" man, are John Wallace, Herring Sivell, Henry Mobley and Tom Strickland.

Wallace and Sivell are big-scale dairymen. Mobley is a farmer and a friend of Wallace, Strickland is Wallace's cousin. Three others are accused of being accessories in the death of Turner, who had just been released from the Meriwether jail at Greenville on a charge of stealing a cow from Wallace. These are Mozart Strickland, uncle of Wallace, and two of Wallace's Negro farm hands, Robert Lee Gates and Albert Brooks. All have denied the charges. The sharecropper's death is alleged to have occurred after he drove across the county line into a tourist court at Moreland on April 20, crying for help.

Spartanburg Herald, Herald Journal - Tuesday, June 1, 1948
Sheriff, seven men indicted in Murder Case

Newnan, Ga - A Coweta county grand jury Monday indicted the sheriff of a neighboring county Monday as an accessory in the murder of William Turner, a share-cropper who was abducted near Newnan and beaten to death.

The jury also indicted 7 men on murder charges in the case.
The state charged that Sheriff Hardy Collier of Meriwether had arrested Turner on a cattle theft charge 2 days before he was slain. He released the prisoner for lack of evidence, the state said, and within an hour Turner met his fate.

Collier was indicted as an accessory and legal experts said that conviction on that charge in Georgia could bring the death penalty. Judge Samuel J. Boykin said he would allow Collier to make $10,000 bond.

Those indicted for Turner's actual murder were John Wallace, Herring Sivell, Henry Mobley, Tom Strickland, Mozart Strickland.
Albert Brooks, Negro; and Robert Lee Gates, Negro.

Eyewitnesses identified Wallace and Sivell as the 2 men who seized

Turner at a tourist camp just inside the Coweta County line from Meriwether County. When last seen, Turner was being savagely beaten by Wallace, the witnesses said.

St. Joseph, MO Gazette Tuesday, June 1, 1948
7 indicted for Georgia Killing.
(This one actually reported Turner was AWOL).

The Coweta county grand jury indicted seven men for murder today in the slaying of a tenant farmer William Turner. The Meriwether County sheriff was indicted as an accessory.

Murder indictments were returned against John Wallace, Meriwether County dairy operator; Herring Sivell, Chipley Dairyman; Henry Mobley, a farmer, Tom Strickland, Wallace's cousin; Mozart Strickland, Wallace's uncle; Albert Brooks and Robert Lee Gates, workers on Wallace's farm.

Sheriff Hardy Collier of Meriwether county was indicted as an accessory to the murder Sheriff Collier arrested young Turner on a cattle theft charge but released him from the Greenville jail three days later.

Authorities said Turner was killed within an hour after his release.

Turner was the object of a three-county search last month after he disappeared. Sheriff Lamar Potts of Coweta County said witnesses told him they saw Wallace and Sivell brutally beat the young tenant farmer, toss him in a car and drive away.

A pile of charred bones were found on Wallace's farm. The bones were identified by Sheriff Potts as Turner's remains. The search was complicated by the fact that Turner was known throughout the county as Wilson Turner. It developed that William had taken the name of his brother, Wilson, when he was awol from the army.

The Tuscaloosa News   June 1, 1948
Eight Indicted in Man's Death after 2 hours.
(This one even goes on to say that the grand jury heard from the widow and child of Turner before returning the indictments.)

Newnan, Ga - It took a Coweta County grand jury only two hours to indict eight Meriwether countians, including Sheriff Hardy Collier, on charges arising from the death of a share-cropper.

Charged yesterday with murdering the tenant farmer, William Turner, were five well known white men - John Wallace, Herring Sivell, Henry Mobley, tom Strickland and Mozart Strickland.

Similarly accused by the grand jurors were two Negro farm hands, - Albert Brooks and Robert Lee Gates.

Sheriff Collier was named as an accessory - a charge which Assistant prosecutor Myer Goldberg said could, if sustained, lead to a death penalty. Superior Court Judge Samuel J. Boykin said he expected Collier to come over with attorneys and post $10,000 bond to await trial. Solicitor-General Luther Wyatt explained that the seven named for murder could not get bond and must remain in jail here.

The grand jury heard the widow and child of Turner before returning the indictments. Mrs. Turner had testified at an earlier hearing that her husband's death climaxed trouble over liquor between him and Wallace, a dairyman for whom he once worked.

Just before he dropped from sight, Turner had been held in the Meriwether county jail at Greenville on a charge of stealing a cow from Wallace. When he was released on April 20, Coweta county Sheriff A. Lamar Potts said, Wallace and Sivell, both big dairymen, were waiting for him.

The Newnan Times-Herald   June 3rd, 1948
Hearing in Murder Case to Be Held Next Monday.

Monday morning, June 7th Judge Samuel J. Boykin will hear the pleas of eight men at the arraignment hearing. If there is any among the group who pleads guilty, the judge will sentence him immediately. If not, the regular trial is set for June 14.

Last Monday a Grand Jury indicted seven men for murder; Henry Mobley, Tom Strickland, Herring Sivell, John Wallace, Mozart Strickland and two Negroes. Sheriff C. H. Collier of Meriwether County was also indicted as an accessory before the fact.

The indictment of Collier came as a surprise and he is presently out on $10,000 bond. His connection with the murder of William (alias Wilson) H. Turner has been rumored and speculated upon at great length. Should the trial prove the veracity of these statements, it is conceivable that the penalty will be severe. Either the death sentence or life imprisonment could be asked. This depends on the recommendations of the Jury.

Collier, head law enforcement officer in Meriwether County, apparently did not participate in the search for the body, nor make any noticeable attempts to solve the murder mystery that horrified the State of Georgia some time ago. Sheriff Potts described the situation in Meriwether as "complete lack of cooperation." It was this lack that caused Sheriff Potts to go to the Governor and the Georgia Bureau of Investigation for aid.

Luther M. Wyatt, Solicitor General, and Myer Goldberg, will prosecute for the state. On the other hand, there is a whole battery of attorneys for the defense. William Schley Howard, Atlanta attorney, is not handling the case of John Wallace, He is, however, aligned with the defense. Others include: Al Henson, Atlanta; Gus Huddleston, Greenville; Kiser Whatley, LaGrange; and Fred New, Columbus.

Warm Spring Mirror – June 4, 1948
Coweta Sheriff Indicts Sheriff Collier in Wallace-Turner Case
The Coweta Superior Court Grand Jury which convened Monday in Newnan, indicted Sheriff Collier of Meriwether County, charging him as an accessory to the murder of William Turner. Sheriff Collier, who has been in ill health for some time, did not go to Newnan Monday, but was allowed to make $10,000.00 bond by Judge Samuel J. Boykin. Mr. Collier has been elected to the sheriff's office of Meriwether County for four, 4-year terms; his present term expires Jan. 1.

At the same time, indictments were returned against John Wallace, Herring Sivell, Henry Mobley, Tom Strickland and Mozart Strickland, who are accused of the killing of Turner.

The Coweta Grand Jury also indicted two Negroes, Albert Brooks and Robert Lee Gates, also charged with taking part in the murder.

The Coweta Superior Court is scheduled to convene Monday, June 14, at Newnan to take up the trial of the defendants.

The Newnan Times-Herald June 17th, 1948 - Thursday
Photo caption: CROWD PACKS COURT HOUSE FOR WALLACE's trial - Spectators fill all available space in the Coweta county court house at Newnan, GA., for the trial of John Wallace, charged with the tourist camp murder of William Turner. The prominent Meriwether county dairyman is accused of killing the former sharecropper on the Wallace farm after a dispute over moonshine liquor. Indicted along with Wallace are four other white men, two Negroes, and Sheriff Hardy Collier of Meriwether county, named as an accessory. (AP Photo).

Wallace to Testify in Thursday Session
Prosecution nears End in Presentation of Evidence

The most sensational murder trial to ever take place in the Coweta county Court House, presently acclaimed throughout the State, enters a crucial phase of the testimony today as John Wallace takes his place on the stand for the first time in this case.

A "packed house" greeted the principals of the case much of the three days, and the usual crowd was swollen by the Wednesday afternoon curfew in Newnan.

Wednesday afternoon the defense council made 35 consecutive objections as the prosecution, led by Luther Wyatt, Solicitor General, and assisted by Myer Goldberg, exhibited 41 bits of evidence. The judge sustained only three of these objections.

Among the evidence were: the floor mats of Sivell and Mobley's cars, guns, blackjacks, parts of the automobile doors, clothes, etc.

Court opened at 10am on Monday morning, but spectators were there as early as six thirty, and had brought lunch and a will to see it through irregardless of the difficulties. Much of the court room space was reserved for witnesses and jurors on that first day.

The judge stepped into the court and everyone stood up expectantly. They relaxed to the calling of over 125 names. In an amazingly short time the jury was chosen and the others were excused. Six more panels must be drawn from the list, however, and the excuse is a temporary one.

That first morning featured two long recesses, and a dinner call. But the trial got underway early in the afternoon. The prosecution was immediately bogged down in legal argument that had to be decided in chambers. This discussion involved the legality of the Sheriff summoning the jury, after having taken an active part in the prosecution. The judge overruled the objection, and the trial went on.

Early testimony told of the cattle thieving and of the catching of Turner by Wallace and Collier. The prosecution introduced witnesses in a sequence which gave the picture of the acquisition and assault on Turner in an orderly manner.

Most pertinent, perhaps, of the testimony was given by Negro "hands" from the Wallace farm who told the story of getting the body of Turner, which they positively identified, from the well -- of transporting it to the pit where it was placed beneath a cord of wood and set afire.

J. H. Turner, father of the deceased, was brought to the stand and spoke of the boy's fine record before he deserted from the army. Judge Boykin forbade the defense their persistence in a chain of questioning which was designed to establish the fact that William Turner had used the draft card of Wilson, and also his name, in order to successfully dodge the army authorities.

The state has introduced witnesses which include a man in jail with Turner in Carrollton, right on up to the point of his assault at the Sunset tourist court. Highway workers identified the truck and cars involved in the chase from Greenville up to the Tourist Court.

Today the state about finishes its presentation of evidence, and upon completion of this, Wallace is expected to take the stand.

Metropolitan journalists have taken up residence in Newnan and wait Thursday morning's developments expectantly. Probing into the case from every conceivable angle, these men are looking to Thursday morning's testimony for a reach break in the case.

Lamar Potts was repeatedly called to the stand and almost every bit of testimony which he attempted to give was objected to strenuously by the defense. Questions of the prosecutions were also receiving careful consideration by the defense, and often the objections were sustained by the Judge as a result of "leading questions" being asked.

Mayhaley Lancaster, "Oracle of the Ages," took the stand the first day of the trial and "stole the show" as far as morning press accounts of the trial were concerned. She testified under oath that many of the law enforcement officers had come to her seeking some lead to solving the crime. Introduced by the prosecution, she also said Wallace had come to her twice. Once in connection with the loss of his registered cattle; another time to ask whether or not the body would ever be found. Mayhaley also stated that she couldn't be sure just what law enforcement officers had come to her. Henson asked whether Lamar Potts had been to pay her a visit. And how about Myer Goldberg?" She said she couldn't say for sure, but she did remember a Mr. Hancock.

(Hancock was the GBI man who actually found the only remaining traces of the body.) Confronted with this bit of testimony, Hancock denied solemnly that he had ever been to the "Oracle" with his troubles.

Dr. Herman Jones testified that the blood found in the cars of Mobley and Sivell was human blood. He also said there were fragments of human bone in the match box of ashes which Sheriff Potts sent to him.

Charles H. Hickson, Negro station attendant who cleaned the car of Herring Sivell the day before Gus Huddleston came to Newnan with Sivell and Wallace, testified that he had seen a puddle of blood on the floor of the car. Henson, leader of the defense, stated that there would be no blood on the floor that could be described as the witness had described it, after so many days.

The problem then arose as to whether the blood flows from a dead man after his heart stops beating. Placed on the stand to help determine this question. Dr. Jones said that there was no guiding rule about this. In some cases the blood ceased to flow. In others it would come very close to draining.

Photo Caption: WIFE WITH JOHN WALLACE AT TRIAL - John Wallace (left), prominent dairyman, talks with his wife, Josephine, and her father, J. W. Heath (center), in the court house at Newnan, Ga. Wallace is on trial for his life. He is charged with murdering William Turner, alias Wilson Turner, a former tenant on his farm. His father-in-law is a former judge in Calhoun County, Florida. (AP Photo).

Photo Caption: Wallace talks with fellow defendants in court - Just before the opening of his trial on charges that he murdered William Turner, John Wallace (standing second from right) talks with his fellow-defendants in the Coweta county court house at Newnan, Ga. Henry Mobley, Herring Sivell and Tom Strickland (seated left to right) are indicted jointly for the tourist camp slaying, but they are not on trial at present. The woman talking with the defendants is Mrs. Herring Sivell. At extreme right is E. J. Hancock, state revenue agent from Columbus who found charred fragments identified as the remains of Turner's body on Wallace's farm. (AP Photo)

Photo Caption: ON TRIAL - John Wallace, prominent dairyman of Meriwether County, Georgia, enters court at Newnan, Ga., to stand trial for his life on indictment for murder in the death of William Turner, a tenant farmer. The dairyman is accused of killing the sharecropper after a dispute over moonshine liquor. (AP Photo)

Photo Caption: TURNER FAMILY AT WALLACE TRIAL - Wilson Turner (left), brother of the slain William Turner, talks in court chamber at Newnan, Ga., with his father, J. H. Turner (center), and Mrs. Julia

Windom Turner, William's widow. John Wallace, prominent dairyman of nearby Meriwether County, is on trial for his life at Newnan for the slaying of young Turner, Charred fragments dug up on Wallace's farm, were identified as the remains of the slain man's body. (AP Photo).

Daytona Beach Morning Journal June 17, 1948
Crime- State Ends Case on Wallace

Newnan, Ga - The State completed its court room picture of how share-cropper William Turner was battered to death and burned to ashes and bone chips at an old still site in a swampy woodland. Its closing evidence was 41 grisly exhibits of articles allegedly used in Turner's death and his cremation on the 2000-acre farm of a wealthy dairyman on trial for murdering him.

Next is the defense testimony, and a different picture of the tenant farmer's demise was promised the Coweta County jury when that starts, probably today.

Attorney Gus Huddleston announced that Dairyman John Wallace of Meriwether county, the defendant, would take the stand and deny that Turner met death in a savage clubbing at a Coweta County Tourist camp as the prosecution contends.

Instead, said the lawyer, Wallace will testify that his former employee died on his Meriwether County farm. Details were not disclosed but Huddleston's statement was taken to mean that the Coweta County court's jurisdiction to try the case might be challenged.

Through its witnesses, the State sought to show that Wallace determined to kill Turner after falling out with him over liquor making and accusing him of stealing a valuable cow.

The witness told how Turner, after being released at Greenville on the cow theft charge, fled headlong out of Meriwether County in a truck on April 20. Wallace and Herring Sivell of Chipley, also indicted for murder, were hot after Turner, they said, overtook him at a Moreland tourist camp, beat him severely, threw him in a car and drove off.

The State's exhibits included a blood-stained pole an investigator said he found at an old well from which the two Negroes said they helped haul the body before its burning.

Also, exhibited was another green pine sapling with a cord attached. It was to this pole, the prosecution held, the body was tied as it was hauled

140

from well to "fire pit."

"White chips" Coweta Sheriff A. Lamar Potts said he picked up near the pit also were displayed. Dr. Herman L. Jones, Fulton County criminologist testified there were human bone fragments.

Dr. Jones also said that spots found on the shirt and trousers of Wallace were made by human blood.

Daytona Beach Morning Journal   June 18, 1948
Wallace Says Killing Was "Accidental"

Newnan - Dairyman John Wallace told a packed Coweta County courtroom yesterday that he "accidentally shot" William Turner while trying to "bluff him into telling me where my stolen cows were."

Dramatically closing six and a half hours of almost unbroken testimony, Wallace said Turner suffered only a cut ear at the Coweta county tourist court where the State charged he had been beaten to death.

Turner's death came some time later, Wallace said, near the scene of Turner's first alleged cow-stealing crime. Wallace said he took Turner there in an effort to get a confession from him.

Wallace, owner of a 2000 acre farm in Meriwether County said he was standing about five feet from Turner beside an old well when --
"I heard somebody holler down by my right . . . I turned my head in that direction and transferred the shotgun from my right and laid it in the bend of my left arm.

At that instant, the gun fired. I didn't see Turner when it fired. I didn't see his face. I had no control over the gun. It blew off the top of his scalp and when I looked the man was lying full length with the top of his scalp torn off."

Wallace said only his uncle, Tom Strickland, witnessed the shooting. Wallace made it clear that the shooting occurred on the farm of the Chattahoochee Valley Lumber Co., in Meriwether county.

Wallace and four others have been charged with murder in the slaying of the young tenant farmer. Wallace was the first to be tried.

"I got into this trouble, gentlemen," the prosperous farmer-dairyman told the jury, "trying to help a young man get a start in life."

Wallace's testimony, delivered calmly and with dramatic pauses for emphasis, was expected to be his only defense. Herring Sivell and Henry Mobley, two others indicted with Wallace, refused to testify on grounds it might incriminate them.

"I'm not afraid to die," cried Wallace. "If it means my death to tell the truth. I'll die telling you the truth. I didn't intend to kill Wilson Turner. I'm an average church-going man, and I love my God like you love your God. Your God is my God. I'm no cold-blooded head-hunter."

The defendant made an impassioned plea to the jury to understand his position as a hard-working farmer who struggled for two years against Turner's houndings "as a law-breaker and cattle thief."

When he went to "talk" to Turner that last time, Wallace said: "I had a shotgun in that car. I'm not going to lie to you, gentlemen. I didn't take that gun to kill anybody with. I had no idea of killing anybody. I didn't leave my home with murder in my heart."

The Miami News June 18, 1948
Tenant-Slaying Case Near Jury
Newnan, Ga, - The murder trial of Dairyman John Wallace, who admitted slaying a tenant farmer "accidentally," is expected to go to jury today. Wallace, in an impassioned plea, declared that he was trying to bluff - William Turner into admitting a cattle theft when his shotgun accidentally discharged.

The state contends that Turner was beaten to death, his body hidden in a well and later burned on a huge funeral pyre and his ashes scattered in a creek.

Wallace exonerated Herring Sivell and Henry Mobley, two of eight men indicted in the Turner slaying. He said that the only witness was his uncle, Tom Strickland, also under indictment.

The Tuscaloosa news - June 18, 1948
John Wallace Takes Witness Stand at Trial
Newnan, Ga - The trial of wealthy Dairyman-Farmer John Wallace on murder charges in the death of William Turner was expected to go to a Coweta County jury today.

Wallace told a packed tense courtroom late yesterday that he "accidentally shot" Turner a share-cropper, while trying to "bluff him into telling me where my stolen cows were."

He said the tenant farmer suffered only a cut on the ear at the Coweta County tourist camp where the state alleged he was killed.

Wallace made it clear that the "accidental" shooting of Turner occurred sometime later on the farm of the Chattahoochee Valley Lumber Co., in Meriwether County.

Court attendants pointed out that the jury, if believing Wallace's story of the death occurring in Meriwether County, could either find him "not guilty," or it could declare a mistrial.

In the event of a mistrial, Wallace could be retried in Coweta County or in Meriwether County - depending upon the jury's recommendations. A verdict of "not guilty" would mean that Wallace could not be brought to trial anywhere on the same charge.

Wallace said he took Turner to the scene of one of the alleged cow stealings in an effort to get a confession. He said he and Turner were accompanied by Tom Strickland, Wallace's uncle.

The defendant said he and Turner were standing near an old well when "I heard somebody holler down by my right. I turned my head, and transferred the shotgun from my right hand and laid it in the bend of my left arm.

"At that instant, the gun fired. I didn't see Turner when it fired. I had no control over the gun. It blew off the top of his scalp. When I looked, the man was lying full length with the top of his scalp torn off."

In his nearly seven hours on the stand, Wallace exonerated Herring Sivell and Henry Mobley. They, and two Negroes, had been charged together with Wallace, of Turner's murder.

Special Prosecutor Meyer Goldberg said the state was prepared to put several rebuttal witnesses on the stand in an effort to disprove some of the denials of Wallace's testimony.

The Evening Independent June 19, 1948
Dairymen Given Chair in Georgia Cremation Killing
Newnan, Ga - John Wallace, prosperous farmer-dairyman, is under sentence to die in the electric chair July 30 for the fatal beating of William Turner, his former share-cropper.

In convicting Wallace, 52, of murder, yesterday, the jury made no recommendation of mercy, which made the death penalty mandatory under Georgia law.

Wallace and four others were accused in the case which had 200 law enforcement officers combing three counties in search of a corpse. Turner's body was found on Wallace's 2000 acre plantation. The body had been tossed onto a funeral pyre, leaving for burial only a few charred bones.

In an unsworn statement, allowable under Georgia law, Wallace admitted slaying Turner, 24, with a shotgun blast; but claimed the shooting was accidental. He said he had quarreled with the farmhand over the manufacture of illicit whisky on his property and the theft of several cows. The state contended Wallace and other men chased Turner in an automobile across Meriwether County after Turner had been released from jail on cow theft charges.

At the end of the chase, witnesses said, Turner was beaten into unconsciousness and tossed into the back of his pursuer's car. That was the last seen of Turner until his bones were found on the pyre.

Three co-defendants - Tom Strickland, Herring Sivell and Henry Mobley - will be tried on murder charges in the case Monday. Wallace exonerated Sivell and Mobley in his statement to the court.

Chicago Daily Tribune June 19 1948
Georgia Plantation Owner Sentenced to die for murder

The Rock Hill Herald June 22, 1948 Tuesday
Three Get Life Sentences for Slaying Farmer
Newnan, Ga - Life sentences were given yesterday to three men charged with killing William Turner, a tenant farmer, John Wallace, operator of a large dairy farm, previously had been convicted and sentenced to die for the slaying. The state charged that Wallace and Herring Sivell followed Turner after he was released from Jail, beat him and threw his body in a well. Prosecutors claimed Turner's body later was burned in a fire pit on the Wallace farm.

Sivell, Henry Mobley and Tom Strickland were given life terms today after attorneys agreed to a consent verdict of murder without trial. Murder charges remain against three others and still another is charged with being an accessory.

Wallace told the jury he accidentally shot Turner with a shotgun while

144

trying to force a confession of cattle theft from him.

St. Petersburg Times June 23, 1948
Three Given Life terms for murder

Newnan, Ga - Three men were sentenced to life imprisonment yesterday for the murder of William Turner, a sharecropper. Their attorneys had agreed to a consent verdict without a trial.

Herring Sivell, Henry Mobley and Tom Strickland were given life terms. John Wallace, operator of a large dairy farm, was convicted of murder in the case last week and sentenced to die on July 30.

Attorneys for Wallace filed a motion for a new trial and Superior Court Judge Samuel J. Boykin set Aug. 14 for hearing the plea. The motion automatically stays Wallace's execution until after the hearing.

Talbotton New Era - June 24, 1948
Three Plead Guilty; Draw Life Terms in Turner Slaying

NEWNAN, Ga., JUNE 21 - Three men charged with helping John Wallace kill young William Turner were sentenced today to life imprisonment.

Counsel for Herring Sivell, Henry Mobley, and Tom Strickland agreed to a consent verdict of guilty of murder with a recommendation of mercy for each of the men, thus making the life term sentence mandatory.
Today, Wallace's attorneys entered a motion for new trial, and Circuit Judge Samuel J. Boykin set a hearing date for Aug. 14 at 11 a.m. This automatically stays the scheduled execution date of July 30 for Wallace.

Indicted With Wallace
The three men sentenced today were indicted jointly with Wallace for beating the young tenant farmer to death April 20, after they chased him from Meriwether county jail into Coweta County.

Testimony in last week's trial revealed that Turner's body was hidden in a deserted well on rented farm property in Meriwether county belonging to Wallace and was cremated shortly afterward in a swampy pit.

All three of the men sentenced today are well-to-do dairyman Sivell, 39, lives near Chipley in Harris county, is married and has three children. He also has an automobile dealership in Chipley.

Strickland, 61, a cousin of Wallace, lives in Meriwether County. He is married, but has no children. Mobley, 37, is a resident of Harris County and is also married with no children.

Two Negroes - Robert Lee Gates and Albert Brooks - charged with murder in the death of Turner, also probably will not be tried until the next term of court.

It is expected that the charges against them will be reduced to accessories after the fact.

Attorneys explain that the accessory after the fact charge is a misdemeanor offense, and Judge Boykin said the maximum sentence is 12 months.

The eighth man indicted in connection with the killing of Turner is Sheriff C. Hardy Collier of Meriwether county, who is charged with being an accessory before the fact.

Observers question, however, whether the aging law enforcement official will ever be brought to trial because of his ill health.

Some seats were empty in the courtroom today for the first time since the trials opened a week ago. The first 12 jurors called were impaneled. Court adjourned at 10:20 a.m.

Harris County Journal - June 24, 1948
Law Moves Swiftly in Newnan Trial; Wallace Sentenced to Chair; Three Go up For Life

NEWNAN, Ga. - Three defendants in the William Turner murder case agreed Monday to consent verdict of murder with recommendation for mercy and were immediately sentenced to imprisonment.

In less than ten minutes, a Coweta jury was impaneled and counsel for Herring Sivell, Henry Mobley, and Tom Strickland, charged with murder in the death of the young sharecropper, agreed to life sentences for each.

This action followed the drama-packed trial of John Wallace, prominent Meriwether county dairyman who was convicted Friday of murdering Turner and sentenced to die in the electric chair.

Wallace's attorneys have entered a motion for new trial, and Circuit Judge Samuel J. Boykin set a hearing date for Aug. 14 at 11 a.m. This automatically stays the scheduled execution date of July 30 for Wallace. The three men sentenced Monday were indicted jointly with Wallace for beating the young tenant farmer to death April 20 after they chased him from Meriwether county jail into Coweta County.

Testimony in last week's trial revealed that Turner's body was hidden in a deserted well on rented farm property in Meriwether county belonging to Wallace and cremated shortly afterward in a swampy pit.

All three of the men sentenced are well-to-do dairymen. Sivell, 39, lives near Chipley, in Harris county, is married and has three children.

Strickland, 61, a cousin of Wallace, lives in Meriwether County. He is married, but has no children. Mobley, 37, is a resident of Harris County and is also married with no children.

The wives of the three men, apparently resigned to the prison terms for their husbands, were expressionless as they talked with them before Sheriff A. Lamar Potts returned the defendants to Coweta jail after the sentences had been pronounced.

After conferring with defense counsel as the morning session opened, Solicitor General Luther M. Wyatt told the court, "the end of justice will be met to allow the defendants to. Consent to a verdict of guilty of murder, with recommendation of mercy."

The three were called before Judge Boykin and separately declined to make any statement. The judge said they would be confined to prison "for and during your natural life."

He reminded the defendants, however, that they would have the opportunity "to make amends for your crime" and appeal for parole. Under Georgia law, they would be eligible after seven years' imprisonment.

The Newnan Times-Herald   June 24, 1948
Photo Caption: THREE GET LIFE TERMS FOR SHARECROPPER"S DEATH -- Three men under sentence to life imprisonment for the murder of William Turner, a sharecropper, are led from the Coweta County courthouse at Newnan, Ga., by Sheriff Lamar Potts (extreme left) and a state trooper. The prisoners are Herring Sivell (at left behind the sheriff). Henry Mobley (right foreground), and Tom Strickland (at right beside state trooper). Judge Samuel J. Boykin sentenced them after they agreed to a consent verdict with a recommendation of mercy. Last week, John Wallace wealthy dairyman, was sentenced to death in the electric chair for participating in the slaying of young Turner. (AP Photo).

Sivell, Mobley and Strickland Plead Guilty; Get Life Sentences

Monday at 10am the gravel dropped to open the shortest session of the
Turner murder case at the Coweta County Court House since the opening
of court. It resulted in a life sentence for Herring Sivell, Henry Mobley
and Tom Strickland.

Advised by their attorneys, Sligh Howard, his son, Pierre, and Jack Allen,
the three made a plea of guilty whereupon the first panel of jurors gave a
verdict of guilty with a recommendation of mercy and they were
sentenced in a little over ten minutes.

Arrangements had previously been made with solicitor-General Luther
Wyatt and special prosecutor Myer Goldberg by the defense attorneys for
a recommendation of mercy if the defendants should plead guilty.

The September session of court will find C. H. Collier, Sheriff of
Meriwether County, on trial along with Mozart Strickland and the two
Negroes who testified against Wallace; Brooks and Gates.

Strickland, Gates and Brooks are presently held in the Coweta county jail.
Collier, who is ill, is out on $10,000 bond. The case of Mozart Strickland
has been postponed because of the mysterious disappearance of a witness,
Ted Turner, who is a Negro hand on the Strickland farm.
The notification for a new trial which was made by Gus Huddleston,
attorney for John Wallace, immediately after he received the death
sentence, has received some action. A hearing on the new trial request is
set for sometime in August.

The Newnan Times-Herald   June 24, 1948
WE COMMEND OUT COURTS (an editorial)

The major portion of the trial in the bizarre murder of William H. Turner
is over. Four men were indicted by the Grand Jury. Only one was
sentenced to death, the others entered pleas of guilty and were sentenced
to life imprisonment. Their pleas verified the side of the prosecution and
we rest with the confidence that justice has been upheld.

The murdered man and the accused were not residents of Coweta County,
but the crime having been committed here; it is set by law. We heartily
commend Sheriff Lamar Potts, his deputies, and the attorneys for the state
for the efficient manner in which the evidence was prepared and presented
to the Judge and jury. We are justly proud of the quiet manner in which
this all important trial was administered.

The county seat has been the scene of a most sensational murder case. Press wires were hot, mobile telephoto units were brought into play for coverage, and the lobbies and restaurants were filled with metropolitan journalists who were here to carry the story of the Wilson murder to thousands of readers.

With such attentions, this trial could easily have degenerated into a gaudy spectacle, a pageantry of tomfoolery in a circus atmosphere and a blight on our record, instead of typifying the dignity of justice. Guided by the steadfast manner of Judge Samuel J. Boykin, and the singlemindedness of the attorneys for both the prosecution and the defense who sought only to see that justice was administered, the trial now stands as a tribute and a credit to the law and the people of this community.

Talbotton New Era – July 15, 1948
Sheriff Collier Dies in Making Arrest of Man

GREENVILLE, July 12 – Hardy Collier, 64-year-old veteran indicted sheriff of Meriwether County, died near here Monday night as he was taking a man he had just arrested to his car.

Death came instantly from a heart attack, his doctor said.

His prisoner, John N. Wright, Woodbury, escaped when the sheriff fell dead but was captured little more than an hour later by state police six miles west of Greenville. Wright was wanted on a warrant charging drunkenness and threatening to murder.

Collier's death came just a month before he was to stand trial as an accessory before the fact in connection with the murder of William Turner in Neighboring Coweta county.

Collier had only the remainder of the year to serve as sheriff, having been defeated for re-election this summer by a 32-year-old war veteran.

He was to face trial in the Turner murder case in about a month. Collier was indicted by the Coweta county Grand Jury about two months ago, and was out at the present on a $10,000 bond.

John Wallace, Meriwether co., dairyman, already has been sentenced to death in the Turner case, and three other men, Herring Sevill, Henry Mobley of Chipley, and Tom Strickland, also of Meriwether have received life sentences and Wallace has entered an appeal.

Turner was killed at a Moreland tourist camp on April 12, 1948 when he was struck on the back of the head with a shotgun, Wallace having dealt the blow, testimony in Wallace's trial showed. His remains, only a handful of bone, were found 12 days later on Wallace's farm after the body had been burned in an old whiskey still pit on a pile of wood. Personal differences were blamed for the murder.

Sheriff Collier is survived by one brother, Jim Collier of Manchester. He was a widower, but had no children.

The Newnan Times-Herald   August 19, 1948
WALLACE HEARING RESET FOR SEPT. 10

The trial of John Wallace which was scheduled for Newnan Court House, Monday, August 9, was rescheduled for September 10, at 10am, according to Judge Samuel J. Boykin.

Gus Huddleston, attorney for the defense, stated that he had received final copies of the testimony the preceding Wednesday and the reports were so voluminous that the defense had not sufficient time to go over the records.

Over a thousand pages of testimony were recorded during the first trial. 150 pages of Wallace's statement alone on legal pages approximated 55,000 words. The Judge granted the postponement at the request of the defense.

Myer Goldberg, special prosecutor for the state, was in court and anxious to carry on. "I am not only ready but anxious to get on with the trial," said Goldberg, who appeared in court early Monday morning and had not been advised of the deferment. Goldberg was the sole representative of the state in the Court House Monday morning.

Harris County Journal – August 24, 1950
Wallace Told to Pay Wife of Slain Man

John Wallace, Meriwether county farmer facing electrocution, has been ordered to pay damages to the widow of Wilson Turner, in connection with whose death he was convicted of murder.

A Meriwether county Superior court jury Monday awarded Mrs. Wilson Turner $7,500 damages against Wallace and Herring Sivell, who is serving a life sentence in the slaying. Court officials said it did not matter whether the defendants "pay half and half or not."

Wallace received news of the verdict in his cell in Fulton Tower with blank amazement.

"I'm absolutely flat," the balding prisoner declared. "I'm devoid of funds to pay any part of it. Where I'm sitting now, I simply haven't any way of figuring out where to get any money.

"In fact," Wallace added with grim amusement, "I'm not too sure that I'm not entitled to some damages myself ... from what I've been through."

Mrs. Turner sued four men for $74,280, or two thousand dollars for each year of her husband's expected life. The jury dismissed the claim against two of the men, T.P. Strickland and Henry Mobley, both of whom are under life sentence for implication in the April, 1948, slaying.

The Manchester Mercury – August 24, 1950
Turner Widow Awarded $7,500 by Court Tues.
Greenville – The widow of Wilson Turner was awarded $7,500 damages against John Wallace, Meriwether county planter facing electrocution, and Herring Sivell, Chipley man who is serving a life sentence, by Meriwether County Superior Court Tuesday in the second day of its August session. The verdict for Mrs. Turner was made in connection with the slaying of her husband in April, 1948.

In his cell at Fulton Tower in Atlanta, Wallace declared that he was totally without funds to pay any part of the damages. Court officials said that it did not matter how the two defendants divided the damages between them.

Mrs. Turner sued four men for $74,280, or two thousand dollars for each of her husband's years of expected life. The jury dismissed the claim against two of the men, T.P. Strickland and Henry Mobley, both of whom are under life sentence for the slaying.

Bob Sparks, of Greenville, and Alton Parker, of Carrollton, represented Mrs. Turner and the defendants by Gus Huddleston and Jack Allen, of Greenville, and Mr. Tilly, of Atlanta.

A few minor cases and several divorce suits were disposed of Monday before the Turner-Wallace case was taken up.

A large crowd was present from all parts of the county for the court and they enjoyed a splendid barbecue dinner served on the courthouse grounds Monday by the ladies of the Greenville Methodist Church.
The grand jury returned a total of 50 "true" bills and eight "no" bills.

The Newnan Times-Herald   September 16, 1948
JUDGE TO REVEAL WALLACE DECISION

The sensational Coweta murder case of John Wallace vs the State of Georgia appeared on the newsstands this week in its first adaption in "Front Page Detecieve" and newstands in Coweta County cannot supply enough copies to last more than a few hours; the demand is so great. But subsequent developments promise to be even more sensational.

John Wallace, who was sentenced to die by electrocution on July 30th, won a reprieve when his attorneys entered a motion for a new trial. Scheduled for hearing August 10th, another postponement was granted when court recorders found the records so voluminous they could not be completed soon enough to give attorneys sufficient time to prepare their case.

Last Friday, the hearing finally took place quietly without crowds and fanfare at the court house and again no action was immediate. The defense presented Judge Samuel J. Boykin with a well-prepared amended motion for a new trial, together with records and briefs that will call for extra time before a decision can be handed down. The Judge asked the lawyers if they would like to indulge in oral debate. All declined.

Al Hinson, leading the battery of defense attorneys, then stated his foremost argument as being "the use of non-expert witnesses to prove scientific facts, and requested the Judge to give him additional time to do further counter-scientific research.

Judge Boykin granted this time and called for the defense and the prosecution to exchange their briefs by the 24th. After consideration, the Judge will then register his decision with the Clerk of Courts, Wallace Gray, in Coweta.

Over twenty pages of prepared document included 11 major points of contention by the defense. The first three concerned the testimony of Steve Smith. The fourth, fifth and sixth provisions were in refutation of the testimony given by Doctors Elliott, Tribble, and Kinnard, in reference to the blow which allegedly killed Turner.

Sections seven and eight had to do with the testimony of Mrs. Merle Hannah. Provisions nine and ten dealt with the photographs which were used as evidence in the trial. The final section discussed the courts allowing the ashes exhibited to influence the jury.

The written motion for a new trial quoted Steve Smith as having testified:

152

"From the force of that blow, the kind of weapon that was used, the conduct of the man before and after he was struck, the size of the man who struck him, and the force with which he was struck, it is my opinion that the blow that struck him back of his head was a mortal wound sufficient to cause death and did cause death."

The movant in his motion; who is John Wallace, then is quoted as having presented the following to the Judge: "Movant insists that the State depended solely upon the testimony of said non-expert witnesses and solely upon opinion-evidence of such witnesses to establish the allegations that the crime was committed in the county of Coweta, as charged in the indictment. And movant contends that a substantive fact, such as proof of venue, the same being a material and controlling allegation in the indictment, cannot be established solely upon the opinion-evidence of non-experts."

Regarding the discovery of the ashes and their presentment to the jury and court, the motion read: "the admission of said evidence was error beyond question, that it caused the jury to be confused with wholly extraneous" matter calculated to create in the minds the idea that some character of scientific precision, beyond the ken of ordinary minds, had fixed guilt upon him and tended to magnify the state's case and vault if above ordinary cases; that it confused the jury by creating a maize of riddles and to them wonders of science, particularly since the very admission of the same was calculated to cause them to suppose that highly scientific techniques not understandable by ordinary laymen had approbation of the law and the courts; that somehow, the court could fathom, if they could not, the weird and seemingly unnatural thing of scattering a handful of ashes in a flowing stream, then a few days later, find them all huddled together again 100 yards downstream isolated from other muck and dust."

Judge Boykin said he would consider this amended motion for a new trial, along with the additional briefs under preparation by both the prosecution and the defense, will pass on them the early part of October. There will be no further court sessions.

The Newnan Times-Herald   October 21, 1948
WALLACE CASE REACHES HIGH COURT NOV. 15th

The case of the State of Georgia versus John Wallace has been assigned for argument before the Supreme Court in Georgia, according to Myer Goldberg, well known local attorney and special prosecutor in the Wallace case, who was notified of the date this week. It is scheduled to begin on November 15th.

Colonel Goldberg and the attorneys for the defendant, Gus Huddleston of Greenville and Al Henson of Atlanta, will appear before the Supreme Court on that date to begin their arguments. It is expected that the Court will render final decision on the case approximately ten days thereafter.

The Newnan Times-Herald Jan 13, 1949
WALLACE DEATH SENTENCE UPHELD

The Supreme Court of Georgia Tuesday afternoon unanimously upheld the death sentence of John Wallace, wealthy Meriwether county farmer.

Wallace was convicted and sentenced to die in the electric chair for slaying William H. Turner (alias Wilson Turner) in Coweta County.

In affirming the verdict of the Coweta county Superior Court, the Supreme Court said: "it was not error to admit the opinion evidence of the expert and non-expert witnesses; and the jury was authorized to find that the final injuries of the deceased were inflicted upon him by the defendant in Coweta County."

Wallace testified that he "accidentally shot" Turner to "bluff him into telling me where my stolen cows were." He claimed that the slaying happened in Meriwether County, instead of Coweta County, as the state charged and where he was tried. The case was described as "a lynching" in the 1948 lynching report by Tuskegee institute.

The Newnan Times-Herald   Feb 3, 1949
GIVEN 30 DAY RESPITE

Governor. Herman Talmadge Wednesday granted a 30-day stay of execution to John Wallace, Meriwether county farmer convicted of slaying William Turner, his tenant farmer.

The governor acted upon the request of the State Pardon and Parole Board which said it needed that time to hear an appeal by Wallace's attorneys.

Wallace was to die in the electric chair February 11.

Newnan Times-Herald - October 26, 1950
Wallace Denied Commutation of Death Sentence

The State Pardon and Parole Board Wednesday refused to commute the death sentence of John Wallace, Meriwether County farmer for the 1948 slaying of Wilson Turner, a tenant farmer. The board's action was unanimous.

A desperate last-ditch stand for his life was made earlier this week as Wallace's attorneys, Guy Huddleston and Al Henson, pled for the second time since last February for commutation of sentence of life imprisonment.

Earlier, both attorneys had charged that unfavorable publicity from "biased newspapers" had brought about Wallace's conviction.
Both Wright Lipford, solicitor general, and Myer Goldberg, special prosecutor, said Wallace was treated and tried fairly in Coweta County, and there was no truth to charges that evidence was suppressed in the case.

Monday, Goldberg told the board: "It would be a crime equivalent to the crime of Wallace if he were ever turned out on the public again."
Lipford declared that if the sentence was commuted, "we might as well abolish the Superior Courts of Georgia, the Supreme Court of Georgia, and the Supreme Court of the United States."

Wallace is slated to die in the electric chair November 3.

The following are from the Troup County, Georgia newspapers, LaGrange Daily News

LaGrange Daily News - October 25, 1950
Wallace is Turned Down In Bid to Escape Death

ATLANTA, Oct. 25 - (UP) - John Wallace, once-wealthy Meriwether County farmer, was turned down by the State Pardons and Parole Board today in what apparently was his last hope of escaping death in the electric chair for the 1948 slaying of a tenant farmer.

The board refused to rescind or amend its order of last year that Wallace be electrocuted for the "premeditated" murder of Wilson Turner.

Wallace had fought through every legal means at the disposal of American citizens, and is [sic] so doing had exhausted his personal fortune, in an effort to keep from taking those few steps from the Tattnall prison death cell to the electric chair.

Just last week, the United States Supreme Court refused to intervene in his case. Prior to that appeal to the nation's highest tribunal, Wallace had sought three times to have the Georgia State Supreme Court grant him a writ of habeas corpus. His entire appeal was based on the claim that his conviction stemmed from "perjured testimony" by two witnesses. He charged they were induced by Coweta County Sheriff Lamar Potts to give "wholly false" testimony.

UNANIMOUS
Parole Board Chairman Ed Everett said today's decision was unanimous and was made after a study of evidence at a hearing two days ago.
The 1949 order said that Wallace was guilty of murder, that "the slaying was premeditated rather than accidental," that there were no "extenuating or mitigating" circumstances and that Wallace was denied none of his constitutional rights at his trial.

After last week's Supreme Court decision not to consider the case, Wallace's lawyers said the pardons and parole board was their last avenue of hope. Wallace's execution is set for Nov. 3.

The Turner murder was a sensation in the spring of 1948. The setting was the Sunset Tourist Camp south of Newnan. A dozen persons were idling about the camp when a car drove up and a harried figure jumped out and sought shelter in the camp office. A pickup truck raced up and four or five men jumped out. The occupants seized the man, according to witnesses, clubbed him savagely about the head with a rifle butt and drove off with his inert body in the truck.

Wallace was identified by eyewitnesses who testified he was the ring leader of the abduction group. Other witnesses identified the victim of the attack as Turner who was then found to be missing from the farm where he worked. A search was started for Turner. Two Negroes living in the area led Sheriff Potts and state officers to a spot where charred fragments of clothing and pieces of burned bone were found.

The bones were identified as human and the clothing as Turner's.
The Negroes who led to the discovery, identified as Robert Lee Gates and Albert Brooks, then admitted they helped burn the sharecropper's body.
At Wallace's trial he admitted killing Turner but said he did it in self defense.

LaGrange Daily News - November 1, 1950
Time Running Out for John Wallace

REIDSVILLE, Nov. 1 (UP) - Time was running out today for John Wallace, Meriwether County planter and convicted slayer of tenant farmer Wilson Turner. Sometime Friday before high noon, Wallace is scheduled to walk from his death cell in Tattnall prison to a straight-backed electric chair. Wallace's lawyers are trying desperately to pull something from their bag of legal maneuvers that will stave off his execution once more. They have been successful several times since Wallace's conviction and sentence for the 1948 slaying.

The convicted man, however, apparently has resigned himself to death. Tattnall Warden Robert Balkcom said Wallace is "peaceful and calm." He still maintains that he is innocent of willful murder although he has admitted killing Turner "in self defense."

Balkcom said three Protestant ministers spent several hours with Wallace yesterday. His only other visitors, the warden said, have been business associates. Wallace, once considered a wealthy man, has spent most of his fortune trying to escape execution.

The LaGrange Daily News - November 3, 1950
John Wallace Executed in Electric Chair by William M. Bates

REIDSVILLE, Ga. Nov. 3 - (UP) - John Wallace, Meriwether County cattleman and farmer, died in Georgia's electric chair today with prayer on his lips for those who had failed to grant him clemency.

The stocky, 54-year-old condemned man walked firmly and calmly into the death chamber at Georgia State prison here, knelt before the white-painted electric chair and prayed for "our good Governor on whom I had placed my hope for life" and the state pardon and parole board, which twice refused his plea for clemency.

Gov. Herman Talmadge was never asked formally to act on Wallace's case. A spokesman said the Governor could act only on a recommendation from the Pardon and Parole Board, which did not relay such to Talmadge in this instance.

Wallace was convicted of the murder of William Turner, his ex-tenant farmer, in 1948. He staved off the death penalty for more than two years with intricate legal maneuvering, and said in a death-cell interview this morning that he had spent everything he had in the fight.

Wallace was led into the death chamber at 10:36 a.m., EST. A single jolt of electricity was turned into his body at 10:43 and he was pronounced dead six minutes later.

Warden Robert Balkcom said Wallace was "the calmest man in the death chamber I have seen in 11 years of penal work."

After he knelt in prayer, Wallace sat down in the electric chair and the Rev. W.L. Higgins, prison chaplain, held his hand and recited the 23rd Psalm - "The Lord Is My Shepherd ."

LOVED EVERYBODY
Wallace's last words were "Goodby, [sic] men, I love everybody. I know I'm on my way to Heaven."

He spoke them - and the prayer that preceded [sic] - in a clear, firm voice that did not crack or break.

About 40 persons witnessed the execution. Among witnesses to the execution were several life-long friends of Wallace, but no members of his immediate family. No relatives of Turner, the victim, were present.

Wallace maintained to the last that he was not guilty of murder. In a death-cell interview less than three hours before he died, the stocky, bald, 54-year-old condemned man admitted shooting Turner accidentally, but he denied that he intended to harm him, that he struck Turner a mortal blow, or that he destroyed Turner's body, as the state charged.

"I am facing death for a crime I never committed at any time, at any place or in any manner," Wallace said. "I was convicted on perjured testimony." A reporter asked if he would be afraid to face Turner in heaven. "If I saw Turner anywhere, I would not be afraid to face him," Wallace replied firmly.

NO CLEMENCY
Wallace's execution came only after he had executed every possible legal avenue for clemency or a new trial. Twice he carried his plea to the U.S. Supreme Court and twice he appealed to the state board of pardons and paroles. All were denied, but the process caused five postponements in his scheduled execution. Wallace was led into the death chamber by Warden Balkcom, Deputy Warden W. T. Wallace and the Rev. W.L. Higgins, prison chaplain.

At his own request, Wallace's body will be embalmed at Metter, Ga., instead of at the prison. Funeral services will be held at the Chipley, Ga., Methodist church at 3 p.m. tomorrow. Wallace will be buried at Chipley. From the beginning, the murder case of William Turner was a weird and tangled story.

SPRING OF '48

It broke in the spring of 1948, at the Sunset Tourist Camp in Coweta County south of Newnan, Ga., about 40 miles below Atlanta. A dozen persons were idling about the camp when a hurried figure jumped from a car and sought shelter in the camp office. A moment later a pickup truck arrived and five men jumped out, seized the fugitive, clubbed him savagely on the head with a rifle butt and drove off with his inert body in the truck. Witnesses later identified Wallace as the leader of the group and swore that the blows were enough to kill the victim. They identified the victim as Wilson Turner, a tenant on Wallace's farm.

After a long search, officers found on Wallace's farm charred fragments of clothing and several small pieces of burned bone. They were identified as the remains of Wilson Turner. Wallace was brought to trial. Turner's father startled the court by announcing that Wilson Turner was alive and well. It turned out that the bones belonged to a brother, William Turner, who had assumed Wilson Turner's identity and draft card during the war. Wallace finally admitted that he shot Turner, but said it occurred on his farm in Meriwether County.

LaGrange Daily News - November 3, 1950
John Wallace Dies; Funeral Set Tomorrow

John Wallace, 54, former Meriwether County farmer, died at 10:49 a.m. today. Funeral services will be held at 3 p.m. tomorrow at the Chipley Methodist Church with Dr. Charles Allen, pastor of the Grace Methodist Church of Atlanta, officiating. Burial will be in the Chipley cemetery with Holmes Clements, Roy Askew, Roy Harrell, Otis Cornett, Harvey Anderson and Pope Davis serving as pallbearers.

Mr. Wallace is survived by his wife, Mrs. Josephine Leath Wallace of Meriwether County, a sister, Mrs. J. W. Mozeley of Atlanta; an uncle, Mozart Strickland of Meriwether County; and an aunt, Mrs. Louie Harrell of West Point. Mr. Wallace was born in Meriwether County and had lived there most of his life. He was a member of the Chipley Methodist Church, a member of the Chipley Lodge, F and AM, and was a veteran of World War I. Maddox Funeral Home is handling arrangements.

~~~~~~~~~~~~~~~~~~~~~~~~~~~~~~~

In 1995 it was reported as:

The trial in the Newnan courthouse was a 10-day wonder.

In actuality it appears to have been a five-day wonder.

View from the Meriwether courthouse to the jail and vice versa.   The health center blocking the view was built in 1951.

A view showing the streets surrounding the courthouse.

The Old Meriwether Jail

Chapter Seven

The Trial

The State vs John Wallace   June 14, 1948

1pm after recess the jury is drawn

First witness: Mrs. William Turner

She states that her husband was William H. Turner but he stated his name was Wilson. The first time she met John Wallace was when her husband went down there from Carrollton. "That is before we moved to his place, went down from Millard Reeves and bought some hogs from him, and I went down there with him to get them.

q. Did you later move down there on the defendant's place?

a. Yes, sir, that was two years ago, this past October. We moved away the last of November or the first of December two years after that.

q. Why did you move from John Wallace's place?

a. My husband said John Wallace threatened to kill him. That's what he told me. Wallace told me - said that my husband ought to have had better sense than to have got O. C. Hataway to move the still for him over on the other place. I told him I didn't know anything about it. He said O.C. Hataway would talk, and he was not going back to the State penitentiary, that he had already been out twice and he was out under twenty years suspended sentence, and that is what he said, and I said. "I wish if you had anything to say about it, say it to my husband" and he nodded to me and he said he was.

q. What was in the barn? Did he tell you anything about that?

a. No sir

the witness is excused but will be called back
****

Call Earl H. Lucas, investigator of the alcohol tax unit, treasury department.

Direct Examination

"On October 22 John Wallace and I had a rather lengthy conversation and he stated that Turner was causing him a lot of worry, and was making liquor all around him all over his place, and he could not do anything with him. He said that he thought about killing him several times, and on one occasion met him in the road up there and he had his wife with him, and said he could not go through with it. He felt like killing him at that time, but his wife looked so pitiful he couldn't do it. Mr. Wallace told me that Turner had been threatening him.

Cross Examination

By Mr. Henson: Did you talk about the threats at that time that Turner had made all over the county about Wallace?

a. Yes, we did.

q. And each one of them was talking about shooting the other?

a. Well, I didn't talk with Turner. I don't know what he had to say about it. Mr. Wallace there did talk to me about Turner threatening him.

q. Yes. Did Mr. Wallace at that time tell you about Turner stealing his

cattle?
a. No, sir.

q. Did he mention any cattle stealing?

a. No but he did say that in spite of everything he could do that Turner was making liquor on his place and he could not stop him. He told me that they had to pull Turner off the train at Greenville to keep him from killing Wallace. Wallace was worried about the man, always said this: he had been to the penitentiary twice about making whiskey and said he didn't want to go again, and it looked like Turner was going to send him back to the penitentiary. He said he was not in the liquor business and had absolutely quit. He told me that Turner was making the whiskey.

q. You didn't make any cases against Wallace?

a. We have now, since this occurred. Wallace had promised the Federal Judge that he was going to quit, and he wanted to be sure that there was no more whiskey made on his farm and that he didn't want to go back to the penitentiary, and that is the reason he reported this. He wanted the liquor business broke up, he said, because his best friends thought he was in the liquor business, and he was not. I talked to Mr. Wallace near LaGrange about a year and a half ago. I talked to him on October 22 and a few days later. I don't recall the exact date. I went there with a special investigator, and John and Mozart Strickland was there in the yard.

q. When you heard about Wallace's being charged with the Turner murder then it was after that you went back and found some liquor was it not?

a. Yes. We developed his conspiracy case after that.

q. Why would you do that? You did all your developing after they jumped on John Wallace here about this occurrence down in Meriwether County, didn't you?

a. Well, the case was assigned to special investigator Swan. It is not my job to develop a conspiracy case. It is assigned to a special agent. I furnished all the facts I had in connection with it, and I sat down the next day after I talked to him and wrote the office and made my report on it. There was no warrant issued until recently.

q. Now after all this happened and John Wallace was connected with it through the newspapers, then it was that you went down there and begun to, as you say, develop your facts?

a. I said I didn't develop the case at all. Special Investigator Swan did. I assisted in it. Furnished some of the evidence and facts.

q. Why did you wait until after this occurred, and who did you talk to after its occurrence that caused you to go down there?

Interrupted by the Court: What does that have to do with this case?

By Mr. Henson: It shows interest or want of interest in this witness.

By The Court: I disagree. Don't follow that line of questioning. You may ask him any question with reference to his interest in the case or what prompted his entry, but anything that transpired after Mr. Wallace was charged with this crime, I rule out.

By Solicitor Wyatt: We have no objection to the defense going into that.

By The Court: We will be here for just about a month if you do that. Go ahead.

By Mr. Henson: As a matter of fact, Your Honor, it doesn't appear that any of his testimony is relevant up to this time.

By The Court: I am inclined to agree with you.

By Mr. Henson: All right now, Mr. witness, isn't it true that you went down to John's place with a man named Bob Hart? Was it Bob Carter that was in this conversation at LaGrange?

a. No, sir. It was at a filling station somewhere between LaGrange and Chipley. I don't recall where it was. I didn't know John Wallace at that time, and Mr. Carter --

q. When was it they gave you this thermos jug full of cool water?

a. That was the day or night we watched this big still that John reported.

q. He gave you a drink?

a. Yes, sir.

q. And that is the still John wanted you to get off of his place?

a. It was not on his place. It was one he wanted destroyed.

164

q. When?

a. In this conspiracy case.

q. That was after this trouble?

a. Yes sir

q. Do you remember telling Mr. Wallace about this taxi driver that was hauling liquor from Turner's house and selling it?

a. Yes sir. I remember talking to him about Bill Ernest, the taxi driver. He said he was hauling a woman that was working there in Chipley. That was his explanation of that.

RE DIRECT EXAMINATION

By Solicitor Wyatt: Do you know when this work started on the conspiracy case?

a. It started that day. The day I seized the still, which was October 23, 1947.

q. What still did this conspiracy involve?

a. It involved this distillery we seized on Oct 23 1947.

q. The one Wallace pointed out?

a. Yes

q And the distillery that he accused Turner of operating?

a. Yes

q. Now you say you found another distillery there in February?

a. Yes sir

q. Where was that still with reference to the defendant's property?

a. It was about 50 yards south of his property line, according to what he said.

q. Is that distillery involved in the conspiracy also?

a Yes

(witness excused)
****

Testimony of Mr. E. R. Threadgill - chief of Police of the city of Carrollton in Carroll County

I first saw John Wallace on Wednesday night of April 13th and again on the following Sunday I believe that was the 17th. I had arrested Wm Turner and me and John Wallace was up there talking to him. He says "Me and Mr. John Wallace used to make liquor" and I told Turner then, I said "Turner, we are not interested in the liquor business now; we are hunting cow. We left. We got down in the lobby of the jail about the front door, and somebody, the boy in the jail I believe, Junior Thompson, hollered and said Wilson Turner wanted to talk to Mr. Wallace, and Mr. Wallace went back up, but he was not gone but a minute or two.

q. What happened after that?

a. We drove back out to the city hall, and Mr. Wallace asked me if it was all right for him to call the sheriff down home to come and get Turner. It was close to twelve, midnight on Sunday night. Sheriff Collier was there about 3 to 3:30 later that morning, Monday morning the 19th of April. They took Turner and his truck back to Meriwether. They came back to Carrollton about eleven o'clock that same day to find the cow.

We went back over where they found the cow tied the night before, and Mr. Wallace and me tracked the cow back across the field where they moved her from. It was about 2 o'clock when they left with the cow. I didn't see them after that. Mr. Collier told me that he didn't know whether he could convict him or not in Meriwether county, and I told Mr. Collier that as much evidence as we had on him I didn't think there was a jury in Carroll County that would turn him loose on me with that much evidence.

q. Did you see them again on Tuesday, April 20th?

a. A few minutes after five.

q. What time did the sheriff and Wallace leave with Turner to take him back to Meriwether?

a. I could not say what time they left.

166

q. What did Sheriff Collier say to you on Tuesday April 20[th?]

a. He had talked to the solicitor and decided that they didn't have enough evidence to convict him in Meriwether County and would I prosecute him in Carroll County and he would turn him loose. Wallace didn't have much to say.

CROSS EXAMINATION

By Mr. Henson: You told the Sheriff that you had plenty of evidence to convict him in Carroll County, as a matter of fact you found where he had stolen the cow and brought it to Carroll County, didn't you?

a. Yes sir. Mr. Wallace brought up the cows registration to show it's pedigreed.

Registration paper is marked D for identification

By Mr. Henson: State to the jury whether the cow had been stolen and how you know it.

a. Somebody called on Monday morning, the 12th of April, and gave me a description of two cows that had been taken from Mr. Wallace's farm. I found one there in Carrollton.

q. Did Turner admit to stealing the cow from Mr. Wallace?

a. Yes sir

q. How many other cows did he say he had stolen from Mr. Wallace?

a. Two of them. I never did see the other one, but the other one left there a few days -- well, she had gone when I caught Turner, I found out later.

q. Turner was in your custody or the Sheriff's custody over there? The sheriff of your county.

a. He was in the county jail.

q. Was he there as your prisoner?

a Yes sir

q. And you told them that you would let them take him back provided they brought a warrant.

a. Yes sir

q. Later did you turn Turner over to the sheriff of Meriwether County?

a. I was at home well, I was fixing to go to bed when they called me and said the sheriff was there, and I told them to let them have him, told Mr. Wallace if Sheriff Collier had the warrant to take him back and he said, I suppose he has; I told him to get a warrant and come get him. I didn't see him take him back but I was under the impression he took him back.

q. Do you know a chap named Windham?

a. No sir. I found where a boy by the name of Tommy Windham was connected, but I would not know him if I were to see him.

q. How about a man named Rigsby?

a. Yes sir.

q. Do you know anything about their connection with this fellow Turner in the theft of a large number of cows?

a. It seemed Rigsby and Windham was connected with Turner.

q. How many cows did you find stolen by this gang?

a. Well that's hard to say. I have got a report and description on several.

q. About how many?

The prosecutor and court interrupts refusing to allow the question

q. How many were Wallace's?

a. Two at this time.

q. How many at other times?

a. It seems there was one and a call before.

q. How long a period of time did this cow stealing cover?

a It must have been for sometime. I could not answer.

q. Would you say two months or three?

a. It had been that long.

q. Three months
a Yes sir

q And you continually got these complaints for three months?

a Yes sir. I would not say just how long, but for some time back.

q. And they were identified as Mr. Wallace's cows?

a Yes sir. These two.

q. Stolen by Turner?

a Yes sir

RE DIRECT EXAMINATION

q. Did you help Mr. Wallace locate his cows?

a. We watched one of the cows for practically a week.

q. What did Turner do with reference to leaving your automobile?

a. Turner, when we first arrested him, he tried to get away, run back in the truck and had a little fracas, but after we got a hold of him he begun to tell me, said "get me away from here, they would kill me, and I began to want to know who was with him, and he kept looking back across the hill.

q. What did he do after Wallace got there?

a. The first time I seen Mr. Wallace I drove up on the square with Turner in the car, and there were four policemen there, two in the car and two on the ground. I told them to come get the boy and put him in the county jail, and when I looked around, Turner jumped out and ran when I turned around talking to the police, and I ran him around in the alley and caught him.

q. Was Mr. Wallace there at the time?

a. Mr. Wallace came up just as we caught Turner.

169

q. Just as you caught him?

a Yes sir. That is the first time I had seen him, that night

witness excused

****

Archie Hodges sworn in

q. Were you in the Carrollton Carroll county jail when Wilson Turner was put in there?

a. Yes sir.

q. Did you see Mr. Wallace come in?

a. He came in there somewhere around one or one thirty at night on Sunday night.

q. What did Wallace say and what did Turner say?

a. Well, Turner -- Wallace was talking to Turner about the cow, claimed that Turner stole his cow, and Turner said he didn't steal no cow. He said he thought it was a gang up on him to kill him, he had been threatened.

q. What is that?

a. He said he had already been threatened by him to kill him, and he thought it was a gang up to kill him.

q Who said that?

a. Turner to Mr. Wallace.

q. What did he say?

a. Well, he was trying to get Mr. Wallace to turn him out.

q. What?

a, Trying to get Mr. Wallace to turn him out of jail, said he didn't want to go to Greenville.

q. Didn't want to go to Greenville?

a. No, Mr. Wallace said he was going to carry him back to Greenville, and he didn't want to go. He said he was scared to go to Greenville jail, it was a gang up on him to kill him. Turner told Wallace that if he didn't turn him out the next morning he was going to tell them about that big still he had on his place. He said you know you have 300 sacks of sugar working now. Wallace said if that is all you have to tell them, I don't want to hear nothing. About 3 or 3:30 in the morning the sheriff come from Greenville up there and got him. Turner was asleep. Me and Junior Thompson woke him up. The sheriff didn't come up in the jail.

CROSS EXAMINATION

By Mr. Henson:
q. Archie, what were you in jail for?

a. Well, that has nothing to do in this case. I was just in jail.

By The Court: Wait a minute. If that happens again I will have to clear the court room. Now I have no objection to you smiling, but if that happens again I will clear the court room. All right, go ahead.

q. So you don't want to tell the jury how often you go to jail nor what they put you in jail for?

a. Well, it is not concerning this case.

q. I am afraid I will have to ask you to tell. Did you steal something?

a. No sir, they had me accused of persuading under aged children out of the county.

q. How many times have you been in jail for stealing?

a. Nary a time, no sir. I was put in a month for drunk.

q. How old were you the first time they put you in jail?

a. About five or six years ago.

q. Where do you live when you are not in jail?

a. LaGrange for the past six months. I lived in Heard County before that with Wigley.

171

q. What made you leave Grady?

a. Just because I wanted to.

q. Are you sure that is it, or because Grady wanted you to?

a. Because I wanted to.

q. Are you still in jail over at Carrollton?

a. No sir. I had a trial over there and come clear.

q. So you are between jail terms now. And you talked to Turner about the cows?

a. Yes sir. Turner told Chief Threadgill that this gang of cattle thieves were liable to kill him.

q. He wanted Mr. Wallace to sort of protect him from this gang he was stealing cattle with?

a. He didn't want to go back to Greenville, and Mr. Wallace wanted to carry him back to Greenville.

q. Do you tell this jury he was afraid Wallace would kill him, and yet wanted Wallace to turn him out and go off with him?

a. He didn't want him to take him to Greenville, said they would gang up to kill him.

q. Which gang?

a. He didn't say.

q. Did you hear Turner tell the officers about stealing cows?

a. No sir. He said he never stole cows.

q. You know he took him to the cows that had been stolen?

a. No sir. The Chief said he stole the cow, and said he had been watching the cow for a week, and he asked him why he didn't get him there when he put the cow there.

q. Who have you talked to about the case?

a. Nobody

q. Not a soul on earth? They didn't know what you were going to swear?

a. Yes, I told the law here what I was going to tell.

q. When did you tell this law here?

a. I told them after I got out of jail.

q. When?

a. Right after I got out of jail in Carrollton.

q. What gang was threatening to kill him?

a. He said he never stole no cow, never had stole a cow in his life. I heard him tell Mr. Wallace that.

q. How many of you boys -- while he was telling you that did you tell him you never did lure any children away?

a. I did not.

q. All you boys got together and told how innocent you were?

a. No sir. They taken me out of the bull pen pretty soon after they put him in, away from him.

q. Are you pretty sure that Turner asked Mr. Wallace to take him out of jail?

a. Yes, sir, asked him to have him turned out the next morning.

q. Did you hear any talk between him and the sheriff?

a. No sir. they were down -- the sheriff was downstairs, and I was up on the run around. I didn't go down. I don't know what was said.

q. Do you know Mr. Threadgill, the Chief of Police, over there?

a. No sir but they told me who he was.

q. What did Threadgill tell Turner and what did Turner tell him?

a. Threadgill told Turner that he had been watching him for a week and saw him put the cow there. Turner told him he didn't steal a cow, asked him why he didn't get him then when he saw him put the cow there.

q. Did you know Turner before you met in jail?

a. Yes sir

q. And you knew his kinfolks named Windham?

a. Yes sir

q. They were the ones that had some of these cows that had been stolen?

a. I don't know about that

q. Didn't you hear Threadgill tell Turner that?

a. No sir

q. Did you hear Turner tell Threadgill he found the cows at Windhams?

a. No sir

q. When is the last time you have been down to visit the Turner people and Windhams, etc?

a. I have not visited them. I have seen them in LaGrange.

q. Over in LaGrange?

a. Yes sir

q. And talked with them?

a. Yes sir. I talked with them.

q. Who suggested that you come up here and testify? Did you volunteer?

a. I don't know how I got over -- how the news got over here to this law here that I knew it, was in jail
q. but the first thing you know, they came after you

a. Yes sir

q. When did you get out of jail?

a. I got out on Tuesday after the day Turner was killed.

q. That has been about a month and half?

a. That was the day Turner got killed.

q. You have just been out two weeks?

a. I had been in jail two weeks the day I got out.

q. But you have been out about a month and a half?

a. I don't remember what day it was. It was the day Turner got killed.

q. Since you have been out what have you been doing?

a. I cotton milled up to two or three weeks ago. I quit because I wanted to. Didn't want to work.

q. You know how to live without work?

a. Yes sir, I think so. I live here and there. Get a meal from someone.

q. Are you any kin to these Turners?

a. I am a little kin to his wife in a way, by marriage. Turner's wife's mother was my wife's sister.

q. Well, that is the reason you came up here to swear in this case?

a. No sir, it was not.

the witness is excused

****

Willie Page Puckett drives a truck for a living

Direct Examination by Solicitor Wyatt:

q. Were you riding in a truck on the morning of April 20 between Greenville and Sunset tourist camp here in Coweta County?

a. Yes sir. It was round 11:30 in the morning. Been over delivering feed. for the company I work for, Puritan Mills.

q. Who was driving the truck in which you were riding?

a. A Negro

q. A colored boy?

a. Yes sir

q. Now I will ask you to state whether or not you met any cars on that road under unusual circumstances?

a. Well, no sir. I meet them driving that way every day.

q. What car did you first meet that you noticed?

a. The first thing I met was a truck doing about 60 miles a hour. There was a car following in about a hundred yards. It looked to be traveling about the same speed. I recognized Mr. Sivell. I've known him for 20 to 25 years. I would not swear it was his car but he was driving it. Behind this car was another car going in the same direction toward the Sunset Tourist Camp. Henry Mobley was in the third car. I've known him about 18 years. I did not see anyone else in any of the vehicles.

Witness is excused.
****

recess called at 3:30 p.m.
****

next witness Miss Mahaley Lancaster

Direct Examination by Solicitor Wyatt:

She states she lives in Heard County, Franklin Rt 3 about ten miles measured from where they are currently at. She states she knows John Wallace that he came to visit her three times. That he threatened to kill Wilson Turner.

q. Why did Wallace come to your house?

a. Said he lost two cows and bought them in South Carolina, and they cost him $3,200.00 and he wanted me to tell him where he could find the cows, said one was a milker and the other one was dry, and I said, "Turner, I said, "Carrollton, GA, it was in a pasture up there, carried there on a truck, and there was some paint or something put about the truck to keep down identification, and the truck that hauled the cows --, and he informed me he was going to Carrollton that night, and said if he found the cow and Turner he was going to kill him. I said, "don't say that; that is a violation of the law, somebody was to meet you in the road and threatened a life like that, it would be a dead man down there. I said "don't say that?

q. He came there twice about the cows?

a. Yes sir

q. Did he ever come there about anybody else later?

a. Yes, something about finding a dead body somewhere. Something about finding a dead body somewhere named Turner and wanted to know would the body ever be located. He said Turner, and said Turner had lived about him for sometime, and he had a difference and said Turner moved away.

q. And he wanted to know whether that body would be located or not?

a. Yes, sir. I told him it was in a well and green flies was around it.

q. Why was he coming to you and asking you that? What business are you engaged in?

a. He was having trouble. My business is fortune astrology and scientific reading.

q. Scientific reading of the palm, commonly referred to as fortune telling?

a. Yes sir. I don't call it fortune telling. Some people do but I don't.

q. What did he say about the body, Miss Mahaley?

a. He wanted to know where it would be located at.

q. Did he tell you where it was?

a. No, he wanted to know himself.

q. Did he mention a well while he was talking to you?

a. I did to him, and told him there was some nails and green flies there, and they were taking the body out and putting it on a horse's back off of the farm where it was at, and muddied it somewhat so it would not be identified or fingerprints found on the horse.

CROSS EXAMINATION

By Mr. Henson: q. I didn't get your name awhile ago.

a. Well, I would not especially care for my name to get in politics anymore.

q. You think it was in politics?

BY THE COURT; Go ahead and give him your name.

a. It is Miss M-a-y-h-a-y-l-e-y

q. H-a-y-l-e-y

a. L-a-n-c-a-s-t-e-r

q. Caster

a. Lancaster. It is an English name

q. Lancaster. Now you are what folks call a fortune teller

a. I don't like that. I don't care for that so much

q. I know you don't, but us folks that don't know the scientific name, we have to call it that.

a. Really I am called an oracle of the ages. We were born that way. We were not made like school teachers.

q. You were born that way, and you have been an oracle of the ages ever since you were born?

a. Yes

q. And you knew exactly where Turner's body was didn't you?

a. Well, I didn't see it.

q. I know, but you knew?

a. I told the man where it was at.

q. You don't have to see anything to know where it is or what it is do you?

a. Well--

q. Now an oracle of the ages can tell these things just in mind, just out of a clear atmosphere?

a. I don't know so much about that.

q. You did that didn't you?

a. Well --

q. You told right where the man was just by closing your eyes and letting a vision come to you?

a. No, I didn't close my eyes. I kept my eyes open.

q. But you did have to have a vision come to you?

a. No, not so much.

q. Well now, just how does the mind of an oracle of the ages work?

a. Well --

q. How do you know all these things?

a. The wise forseeth and hideth himself.

q. And that's how you got all this information? You are just the wise forseeth, and hideth the information? Is that what an oracle of the ages does?

a. I do many things. I buy oxens and mules.

q. Now did these officers come to you to get their information?

a. Considerably few of them.

q. And the info that they have got there they got it from you?

a. I don't know about that.

q. How many of them went to you? Did Mr. Goldberg come to you to find out just exactly what the truth of it was?

a. I would not know Mr. Goldberg

q. This handsome young gentleman over here, did he come to find out the whole story about this?

a. There was some men over there. I would not testify on oath that was him.

q. Look at him. Did he come?

a. I remember seeing him, but I don't remember talking with him.

q. He came and got from you the info about this case?

a. Well, there was one man named Hancock, but I do not know where he come from.

q. Mr. Hancock?

a. And another man. -- by the name of -- he was a deputy sheriff sometime, and he now lives in LaGrange.

q. Look at this gentleman twirling the hat before you. Did he come and get his info from you?

a. Well, I would not say, because there is so many of them, Mister, I could not keep up with them.

q. Look at him good. How many times did he come to find out about this affair?

a. Well, I didn't keep up with it this time.

q. You didn't keep up with it?

a. No sir

q. Do you know the prosecuting attorney over here?

a. Yes, very well

q. How many times did he come?

a. Not at all

q. Well, you had it all, didn't you? You had all the information?

a. I don't think so. I think some they have not got yet. I don't think so. I think there is some they have not got yet.

q. You mean there is some info you have got yet, and you are an oracle of the ages.

a. Well, you are not paying me to tell you.

q. Well, they are going to pay you the witness fees.

a. I am not dunning them.

q. if I was to pay you to tell me, could you tell?

a. No, I would not do that.

q. You would not?

a. No

q. Well, you know though don't you?

a. Well, you are not examining my brains.

q. You are not going to tell me all you know are you?

a. Well, I will tell you what I do know, a reasonable amount.

q. Are you going to tell this jury all you know?

a. No. I know of things I would not tell them. On the square, I would not tell.

q. Would not even tell this jury? All right now, how many cows did this man Turner steal from Mr. Wallace?

a. Two

q. Just two. How about the four they found over in Carroll County? Did you know the cows were over there?

a. I didn't know anything about it

q. Do you mean to tell this jury that you didn't know where these cows were tied?

a. Well, this man told me that he bought the cows in South Carolina.

q. I didn't ask you that. I asked you this: do you mean to tell this jury that you didn't know there was four cows tied out over here in Carroll County?

a. I never saw the cows in my life.

q. You don't have to see anything to know it, being an oracle, do you? You didn't see these green flies circling around this man's body in the well?

a. I told him there was some there.

q. I know you did, but you didn't see them did you?

a. Well, the wise forseeth evil and hideth himself.

q. What I mean to say, did you see the flies with your natural eyes, the one you are looking at me with?

a. I have an artificial left eye.

q. The artificial eye then, did you see the flies flying around the body?

a. I didn't go to the well

q. How do you know they were there?

a. Well, I saw very well. I saw very well that the body was put in a well and the green flies was swarming around there, and a hand full of nails laying in there.

q. You saw that?

a. Not down there I didn't.

q. Where did you see it?

a. Well, astrology is a science that treats the stars. Presented to me through the stars.

q. Now tell the jury just how it got to you through the stars?

a. Well, the jury is examining a murder case and not the stars.

q. I didn't ask you that. I asked you to tell the jury how the info of this well and these flies happened to get to you through the stars.

a. I am not going to tell the court or anybody else that I saw them flies with my natural eyes.

q. How did you see them? Have you got another pair of eyes you can see them things?

a. Crawfishes eyes are in their tail, and mine is in my head.

q. Tell the jury what pair of eyes you did see this man in the well with.

a. I told you I only had one eye. I didn't see the flies at all, because I was not in that county. I was back up here at home.

q. You never did go down there in your life ever?

a. Yes, I have been in that county

q. You never did go to this well?

a. I didn't have any business there. Not to that well I didn't .

q. Yet you told Mr. Wallace that the man's body was in it didn't you?

a. Well, he knew what they put in there.

q. I didn't ask you. Did you tell him that the man's body was in the well and that green flies were there?

183

a. And they were going to move it. And put it on a horse's back and carried it to another place.

By The Court: let her answer the question. Let her finish the answer.

By Mr. Hinson: Is there anything else you want to say about this? Tell the jury how you knew the man's body was in the well.

a. Through an inspiration of the all wise God that come to me.

q. The all wise God has not dispensed that information to very many people.

By The Court: That is irrelevant, and stay with the evidence

By Mr. Hinson: I want to know the facts.

By The court: Stay right with the facts

q. May I ask you this question: has the all wise God given you more wisdom than the officers that investigated this case?

a. My share.

q. He has? And that is what you base your info on, that extra wisdom that God gave you but didn't give these officers?

a. No. I feel my importance.

q. Are you more important than these officers?

a. Well, if there is anything in the truthful line according to the laws of the State, where I was born and raised, I am so.

(She says more but it's just odd and peculiar)

q. The court wants to know how you can focus your information finder?

a. It would not have any weight with the case.

q. Haven't you said you are of a great deal more importance than these other folks?

a. I would say so if it is my opinion.

By Solicitor Wyatt: I think it would be confined to the questions and answers brought out.

By The Court: I think so. Confine it to evidence brought out by the state on direct examination

By Mr. Hinson: Do you read any newspapers?

a. Sure

q. Did you tell these newspaper reporters what to put in them?

a. No

q. How did they know if they didn't talk to you?

a. I don't know.

q. You don't? Now Mr. Wallace was joking about killing somebody that was taking his cattle?

a. No he said he was going to do it.

q. Well, you knew what was going to happen. You can tell what is going to happen in the future can't you?

a. You ought to get me to tell you sometime and see how you come out.

q. Well, could you do it?

a. I might

q. Well, I want to know could you tell me what is going to happen in the future to me?

a. You may get what Turner got.

BY THE COURT; Let's go to something else

> the witness is excused

By The Court: Anything else this evening?

By Solicitor Wyatt: That is all

By The Court: Gentlemen of the jury, I caution you that you will not permit anyone to discuss this case with you, nor will you discuss it among yourselves at all, now will you permit anyone to discuss it in your presence. Just do not discuss the case at all or permit anyone to discuss it around you. Now counsel have agreed that you may go to the picture show if you wish to, or if there is a ball game here then you may go to the ball game, provided that you are kept together and with your bailiffs. now the bailiffs or the sheriff will take charge of you and take you to your hotel and make you comfortable, and if you wish to take a walk or go anywhere, then that is all right. Counsel have agreed that you may go to these amusement places, and those of you who have not notified your home may do so by telephone, counsel having agreed that you may do that so that you might get whatever things that you might want, these articles. Now we will take a recess until 9:30 tomorrow morning. Let the jury go to their room until everybody gets out.

(Counsel and the defendant agree that the Court may go to his home in Carrollton at night during the course of the trial)

(recess at 4:15 p.m.)

Day Two

The State vs. John Wallace
Filed in office this September 10, 1948 Wallace Gray, clerk

9:30 A.M., June 15, 1848

Mrs. Julia Turner recalled for the State, testifies further as follows:

Direct examination by Solicitor Wyatt: When you and your husband moved away from the defendant's farm in the fall of 1947 did you have a crop that you left there?

a. Yes sir. We gathered I would say right about half of our corn, and the other half we sold in the field to Broughton Myhand, just for what he wanted to give us for it.

q. You sold it to Broughton Myhand?

a. Yes sir

q. And you left that part of the crop there?

a. Yes sir

q. Now I hand you the photograph and ask you to state whose photograph that is.

a. It is my husband, the real William H. Turner.

By Mr. Henson: before they can introduce that, there is a certain foundation they have to lay.

By The Court: It has not been introduced.

By Mr. Henson: I know that.

By The Court: Wait until they introduce it.

By Mr. Henson: If they interrogate her, that is tantamount to introduction.

By The Court: Wait until they offer it, then I will rule on it.

By Solicitor Wyatt: When did you last see your husband, William H. Turner?

a. On Sunday afternoon, April 19th. I think. Yes, April 19th.

q. Can you look at the calendar there and tell us what date it was? What day of the week it was?

a. Sunday

q. Was that on Sunday prior to the day he was killed?

a. Yes sir. It was Sunday before he was killed on Tuesday.

q. Have you seen or heard from him since that time?

A. No sir

q. Where was he in jail?

a. They locked him up in Carrollton first then carried him to Greenville in Meriwether.

q. Did you ever see him while at Greenville?

a. No sir. I went down there to see him, but Sheriff Collier was not there, and Mrs. Mathis would not let me see him Monday afternoon.

q. Did you see his truck there?

a. Yes sir. It was parked on the right hand side of the jail as you go in the front. It was parked on the right hand side up in the driveway kind of in behind inside of a fence. In was inside the fence that was around the jail.

q. Did you telephone down to the jail?

a. Yes sir I telephoned the first time Tuesday morning around 7 a.m.. I talked to Mrs. Mathis, and she said --

By Mr. Henson: Just a minute. I object to conversation.

By Solicitor Wyatt: We don't insist on it.

By the Court: I sustain the objection.

By Mr. Henson: I wish to reserve my right to recall her, because subsequent developments might make it unnecessary for me to go into a long investigation and it will save time I think.

By The Court: You don't care to cross examine her at this time?

By Mr. Henson not at the present time.

the witness is excused
<<<<<<<<<<<<<<<<<<<<<<<<<<

Mrs. Eula Baker lives at Greenville

Direct examination by Solicitor Wyatt
q. Do you recall on Tuesday, April 20th of seeing any people there across from your cafe?

a. I saw Herring Sivell and Henry Mobley between 9 and 11am.

q. Where was Henry Mobley when you first saw him?

a. Parked beside the courthouse in his car headed North toward Newnan. I don't know if the person sitting in the car could see the jail or the road by the jail. I have not lived in Greenville long and don't know just where the jail is located.

q. How long have you known Henry Mobley?

a. Twenty years

q. Did he come into your cafe?

a. Yes he drank a coca cola.

q. Did you talk to him?

a. No

q Did you hear anybody ask him what he was doing in town?

a. No

q. You didn't ask him that question?

a. Not that I recall.

q. What did you say to him?

a. I didn't wait on him.

q. Did you say anything to him?

a. No

By Mr. Henson: Conversation of the two people outside of the defendant's presence would not be admissible.

By Solicitor Wyatt: He is a co defendant.

By The Court: They are indicted jointly.

By Mr. Henson. I know but they are not being tried jointly.

By The Court: I know. You can go ahead. It seems she did not have any conversation with him and it could not make any difference.

q. What kind of car was he sitting in?

a. A black Ford

q. Did you see anyone come to his car and talk to him?

a. No

q. Did you see anyone in the car besides Mobley?

a. No

q. What time of day was it when you missed this car?

a. Well, I didn't miss it. I didn't look anymore.

q. Did you go to school with Henry Mobley?

a. Yes

q. Did he drink all the coke?

a. I didn't wait on him. I don't know how much he drank.

q. When you looked out at noon was the car gone?

a. Well, I was very busy.

q. Ma'am?

a. I was very busy. I didn't notice it.

q. Did you ask him when he was in the cafe, "what are you doing up here" and he laughed and said nothing?

By Mr. Henson: That is a leading question.

a. I did not have a conversation with him.

By The Court: She answered that she did not have a conversation with him. Don't ask that question anymore.

By Solicitor Wyatt: q. Where did you see Herring Sivell?

a. Sitting in his car.

q. Was that in the same car Mobley was in?

a. In a green Ford. He was parked across from my place. Just across the street. One car was on one side of the street and the other car was on the other side.

q. Where was it in reference to the Standard Filling Station?

a. Well, down beside it.

q. Just south of it?

a. Yes

q. Now was Mobley's car south of Sivell's car or north of it?

a. Sivell's car was parked beside the filling station and Mobley's car was parked beside the courthouse.

q. Did you see a man standing by Sivell's car talking to him?

a. No

q. Did the see the green car pull off before the black car?

a. I don't now when either car pulled off.

q. How well do you know Herring Sivell?

a. I have been knowing him for twenty-five years. I went to school with him too.

q. Why did you notice these men parked out there?

a. Because I went to school with them. They were from my hometown.

q. Mrs. Baker, you made a written statement about this case, Didn't you?

a. I put down a few words, is all.

q. The statement was read to you?

a. No

q. Made it on the 29th day of April 1948?

a. I could not recall the date. I was very busy.

q. Is that your signature?

a. It is.

q. Will you take that statement and read it and refresh your memory?

a. I think I told the whole truth.

By Mr. Henson: We certainly object to that as leading.

By The Court: I overrule the objection.

By Solicitor Wyatt: q. Won't you read it, Mrs. Baker?

a. I would rather not.

q. You don't want to read it?

a. No

q. Did you make a true statement when you told the officers what was in here and signed your name to it?

a. But I didn't put but very few words.

q. I said was that a true statement?

a. Sure. I didn't write it.

q. Won't you read it?

a. No

By Mr. Henson: I certainly object to their trying to impeach their own witness without laying a foundation for it.

By The Court: He is not trying to impeach his witness at all. I overrule the objection. Go ahead.

By Mr. Henson: Will you let me get all of my objections in the records?

By The Court: Yes get it all in the record.

By Mr. Henson: I object to it because it is an attempt to impeach the witness by proof of contradictory statements.

By Solicitor Wyatt: I would like the right to ask her leading questions, because she made a statement, and be entrapped.

By The court: If you state you have been entrapped I will permit you to lead her. Is that correct?

By Solicitor Wyatt: That is correct.

By The Court: All right. Go ahead

By Solicitor Wyatt: q. Did you state this to the officers on April 29?

a. I can't recall the date.

By The Court: Wait and let him ask the question.

By Solicitor Wyatt: He read the statement to her. She agreed up until the remark. Mobley drank half a coke, walked out and continued to sit in his car.

a. She responds with - I don't know how long he sat there.

q. Did you make that statement?

a. I don't know how long he sat there.

q. I looked out the window around noon and he was gone.

a. I didn't see him anymore.

q. Did you look out the window about noon and he was gone?

a. I noticed over there sometime in the day and the car was gone but I don't know the time when I looked. I was busy serving dinner.

q. Dinner is around noon?

a. Between 11 and 4.

q. While he was in the cafe I asked him what he was doing . . .

a. I didn't have a conversation with him.

q. So that didn't happen?

a. I didn't wait on him and have a conversation with him.

q. Did you tell the office this?

a. I didn't wait on him.

By The Court: Answer his question.

a. I don't think I did.

q. Do you know if you did?

a. I am sure that I did not.

Wyatt continued reading from the statement

q. There was a man sitting in the back seat of Sivell's car, but I couldn't see who he was.

a. I didn't see anybody with Herring Sivell.

q. Did you state this to the officers?

a. I didn't see anybody with Herring Sivell.

.
q. Did you make that statement?

a. No. I didn't see anybody with Herring Sivell.

q. The green car pulled off a good while before the black one did. Did you make that statement?

a. No

q. I did not see these cars anymore after they left?

a. No

q. When I served dinner they were gone.

a. Well, they were gone. I don't know what time.

q. You signed it?

a. Yes

q. Do you know Cecil Perkerson?

a. Yes

q. Do you know what relation he is to Herring Sivell?

a. I think it is his brother-in-law.

q. Was he the Deputy Sheriff in Meriwether before this thing occurred?

a. I don't know.

q. Did you ever see him wearing a deputy sheriff badge and gun?

a. No

q. Were you present when he came in and talked to your son, James L. Baker, Jr?

a. No

q Did he talk to you?

a. No

q. Did you hear your son make this statement around 1 or 1:30? Cecil Perkerson came in the front door and walked back to the kitchen where I was drinking a cup of coffee and motioned for me to come and follow him. (He read the entire sentence made by her son.)

BY THE Court: Wait a minute

BY Mr. Henson: I object to that, because that is a conversation between third parties, not between them.

By Solicitor Wyatt: I am asking if she heard that.

a. I did not

By The Court: I don't think it is proper to go in it that way. You can ask if she heard a conversation between them.

By Solicitor Wyatt: Did you see Perkerson in there on that date?

a. he delivered my milk

q. he comes in there every day?

a. Him or his wife one.

q. Do you recall that day that he came in there and called your son out to talk to him?

a. I do not

q. Do you know whether that did or did not happen?

a. I could not say. I didn't hear it.

q. You could not say?

By Mr. Henson: Let me have that statement, brother Wyatt

By Solicitor Wyatt: Yes sir
CROSS Examination

By Mr Henson:
q. You testified that was your signature, it that correct?

a. Yes

q. Is that your handwriting?

a. No

q. Do you know who wrote it?

a. No

q. Was it all written before they came to your place?

a. No. He wrote just a small piece in my place.

q. A small piece

a. Just a small piece of paper.

q. Did he write all of this in your place?

a. I can't exactly recall.

q. Did he write more than one page while he was in your place, or do you recall?

a. I can't.

q. You do know that you didn't tell him the facts that he has in here don't you?

a. Well, there was three statements made right there together, and I think they are a little mixed up.

q. You didn't tell them to put that in here at all did you?

a. I did not

q. Did they read this over to you before you signed it?

a. No, not all that.

q. If they had read it to you, you would not have signed it?

a. Well, I was very busy.

q. You would not have signed it if they had read it to you because it has incorrect info in it?

a. Well, they told me I was not to come to court, you know.

q. I see, and they told you if you signed this you would not have to come to court?

a. Yes.

q. And they didn't read to you some of the things that is in here did they?

a. I don't recall. I told you exactly what I told them.

q. I know. And you told Mr. Wyatt that some of these things in here you had not told the officer at all didn't you?

a. I didn't see anyone with Henry Mobley or Herring Sivell.

q. And you didn't tell anybody to put in this statement that you did, did you?

a. I did not.

q. Well, either way, there was a lot of people in town that day besides these two fellows.

a. I am sure there was.

q. Parked all around?

a. Sure

witness is excused

James L. Baker lives in Greenville.

Direct Examination

q. Do you remember seeing Herring Sivell on April 20, 1948?

a. Yes sir. He was across the street in front of our cafe between nine and eleven. He was talking to Mr. Mobley. He was standing beside the door and talking to Mr. Mobley for just a few minutes. I didn't keep track of the time.

q. Could you see both roads from where the cars were parked?

a. Yes sir

q. Did Henry Mobley come in the cafe where you worked?

a. Yes sir, he got a coca cola I asked him what he was doing up there and he said messing around.

q. Did he laugh or not laugh when you asked him that?

a. He just smiled.

q. How far do they live from Greenville?

a. approximately sixteen miles.

q. Had you ever seen them there at that time of day?

a. No sir

q. Do you know Cecil Perkerson and what position he held down in Meriwether?

a. Yes I know him. I think he owns a dairy.

q. I mean with reference to the law enforcement?

a. No sir.

By Mr. Henson: I object. This is not relevant.

By Solicitor Wyatt: To illustrate the relation of conspiracy.

By Mr. Henson: He is not alleged to be in any way concerned with this.

By Solicitor Wyatt: Herring Sivell is indicted for murder in this case.

By Mr. Henson: Perkerson is not.

By The Court: I will let that in for the time being. Go ahead.

q. What did Cecil Perkerson say to you about you testifying as to Sivell being in town that day?

By Mr. Henson; I object to conversation between persons, who are not in this indictment at all, a third person outside of the defendant's presence. It would be hearsay and harmful.

By The Court: I sustain the objection

By Solicitor Wyatt; All right, he is with you.

Cross examination

By Mr. Henson:
q. was there a lot of people in town that morning.

a. yes

q. And you just by chance looked out and saw Mobley and Sivell and a lot of other people I would imagine?

a. yes

q. That's about the time the bank opens isn't it?

a. yes sir

q. And you saw -- dozens of cars parked that day with people talking in them?

a. Yes sir

q. Did they read the statement to you for you to sign?

a. No sir, --- oh yes

q. Did they have it already fixed when they got there?

a. No sir

q Did you read it?

a. Yes sir

q. Can you write?

a. Yes sir

q. Did you write the statement?

a. No sir

Re Direct Examination

q. Who took the statement?

a. A little short fellow.

q. Was he an officer?

a. Yes sir

q. Dressed in an officer's uniform?

a. No sir, just had on a suit. He said he was an officer.

q. Did the same man take your statement that took your mother's?

a. No sir

q. Did he read to her the statement before she signed it?

a. Yes sir

witness is excused
****

Statement of Willie Joe Copeland waitress at cafe

I heard Mrs. Eula Baker ask him what he was doing in town. I never heard him answer. He drank part of a coca cola. Mr. Mobley was parked in the curb toward the courthouse. Mr. Mobley went over and talked to Mr. Sivell for a minute. I don't know how long.

No cross examination.   Witness is excused
****

C. E. Miller Commissioner's agent, Department of Revenue

By Mr. Henson: q. Do you know John Wallace?

a. Yes sir. I saw him around noon in the Greenville production credit corporation office in Greenville.

q. Are you sure about the time?

a. Yes I spoke to Sheriff Collier just a few minutes previous to noon and I looked at my watch and it was ten minutes to twelve, and I told him that I wanted to see Clements before he went to lunch, and I had better go on.

q. Where was Sheriff Collier?

a. He was sitting there on the corner at that courthouse right on the northeast corner of the courthouse.

q. Was anybody in this place with John Wallace?

a. Nobody came in with him. No sir.

q. Did you see Herring Sivell there that morning?

a. Yes sir

q. Where was he?

a. He was in the place. He came in soon after I went in.

q Was he in there before or after Mr. Wallace?

a. Before.

q. How long after he was in there before Wallace came in?

a. Oh, several minutes, maybe four or five.

q. Did you ever see the two men together that morning?

a. No sir.

q. What was Sivell doing there?

a. He was attending to some business. I didn't pay strict attention. the lady was waiting on me, and Mr. Sivell came in, and she said "excuse me just a minute. I know what Mr. Sivell wants." I didn't know Mr. Sivell.

q. Did you see Wallace come in while Sivell was transacting business?

a. Yes sir, he came in. He came in the door and walked right on back. I was sitting back behind the rail. The lady was getting some info for me, and I was sitting in a chair by a desk and she was standing up talking to Mr. Sivell.

q. Who was?

a. The lady. I don't know her name.

q. Did Wallace say anything to Mr. Sivell?

a. Not that I know of.

q. Did he transact any business while he was there?

a. No sir, he did not. He walked right on back and opened the little gate and came in and shook hands with me, and passed the time of day, and walked on out.

q. You know whether he walked close to Sivell and looked at each other or not?

a. I just didn't pay any attention. If he said anything. I didn't hear him.

CROSS EXAMINATION

By Mr. Henson:
q. Now Mr. Miller, when Mr. Wallace came in did he ask for Mr. Clements?

a. I didn't hear that. He came right back in there and shook hands with me and asked me how I was getting along, and we talked a second, and he turned and walked out.

q. You work with a gentleman named Cook?

a. Yes sir.

q. Have you and Mr. Cook been concerned with some liquor stills down there close to Mr. Wallace's place?

a. Yes, sir we have.

q. Who has been helping you? Has not Mr. Wallace been asking you to clear out these liquor making places around his place?

a. Lately he did, yes sir.

q. Now that was after he had his last case down at the federal court was it not?

a. I don't know when his last case was.

q. Last year he did call on you and Mr. Cook to help him clear up that liquor making?

a. Along the latter part of November or first of December I believe it was.

q. How many times did he call for help?

a. One time only.

q. You found a big still down there didn't you?

a. Comparatively big. It was not an extra big one.

q. You and Mr. Cook had hunted for that still before hadn't you?

a Yes sir, we had.

q. And Mr. Wallace found it and called you, didn't he?

a. Well, the big still, he didn't call us.

204

q. He gave you directions as best he could about where it might be operating?

a. I could be confused about which still you have in mind.

q. How many did you raid down there, Mr. Miller?

a. Several. I have helped raid several in that vicinity, but the one I think you have reference to Mr. Lucas. Mr. Wallace I think called him, but Mr. Lucas called me in on it later. Yes sir, I didn't see Mr. Wallace any of the time we had this still under observation, the big still.

q. But he did talk to you about the still and about the still generally that he wanted found?

a. Yes sir, twice.

q. Now did you catch anybody at these stills?

a. At the one Mr. Lucas called me in we did not catch anybody. At the one Mr. Wallace -- I took Mr. Wallace in my car and went to a distance of some four or five miles to this other still. We did catch some defendants there, Mr. Cook and I.

q. Who did you catch?

a. We caught a Negro named Charlie Magruder, and while I was going to the still I saw the boy that I knew as Wilson Turner and Thomas Windham leave the still and come up the path toward the road. They escaped in a car before I could get back up and stop Mr. Cook.

q. You saw a boy you knew as Wilson Turner?

a Yes sir. I understand his right name was William. He was parading under a false name all the time. I know three men named Windham they are kin to Turner. Brother-in-law I understand and some of them operated these stills with Turner. They were partly to blame for the trouble down that way. We've caught Turner once with one gallon, the next with 35 gallons.

q. Did you catch his brothers in law with any?

a. No sir

q. Didn't you find these Windhams, Ed and Tom I believe that is their names --

a. Yes sir

q. You saw them once making some equipment for a distillery?

a. We did, yes sir. They were between the barn and the house where Wilson lived. They were making two stills. One would hold approximately two hundred gallons, and the other one about three hundred gallons.

q. What did you do with that equipment?

a. We cut it up with an axe.

q. When was that?

a. I don't know. I could go to my records and find out but I don't know right this minute.

q. Was it in the fall?

a. Yes it was corn gathering time. It was in the fall. Some other people there were gathering corn. In 1947.

q. And that was when Mr. Wallace was appealing to you officers to help him free his place from these people who were making this.

a. No sir, not at that time. Mr. Wallace had not appealed to me or to Mr. Cook to my knowing.

q. Did he appeal to Mr. Lucas?

a. I don't know

q. Did you and Mr. Wallace chase Turner at any time in connection with these operations?

a. The night that I had reference to when Mr. Wallace -- he wrote me a letter, I went to his house by myself, and he and I went to a place, as I told you, where he pointed out that he thought the still was, and in returning to Mr. Wallace's home we met Wilson's car.

He thought Wilson was driving it, and I suppose he was, and he supposed that he had whiskey in his car. I said, if you were not in here with me I would see and he said, "well if you want to chase him I can get out, so I ran him, I turned in, he turned right at Durand into the Warm Springs road. I passed Turner's car. I still didn't know who was driving the car, and drove on out of sight of his car, and then Mr. Wallace got out. I blocked the road and stopped the car and searched it, and Thomas Windham was driving it at the time.

q. Did you find anything in it?

a. No sir. There was a five-gallon can with maybe a pint of whiskey in it, was not enough to make a case out of it. It was a five-gallon metal can commonly used to transport whiskey. You could have used a funnel to pour out small quantities.

q. A kind of vessel they use to retail this rot gut white liquor?

a. Yes sir

q. That is the kind Turner made?

a. Well, white liquor, moonshine.

q. Did you at any time chase Turner? Didn't you chase once and stop him about midnight, and he gave you a dressing down for disturbing him?

a. No, I didn't do that. I carried Mr. Wallace on home that night and as I was returning home Mr. Turner and Thomas Windham came by and blinked the lights two or three times, and I thought they wanted me to stop and I did and he came back and said some words, something to me about searching his car.

q. Let's go back a moment, Mr. Miller, to this big still. There was a still Mr. Collier, the sheriff down there called you in behalf of John was it not?

a. No sir he didn't call me. I knew nothing of the still until Mr. Lucas called me and asked me to join him the next morning.

q. Was there a raid of a still that Mr. Collier and Mr. Wallace interested you in and asked for help?

a. The sheriff had helped us at different times, and I don't know. He didn't give me the source of his information. Now Mr. Wallace might have done that. I don't know.

q. You and Mr. Wallace looked for a still down there on a number of occasions and didn't find it.

a. No sir, we didn't look for one. That is the only other time that I have ever talked to Mr. Wallace in that neighborhood, was soon after we had caught Wilson Turner and we had info there was a big still down in that section and I was doing some walking and after I had walked out the territory that we had info on, I came out at the road near Mr. Wallace's home, walked by his home and back toward where the car was to pick me up, and Mr. Wallace on a horse caught up with me in his pasture, and we talked there a few minutes. That is the only time.

q. Now you found the still about 500 yards from that point didn't you?

a. No sir. You are confused about the time. This was a year previously to that. Then I found the still right close to where Mr. Wallace thought it was the night that I carried him in my car.

q. When you found these people at Turner's house building this still, did you find Turner?

a. No sir he was not there. I never did see him.

q. Did Mr. J. Leonard Williams report any stills to you?

a. Yes sir I know the name but he did not report any stills.

q. Did anyone else report Turner's still?

a. The only one that I know of that was ever reported to us -- well, I am sure of that -- the only one that was ever reported to us, and turned out to be Turners was the one Mr. Wallace carried me to that night, or rather I carried him in my car. That was the latter part of November or in December after we had destroyed this big still over near White Sulphur.

RE DIRECT Examination

By Solicitor Wyatt: Did Mr. Wallace ever ask you to do anything about the stills on his place and around his place until after you had gone down there and found some stills?

a. No sir. He did not. I didn't know Mr. Wallace until after that. Not until we began to get in that community and catch the stills there.

q. The distillery that you saw them manufacturing over there, where was that with reference to Wallace's place

a. It was on Mr. Wallace's land. I was told. I don't know who owned the land. It was a good piece from where he lived. It is sort of hard to estimate the way the road goes, but in a line I would say it was somewhere around two to three miles.

q. And they were making the still in the broad open daylight?

a. Yes sir. Anybody could have seen them if they had walked up there.

q. Did you make the case against Wilson Turner at Greenville for liquor, and the defendant signed the bond?

a. Yes sir

q. When was that?

a. It has been -- it was in 1945 I am pretty sure.

q. 1945?

a. Yes sir

q. This defendant signed Wilson Turner's bond at Greenville for liquor?

a. Yes sir. I didn't see the bond myself.

q. You know who paid the fine as a result of that case?

a. I know what Wilson told me the night I stopped him over there. He said Mr. Wallace paid the fine. Wilson Turner said so. I tried to get him to do some talking, and he said as long as a man stood up to him in the courthouse he would not go back on him.

q. Now has there been a conspiracy case? Have you officers –state whether or not you officers have been investigating a conspiracy case in which this defendant is involved?

a. Yes sir

By Solicitor Wyatt:
q. did you ever hear John Wallace say anything about Wilson Turner?

a. Well, the night I carried him over there in my car he showed me the still, or the territory it was in, Mr. Wallace stated to me that Wilson was the craziest man that he ever got mixed up with, and he had to get rid of him, and he was apologizing for turning up a still. That is the way I took it.

q. What did he say about it?

a. He said he used to fool with whiskey and he didn't want folks messing with him, and he said it in that way, that he was turning that up, just had to get him off his place, get rid of them, that is the words he said, I have got to get rid of him.

q. Got to get rid of him?

a. Yes sir
                    witness is excused

By the court we will take a recess of about five minutes.
recess at 10:45 a.m.

L. F. Garrett Chief of Police of Greenville

DIRECT EXAMINATION

By Solicitor Wyatt:
q. Did you see John Wallace on April 20 and where?

a. Right near the Credit Production office. I've known him for more than 30 years. I also saw him near the library sitting in a car talking with somebody between twelve and 12:15. I looked at my watch as I come out. I was a little late for lunch is how come me to look at it.

q. At the time you saw him in the car did you look at your watch?

a. Yes sir, that was the time between ten and eleven. I was fixing to go to the plant. He was in a grayish sort of car. I thought it was Mr. Frank Hatchett's car. It was near his house, and I thought he was sitting in the car talking to him.

q. How far is that from the road that leads out from the jail that leads to Hwy 41?

a. 30 or 40 feet. I walked out the city hall door, which is the old library and as I come down the steps I saw him and I kept walking. I just could not hardly say it was him, but he was sitting about a 90-degree angle, and I was behind the car. He was in the right hand side and his arm laying up in the door. I did not see anyone else and I could not swear that was him, because I saw the side of his face and ears. It looked like him.

witness is excused

,   ,,,,,,,,,,,,,,,,,,,,,,,,,,,,

Hugh C. Martin
Direct Examination by Solicitor Wyatt

q. Do you know John Wallace?

a. No, only just when I see him.

q. Did you see him on April 20?

a. Yes sir, at the service station he got in the car with Mr. Collier in Greenville around three o'clock or after.

witness is excused

....

Frank Perkerson

Direct Examination by Solicitor Wyatt
q. Do you know John Wallace?

a. I have known him for 25 or 30 years. I saw him mid morning between 10 and noon and again between 3 and 4.

q. What was he doing between 3 and 4?

a. I was sitting at the corner of Hillbrose and LaGrange street and he walked up and spoke to the crowd. He was by himself. After he spoke to the crowd he and Sheriff Collier walked off up the sidewalk.

witness is excused

....

Mrs. Vivian Matthews also seen name spelled Mathis in earlier records. At least I think it refers to the same person. In any event this lady works at the Meriwether jail. She lives in Greenville and does house work at the jail.

Direct Examination by Solicitor Wyatt:
q. You are the wife of the jailer?

a. No sir, I am just assistant jailer.

q. You are the assistant jailer and you live there at the jail?

a. Yes sir

q. How long have you been living and working at the jail in Greenville?

a. 14 years in October.

q. Has Mr. Collier been Sheriff during that time?

a. Yes

q. Do you remember April 20th when Wilson Turner was in jail there?

a. Well, I was not downstairs. I was in the building but I did not see him.

q. When was he put in there?

a. Before I got up in the morning.

q. What day?

a. On Monday.

q. Was it early Monday morning?

a. Yes, sir.

q. About what time?

a. Well, it was before I got up and I generally get up around six, we have the baby that wakes up, it must have been around five o'clock. I don't know.

q. Before six o'clock?

a. I don't have a clock.

q. Who else did you see or hear at the jail that morning?

a. I didn't see or hear anybody.

q. Did you see the truck that was put there that morning?

a. I saw it, yes sir. It was a green truck. It was new. I don't know the make of it.

q. What time of day and what day after that truck and that man was brought there did the truck and man leave the jail?

a. I don't know. Left on Tuesday, but I don't know what time they left. Tuesday, April 20th, I think it was.

q. Did you give anyone any directions about that truck just immediately before Turner was released and left there in the truck?

a. Well, up in the morning where I hang out my clothes in the backyard it was under the clothes line and I told the colored man to back it out, you know, out of the gate.

q. Where you over at Mrs. Jarrell's house that morning?

a. Yes sir. I was over there three different times. I was doing some work. The truck was backed out as I was crossing the road to go over there. I don't know what time it was. I come back to get the hammer to do some work. I was doing some upholstering work for her and I come back to get the little hammer and screw driver. Then I went back. I don't know how long I stayed. There was not a clock in the room where I was and I was just doing the work and I didn't think about any clock. I didn't have on a watch.

q. When you came back over to the jail was the truck there or was it gone?

a. I don't know. I didn't look. It would have been in the side of the yard.

q. Who was it that came over to Mrs. Jarrell's and called you and you told them to move the truck?

a. No one did.

q. Who was the person who backed the truck out?

a. Jack Howard

q. Is that a colored man that works at the jail?

a. Yes sir

q. Did you stay over at Mrs. Jarrell's until about noon?

a. Well, it was close to noon. Yes, it was close to noon.

q. When you went home did you see Jack Howard there?

a. No. I didn't see Jack. I went in the house.

q. Did you see Mr. Collier, the Sheriff?

a. No

q. Had anybody eaten lunch at that time?

a. No sir

q. When did you eat with reference to the time you went in there?

a. Well, I ate immediately because I was going away.

q. Did you prepare the meal that morning?

a. No. Well yes, I always make my -- what I am going to have for dinner make the menu. I had started it, me and the cook together before I went to Mrs. Jarrell's.

q. Mrs. Matthews, did you see any warrant that the Sheriff had there for Wilson Turner?

a. No

q. Was there any record made of his being placed in jail at the time he was placed in jail?

a. I didn't put it down that day because --

q. Was there any record made on April 20th when he was released from jail?

a. No

q. He was released from jail the day you talked about going to Mrs. Jarrell's?

a. Yes sir

q. Up to that time no record was made of his coming into jail or going out.

a. I don't put it down every time as soon as they come in.

q. I say none had been made up to that time?

a. No sir. I did not put his name down that day.

q. Do you know whether there was any warrant pending against Turner over there at the time he was in jail on April 20th, at the time he was released?

a. Yes

q. Was there a warrant for him there at that time?

a. Yes

q. Do you know what it was for?

a. Cow stealing I think.

q. I mean another warrant. Was there any other warrant there?

a. I didn't see one.

q. Do you know anything about a liquor warrant that was in the Sheriff's office?

a. No sir. I didn't look through them. I didn't know whether there was one in there or not.

q. Did you see any warrant about stealing the cow?

a. Yes sir, I saw it.

q. When?

a. Well, that night or morning.

q. What night?

a. Morning.

q. What morning?

a. About two o'clock.

q. Who had the warrant?

a. Mr. Collier

q. I believe you said they got in there before you got up.

a. Well, that was on Monday morning.

q. When did you see the warrant Monday morning?

a. Laying on the table. I saw it Monday morning.

q. How is that?

a. It was on Monday morning. I did not look at it.

q. You know who signed it?

a. Yes. It was Major Irvin.

q. I am talking about who made the affidavit to it. Who else signed it besides Major Irwin? Who swore to it? Who issued the warrant, who swore it out?

a. My husband.

Cross Examination

By Mr. Henson

q. As assistant jailer, it is among your duties to keep the records?

a. Yes.

q. Now you post your records every now and then don't you?

a. Well, I when I have to go in there, I do. If not, I keep it in my mind. I post them if I am in there, if I put them in or if I turn them out but if I am not in the office I don't every time go in there right at that time and do it.

q. But later on you do post the books?

a. Yes, I do.

q. Is it a day or two sometimes before you put a matter on?

a. Yes, that is right.

q. But you did post these records?

a. Yes, I always do that.

q. And they are posted now?

a. Yes

The witness is excused.

Mrs. T. R. Jarrell
She lives in Greenville, just across the street from the jail.

Direct Examination
She confirms that "Mrs. Matthews came to her house early in the morning to fix -- she was going to cover a dressing table for me, and then she went back to get the hammer, and she came back a little later in the morning and you know, did the work. She left my house around 12.00. I heard her tell someone to move the truck. I could not say just exactly what time it was but it had to be somewhere between the hour of eleven and twelve because that was when she was over there but I could not say just what time. I don't know who she told to move it. All I know is who she said to tell. I know she said "tell Jack to do it, but I don't know who was at the door.
No cross Examination. The witness is excused.

Jack Howard
is a prisoner at the Meriwether county jail house and also works there. He does not know the exact time that he backed the truck up but it was

around 11 or 11:30. "I back it out and stops in front of the garage, I get out and put the key in the house and goes to town. I went to get the 12 o'clock mail.

q. Who gave you the directions to back the truck out?

a. Mrs. Matthews

q. Did you know whose truck it was?

a. No sir.

He states that was the only truck there that day.
No cross Examination   Witness is excused.

~~~~~~~~~~~~~~~~~~

Leon Flournoy
works at the State Highway Department.
On April 20th he was on 41 North Highway between Luthersville and Greenville.

Direct Examination
Tell the jury what you saw.

a. All I saw, it was noon time. We were off the road under a shade tree and the truck and car come -- they were running a speed you could hear the tires squawk and we had up a sign "one way drive, and they went by and I thought it was the revenue with a truck load of whiskey. We went back to work at one o'clock, and it was a few minutes after one I seen a green car come back. I saw the green car come back about 40 minutes later. I only saw one man in it. On the way up there were two men. On the way back he had to slow up. We had the road blocked at the time being because we were over the center line tearing out the hole in the concrete highway and he had to slow up when he come back.
                    Witness is excused.
~~~~~~~~~~~~~~~~

Steve Smith testimony

Direct Examination: Tell what you saw.

a. The truck come in there so fast, and the cars, that is what attracted my

218

attention. Turner got out hollering for help. Wallace caught him at my front door. Turner put up a pretty stiff fight. Wallace caught him with one hand and had his gun in the other. Turner had both hands free. Turner was hollering and putting up a stiff fight. I could not see the 20 feet as I came from behind the counter to the front door . . . I didn't know what was happening. When I got to the front door, I saw Wallace dragging Turner to the car. Once they got to the car, Sivell met him around on that side.

(This witness walked 20 feet to the front door, then walked 20 feet back then walked to the side door before Turner and Wallace got from the front door to the car.)

When he stuck his head out the side door, Wallace and Turner were 10 or 12 feet from his front door. Wallace held the stock of it in his hand and hit him. He would have had to hit him with the barrel. Turner fell with his head down in the car, and they got him by the heels and piled him up in the car. Before Turner was knocked in the head, he braced himself up against the car trying to keep himself from being put in. He had one foot against the running board. He had his foot on the running board with his head down and Wallace knocked him in the car.

By Mr. Henson: If he had his foot on the running board pushing against the car, his head would be higher than the car and they could not knock him in the car.

a. They did knock him in the car.

q. Knocked him in the car. Then what kind of instrument was it you swore this morning Wallace was hitting him with after he got him in the car?

a. I don't know. I didn't pay much attention to it. (He thinks it was dark and about five inches long and an inch and a quarter in circumference.)

q. You swore to the Justice of the Peace in the case before that he had nothing in his hand. Didn't Mr. Huddleston ask you the following question, on page 12? "Do you know what he was beating him with?" You answered: "I could not see anything but his fist."

a. I meant I could not see what was in his fist.

q. Don't you know you swore before the Justice he had nothing in his fist, and you come before this jury and swear he had a cylindrical object an inch and half in diameter and five inches long? Who told you to say he had something in his fist?

a. Not anybody.

q. Who talked to you about the case?

a. Not anybody.

q. Nobody at all? Not the officers? You have not talked with Mr. Goldberg about it? You did not give Mr. Hancock a statement. You did not talk to Sheriff Potts?

a. No sir

q. You swear to this jury you have not talked to Mr. Goldberg or Mr. Hancock about this case.

a. No sir, I have not talked with anybody.

q. You swear that you have not talked to Sheriff Potts about it?

a. I talked to him something about it but I have not talked about that.

q. Why didn't you say so awhile ago? Now let's see who did you talk to?

a. Not anybody particularly about what you are talking about.

a. Did you talk to Mr. Goldberg?

a. I didn't talk to anybody about what he had in his hand.

By Mr. Henson: I asked you if you talked to anybody about the case.

a. There has been several people talked to me about the case.

q. Then you didn't tell Sheriff Potts what you saw down there did you?

a. Yes sir

q. What?

a. Yes sir

q. You just swore you didn't?

a. You are talking about what he had in his hand.

q. No. I am talking about what you talked about. Mr. Smith, I am asking you about this case, not what he had in his hand. Now tell this jury who you have talked with about this case and about what you knew, since that.

a. I talked to Mr. Potts about it when he come down there. I called him up and told him what happened down there. That is the only time I ever talked to him about it.

q. I want you to tell this jury how come you swearing on the 27th of April that this man had nothing in his hand, and then you come up here on the 15th day of June and swear he had a great big black object in his hand. Who told you to change your story?

a. Not anybody. I meant I could not see what he had in his hand.

By The Court: Don't ask him that again.

q. Mr. Smith did you ever study medicine?

a. No sir

q. You never observed injured people in the hospital or any other place?

a. No sir

q. This is the first time you ever saw a man hit that hard?

a. The first time I have ever seen one hit hard enough to kill him.

q. That is the first time you ever saw a man hit with a shotgun in all your life?

a. Yes sir

(The whole thing lasted four or five minutes from beginning to end when they drove off he got the tag number of the car by going through his building.)

q. Now you don't know what affect this blow had on this boy at all do you, except just your imagination?

a. I just know he hit him hard enough to knock him down.

q. That is just your opinion, isn't it?

a. Yes sir

q. You don't know at all do you?

a. I didn't get him out and examine him

q. Do you have a lot of prejudice against John Wallace?

a. No sir

q. Did you know that Turner was running away from a cow stealing warrant?

a. No sir

q. Did you know that Turner was using a false name?

a. No sir

q. Did you know he had a false draft card in his pocket?

a. No sir

q. Now about this photograph. You knew Turner had a brother didn't you?

a. No sir

q. Did you know he had his brothers draft card and they looked a lot alike?

a. No sir

q. Who showed you this picture first?

a. They showed it to me up here at the commitment trial that day.

q. Who?

a. Mr. Goldberg or Mr. Potts or some of them. I don't know now.

q. You told me you never talked to him about the case in your life.

a. In the commitment trial he showed me the picture, or some of them did.

q. Have you ever seen Mr. Goldberg before in your life?

a. Yes sir. Around down here a lot of times.

REDIRECT

q. Did you see Sivell there, the man with Wallace?

a. Yes sir

q. Were any weapons in his hands?

a. Yes sir. He had a big white-handled pistol. Shiny. I saw it in his hand and when he went to shut the door and to go around and get in the car. He put it in his right front pocket.

Witness excused

Mr. M. Phillips
saw part of what happened at Sunset Tourist Camp

I saw two men catch one man and carry him back toward the car, pulling him, and when they got to the car with him, this man was hollering "help" all the time, and when they got to the car with him evidently he must have been struck with the gun because the gun fired and -- well, he must have, and he kindly fell in the car, or they pushed him in the car and I saw them as they were pushing his feet in the car but I did not hear him anymore after the gun fired. I recognize Mr. Wallace as being the man I saw.

q. Could you recognize Turner if you saw him?

a. I don't think so.

q. Where were you when this happened?

a. Well, I was sitting at the first booth as you go in right by the window. That is when I saw them when they caught him at the door. They either fell against the door, or had a hold of the door or something. The door rattled and as they turned back this man over here was facing me and I got a good impression of his face. Wallace had a pump gun. I don't know what make. But it looked as though it was a sawed off pump gun.

q. Sawed off pump gun? Was it a short barrel?

a. Yes

q. Did you hear any conversation between Mr. Smith to Wallace?

a. Well, I believe he first asked them did they need any help, then he asked them why they didn't put handcuffs on him. That is all I remember hearing.

q. How long did all this take?

a. Well, I would think they was there about probably a minute and half or two minutes.

(The witness saw Turner's feet being pushed into the car.)

q. Do you know anything else?

a. I would not say it was a row. They just ran up there and overpowered the man and carried him off.

q. Did you know that they had a warrant for him for cow stealing?

a. I didn't know anything.

witness excused

Dr. C. C. Elliot, a practicing physician for thirty-six years. Has an MD. degree from University of Chattanooga.

q. If a man that size (meaning Wallace) were to take a pump shot gun, made in that manner, and struck a man that weighed from 125 to 130 pounds in the back of the head with all his force, that he could apply to that stroke. I will ask you to state whether or not in your opinion that lick would be sufficient to produce death.

Objections made.

a. Yes, it might produce death. It might produce instant death.

Cross Examination
Mr. Henson: And it also might not, might it, doctor?

224

a. It might not

witness excused

Dr. J. D. Tribble a thirty four year practicing physician graduated Emory regular MD course. He was connected with the US Army medical corp for twenty-five years. From a private to a full Colonel. Full Colonel five years.

q. This man over here in the short sleeves leaning back against the railing there. If a man that size would take a pump gun made something like this and strike a man across the base of the brain or the back of his head with all the force he could apply to the blow, could such a blow cause the person's death.

a. Yes sir, it would.

Cross Examination

q. There would be some cases in which the man would survive that blow, wouldn't there?

a. He might for a few hours.

(Must be a mix up in the records here because what the doctor says next doesn't make any sense.)

q. Would he not for a few years in certain areas --

a. Well now, Colonel, I don't know you, and I never saw you before, but don't try it here.

q. Don't try what?

By The Court: Go ahead and answer the question, doctor.

 a. Well, that is the best way I know.

By the Court: Answer the question.

By Mr. Henson: Would you mind answering the question? You are a dignified professional man, and this is not a place for clowning.

By The Court: Wait a minute, Mr. Henson. I ruled on that. The doctor will answer the question. Go ahead.

By Mr. Henson. q. You are a qualified practicing physician?

a. Yes sir. I have a license been practicing for thirty-four years.

q. Well now as such, don't you know that a blow on a man's head, that the result of it would depend somewhat upon the area injured, upon the severity of the blow, upon the physical stamina of the man stricken?

a. Well, all that would enter into the case, yes. The gentleman there described a heavy blow. A heavy blow may not always cause instant death.

q. Some men have had severe blows in the head and survived them.

a. I have heard of them. I don't know of them.
                    witness is excused

Recess called at 3:35 p.m. for ten minutes.

Dr. George P. Kinnard graduated from Jefferson Medical College in 1922. I put two years at Philadelphia General Hospital, one year in Middlesex Hospital, London, England, one up at Harper hospital, Detroit, Michigan and I was a Chief of professional services Station Hospital, Balstall Field for a period of three years, 1933 to 1937. I was chief of surgical services, 110th Evacuation Hospital, E. T. O., from 1944 to 1945.

q. Was part of that teaching in the army, or service in the army?

a. Yes sir, from 1944 to 45.

The same question about size was asked.

a. I would say that blow would cause death in all ordinary circumstances.

Cross Examination

By Mr. Henson
q. Are there circumstances under which it would not?

a. I said in all ordinary circumstances.

q. Would it depend on what area of the skull?

a. A blow of that force will usually involve both areas of the base of the brain.

q. How do you know?

a. Just from past experience.

q. How hard a lick are you talking about?

a. As he described it, it was the lick with the full force of a heavy man.

q. How can you measure any such force as that?

a. It would just be a matter of common experience like a man swinging at a base ball. You can tell from how hard he swings how much he intends to do.

q. Will all men of that same size hit with the same force?

a. No, but as the question was asked me, it said with his full force. I believe if it was their full force with a weighted object it would be sufficient. I have no idea what force was used. It was not asked of me. It was asked if a man of that size struck with full force. I have seen men unconscious recover hours later. I have seen crushed skulls recover.

(Demonstration made by Mr. Henson to show that any such blow would have hit Turner's skull in the back and toughest place.)
Witness excused

Mrs. Merle Hannah
was across the highway of the Sunset Tourist Court

"Around 12:30 on Tuesday this pickup truck came up from toward Greenville, and this car following it. Both came at high speed, and the truck swerved and turned it at the Sunset and parked at the north side of the building, and the car swerved and they come in almost bumper to bumper, the car and truck, and the truck stopped and the driver of it jumped from the truck and ran under the shelter, and he made an attempt to open the front door of the building there, but he missed the door, and he was reaching for the screen. In the meantime, two men jumped from the

Ford, this car, and Wallace had a shotgun and he raised the gun as if he was going to shoot the man and in the excitement I told him not to kill him, and he told me -- he signaled like that -- to hush, and as he did that, he ran under the shelter and grabbed him before he opened the door and they scuffled with him and began to beat him until they got him almost to the car and when they got out, the door of the car was open and he kind of backed back and pushed back as if he didn't want to get in the car and this Wallace drew back with a shot gun and struck him across the head, looked like full force and as he did that the gun went off and at that time Turner slumped like he -- he had hollered once before, "don't let them kill me, but when they struck him he didn't holler anymore. He just fell as if he was lifeless. When he slumped forward, they picked him up and shoved him in the back of the car between the front and back seat in the foot, but his feet were out and this old man Sivell shoved his feet in so they could close the door. Wallace crawled in on him, still in the motion of beating him, and closed the door and Sivell drove off. He drove the car up there. They went around the building and went back the way they came, and him down in the foot of the car on top of Turner.

(She states she had never seen Wallace, Turner or Sivell before. She was asked to point out Wallace. The bald headed man leaning against the rail in the short sleeves.)

q. What part did Sivell take in this attack?

a. Well, he ran with Wallace to catch him at the door, and he helped shove him, and kind of beating on him trying to get him in the car, and he resisted and both had a hold of him.

q. Did Sivell have anything in his hand?

a. I could not say for sure, but I do know he was striking him but the shotgun is what attracted my attention.

q. The defendant left there beating him in the back of the car, could you see his hand and what he had in it?

a. I could not. You could just see the top of his head as the car drove off.

By The Court: State what he was doing.

a. All right. He was beating him when he left. It was not a motion to it. He was beating him when he left. I imagine it would be a motion if you were beating --

By Mr. Henson: I object to what the young lady imagines.

a. If anybody was beating, he would have to be in motion.

By Solicitor Wyatt: What happened to Turner when they hit him in the back of the head with the gun?

a. He slumped over, dropped forward.

q. Had he been saying anything prior to that time?

a. He hollered "Don't let them kill me" after I hollered "Don't kill him" and they grabbed him, and he yelled "Don't let them kill me.

q. Would the blow he received cause his death?

a. In my opinion, he was dead when he left Sunset.

Cross Examination

By Mr. Henson: Why did you change your testimony? At first you said he was in the motion of beating him, then you said he was beating him. Why did you change?

a. Because you wanted me to, because you can't beat anybody without being in a motion.

By Mr. Henson: Will you ask her to answer the question?

By The Court: Wait a minute. If that occurs one more time, I will have to clear the court room. Now don't let it happen again. If it does, I will clear the courtroom for the rest of this trial. Go ahead.

By Mr. Henson: I most respectfully submit she did not answer the question.

By the Court: If you can get a better answer, go ahead.

By Mr. Henson: All right, I will try.

q. Now with the permission of the court, I will ask you again, you just testified you first said he was going through the motion like he was beating him. Then you changed it and swore that he was beating him. Now my last question to you was why did you change your testimony.

a. The last time you made me change it. You asked me if he was in the motion.

q. Did I make you change it?

a. You wanted me to. I still say he was beating him.

q. Did you change it because I wanted you to or because I made you?

a. No. I changed it because he was beating him.

q. Why didn't you swear that to start with?

a. I said it at first. He was beating him, in the motion.

q. Don't you know you didn't say that at first?

a. Well, I want you to know he was beating him.

q. So you want to rest on that now regardless of what you swore before?

a. I want to rest that he was beating him.

q. Regardless of what you swore before?

a. That is right.

q. Now where were you standing, young lady?

a. I was standing beside the highway, the distance of the highway, on the opposite side of the road.

q. Is the highway as wide as from where this little girl is to where that gentleman stands in the door?

a. It is the same width as it is going down the main highway.

(Some discussion follows on how far she was from the men then she was asked if she could hear the conversation of some young girls at the trial.)

a. I could if they were talking as loud as he shouted to me to hush.

(She did not see what part of the head, Turner was hit. Turner was resisting getting into the car.)

q. Now did you see the same thing Mr. Smith saw?

By Solicitor Wyatt: I don't see how she could. That is an improper question.

By Mr. Henson: I will ask you this way. They were not there more than a minute or two?

a. I guess the whole thing occurred in about five minutes, four or five.

q. Were you and Mr. Smith looking at them at the same time?

a. If it just happened once then we were looking at them at the same time.

q. You don't know how bad the man was hurt, do you?

a. No, from my distance I could not tell if he was hurt.

q. How did they get him in the car?

a. They shoved him in after he struck him.

q. Slammed him in? They didn't take that gun and knock him in, did they?

a. They pushed him in, shoved him in.

q. But they didn't take the gun and knock him in?

a. No. They had struck him on the head with the gun.

q. They had already done that before they put him in the car?

a. That is right.

q. Now the blow that they used to strike him on the head was not the blow that knocked him into the car at all.

a. No sir

q. And you saw the same thing Mr. Smith saw, didn't you?

a. It happened one time, and all the witnesses saw the same thing I did.

q. Did you know any of them or why they were taking this man back?

a. I didn't know anything about them.

q. How many times have you talked with Mr. Hancock, the officer, about this?

a. I have not talked with Mr. Hancock about it.

q. How many times did you talk to Mr. Goldberg?

a. Well, we had a few words when we came up to the commitment trial.

q. Has anybody been to see you about this?

a. Just to bring me a subpoena.

q. Have you ever signed a written statement?

a. I have not.

q. You mean that none of these people have asked you what you know about the case?

a. They have asked me some, but I have not signed a statement.

q. Who asked you about it?

a. Mr. Goldberg when he brought the subpoena.

q. He didn't talk to you about the case?

a. No sir

q. He just said "Mrs. Hannah, here is a subpoena?

a. He asked me what I knew about it. I said that --

q. Did you tell him?

a. I told him what I knew.

q. And you all talked about it? He told you about how important it was for this Turner to be dead over there didn't he?

a. No. He didn't talk to me about that.

q. What?

a. He didn't say it. I told him how it happened, and in my opinion he was dead.

By Mr. Henson: I object to it on the grounds that it is a conclusion of the witness based on no facts or circumstances, not being qualified to express an opinion, it being merely the opinion of a non expert without any reason on which to base the opinion.

By The Court: Anything further for this witness

(Jury retires)

By Mr. Huddleston: If Your Honor please, at this time I would like to make a motion for a mistrial, based on the grounds that when Your Honor remarked to counsel examining the witness who just left the stand that it seemed like a good answer to Your Honor -- and we can check the record to see if I am quoting the answer right -- there was a burst of applause in the courtroom, which clearly showed amusement of the crowd, to the jury, and demonstrated to them the feeling of this crowd, and I think if Your Honor please, I would like to insist on this motion at this particular time, that the crowd thinks that was perhaps an expression of Your Honor's opinion in this matter. And the jury might take it the same way, and I think it is irreparable and the mistrial should be granted.

By the Court: Is that all?

By Mr. Huddleston: That is all.

By the Court: Now the court wishes to correct counsel as to being an outburst of applause. There were about two persons applauding , and they were reprimanded by the Court at the time, the court stating that if that happened again, that the courtroom would be cleared. The motion is overruled.

By Mr. Huddleston: If your honor please, in order to preserve my rights, I would like most respectfully to renew my motion for a mistrial.

By The Court: I most respectfully overrule it. Let the jury come back.

(the jury returns to the box)

By the Court: Call your next witness.

233

Wilson Wood

By Solicitor Wyatt
q. Where do you live, William?

a. I live down in Meriwether.

q. Your name is William Wood?

a. Wilson Wood

q. Do you know the defendant, John Wallace?

a. Yes sir, when I see him.

q. Did you have any conversation with him during the time they were looking for the body of a man by the name of Turner?

a. Well, one morning, I forget what morning it was, Mr. Potts said it was Tuesday morning, Mr. Wallace come down the road from toward --

By Mr. Henson. Objection made to what Potts said.

By The Court: Sustain. Don't say anything about what anybody else said.

By Solicitor Wyatt: q. Tell about your conversation with Mr. Wallace.

a. He come down the road from toward Durand. Mr. Wallace in a black pick up truck and I was on my way from the house going to the lot, and there was a little ditch that runs from the road out to it. I had got across the ditch between there and the lot. I could not see the road and truck for the two apple trees. When it got out from behind the apple trees I could see it was near about in front of my house. He stopped the truck. I didn't know who was in the truck until he pushed the door open and stepped out of the truck, and said "I want to see you a minute, Will.

I said, "me?   "Yes" He come in about twelve feet of me and said, "Will" - - I said "sir.   He said, "how many old wells is there back there in that old plantation,   nodding his head just that way.

I said, "which old plantation?"
He said, "back there in that old plantation.   I said, "two, or three or four, I don't know.   Well, I don't know. It has been near four years since I have

been over there hunting. I didn't know, and he turned around and didn't say a word and walked back and stepped in the truck and went on the way he was heading, so I don't know.

q. Did you tell him where the wells were located and what old plantation?

a. No sir. He was referring to the old plantation that led from my house. I don't know what it's known by.

q. Does Wallace have a pasture in back of that plantation?

a. Yes sir

Cross Examination

By Mr. Henson
q. When did Wallace ask you this?

a. It was one morning. I don't know myself for certain, whether it was Tuesday morning or not, but it was one morning, and it was not Thursday and Friday. It was Tuesday or Wednesday.

q. It was not Saturday, it was not Monday and it was not Tuesday?

a. No sir

q. It was not Wednesday?

a. It was Wednesday or Tuesday

q. Which year?

a. This year

q. Which month?

a. I don't know. But it was a little before I heard of this.

q. A little before you heard of this?

a. Yes sir

q. A week or two before?

a. No sir. I goes to Chipley the next day or two --

q. Yes?

a. And coming on back from Chipley I run on some people down by the highway, had some car trouble. I stopped.

q. I am not asking what they said, and I don't want to get hearsay evidence

.

a. I stopped, and those parties said --

By Mr. Henson
q. That is what you can't say.

a. Well, I heard of it.

q. You don't know when it was?

a. No sir

q. And that is all they asked you? You are an old timer down there aren't you?

a. I am sixty years old. I was born and raised right there. I have hunted lots. I don't hunt back there. I am afraid of the wells. Afraid I might step in there. I don't hunt back there. I have not been back there in nearly four years.

q. Nobody going to get you back there is there?

a. No sir, ain't nobody going to get me back there.

witness excused

Mary Turner

By Solicitor Wyatt
q. Where do you live?

a. I live down there with Mr. Mozart.

q. You live on Mozart Strickland's place?

a. Yes sir

q. What is your husband's name?

a. Ted Turner is my husband.

q. Where is he?

a. I don't know.

q. When did he leave?

a. Left Thursday morning.

q. Where did he go?

a. He didn't say. He said he was suppose to go haul wheat, but he didn't go I don't reckon. I have not seen him since.

q. He disappeared?

a. Yes sir. He left to go haul wheat. He told me he was going to haul wheat at Mr. Tom Strickland's.

q. And you have not seen him since?

a. No sir. I have not seen him since.

q. Do you remember on Wednesday night when the defendant, John Wallace and Boy Brooks came up there to Mozart's house?

By Mr. Henson: That is a leading question. and puts the information right in her mind, and tells her all about it. I hope the Court will protect us.

By The Court: Yes. I sustain the objection.

By Solicitor Wyatt:
q. Do you remember anytime the defendant, John Wallace and Brooks came up to Mozart's house?

a. Yes sir. They come up there all the time. Yes sir. I remember them coming up there.

q. Well, what day of the week was it when they came there and got the truck?

a. If I make no mistake, it was on Wednesday, if I make no mistake.

q. Wednesday, what time?

a. I don't know the exact time. It was in the evening. It was late afternoon not soon after dinner. I didn't see nobody with him when he come up there but Albert. That is all I seen. Albert Brooks.

q. That is the colored man you call Boy Brooks?

a. Yes sir.

q. How did they come?

a. Rode up there in a car. The one Wallace rides in.

q. Well, what did they do when they got up there?

a. Well now, I didn't see them do nothing. He spoke to me and told me good evening. That is all I seen him do. He spoke to me. Later I saw the truck turn around in the back yard. I was in the kitchen. That was Mr. Mozart's truck.

q. What did it have on it?

a. Not a thing in the world when I saw it.

q. When did you see Mr. Henry Mobley?

a. Let me see -- I don't know. I reckon it must have been a week or two after then because I didn't see him that day.

q. What did he say to you when he talked to you the next time you saw him after this thing happened?

By Mr. Henson: Pardon me, but what did who say to her?

By Solicitor Wyatt: Henry Mobley

By Mr. Henson: We submit that is hearsay conversation between third parties.

By Solicitor Wyatt: He is a defendant.

By Mr. Henson: I know that he is but because you put the names in a bill don't give you the right to go in extraneous conversation

By The Court: Sustain

By Solicitor Wyatt: Did you see John Wallace on Tuesday?

a. No sir

q. You didn't see him on Tuesday and give him anything?

a. No sir. I have not seen him on Tuesday and give him nothing.

No Cross Examination   Witness Excused

Robert Lee Gates

q. On April 20 of this year where did you live?

a. Lived on Mr. Wallace's place.

q. Where were you about ten o'clock on the morning of April 20th?

a. I was working on the tractor, putting the planter on his tractor.

q. Where were you?

a. Down there to Mr. Wallace's house, right above the barn, the mule barn.

q. Did anybody come to this place while you were there working on the tractor?

a. Yes sir

q. Who was the first man to get there?

a. Mr. Tom Strickland was the first one. About 10am. I guess it was twenty minutes later and Mr. Henry Mobley came by. About fifteen or twenty more minutes Herring Sivell came. After then about half an hour I guess Mr. Wallace come.

q. When Tom Strickland came, what was he looking for?

a. He was looking -- he asked where was Mr. Wallace.

q. What about Henry Mobley?

a. He didn't say. He drove up where Mr. Tom was parked at, and they talked a few minutes and drove on up there about the mule barn near where we were working at.

q. Did Mr. Sivell call for anybody?

a. No, he just come up where they were. He stayed there a few minutes after Mr. Wallace come. After Mr. Wallace got there, they stayed about ten minutes, I reckon it was. Mr. Wallace and Mr. Sivell got in Mr. Sivell's car and left together. Mr. Tom and Mr. Mobley got in Mr. Mobley's car and left together.

q. What did you do for the rest of the day?

a. Worked on the tractor. I saw Herring Sivell between two and three o'clock somewhere along there. He come back there right below where we were working at and called Albert and told him he wanted him to fix a tire, carry a tire to Chipley to have it fixed.

q. What did Sivell give to Brooks?

a. He also gave him two shotguns. It looked like a double barrel shotgun from where I was and a pump gun.

q. What happened to the guns?

a. Albert set them around there in the gear room.

q. What time did you see Mr. Wallace?

a. Around four o'clock I reckon it was between four and five they went up the road from where we were, up north. It left out toward Greenville, but there is a fork up there a little piece from there, takes you out right to hit the highway.

q. Where were you on Wednesday night, April 21st?

a. I was at home. It was round 8pm I was fixing to eat supper. I was sitting down to the supper table. Mr. Wallace and Albert Brooks came up in a pick up truck.

q. What was on the truck?

a. Cord wood and gas. Mr. Wallace told me to get my hat he wanted me to help him a little bit. We drove on down there by the swamp and throwed the wood off, and set the gas off, and come on back down to his house then. It was pine cord wood that we unloaded. Then we got in the truck with him and went on back down to his house and he told us to get the bridle and put on the saddle horse and catch old Nell and we went and caught the horse and put the saddle on, and he told me to get Nell and he got on the saddle horse and told Albert to meet us over there at the pasture fence over there at the Gates place over there at the gap, that if he hadn't been there by the time I got there to wait, he would be there, and Albert come the nearest way and we come through the swamp.

Albert got there first. He opened the gate, Albert opened the gap and we went on up in the swamp. The pasture belonged to Mr. Wallace. We used it to put the wine around there. We went on up in the swamp there and tied the horses, and he told us he had a package that was hid over there he had to find, and we come looking for the package, he said it was in a thick place with some bushes around it, it was in a well, and we looked and looked, and we didn't find no well nowhere, so we come back where the horses were tied at and rested, and sat there.

I reckon a half hour or a little better, and said "well, let's try it again. We looked at his watch and it was 2 o'clock at night and we went on, kept looking, so Albert found the well, and when we found the well he called me, said "here is a well here. I said, "call him and tell him, and we called him and he come with his flashlight and looked. He said, "this looks like the place, but there ain't no water in this well. He said "water is in this well, and we went on then and looked for another well, and we found another one, was not no water in it, so we kept looking then and the next time he looked at his watch it was three o'clock. He said, "we have to find this package if it takes us all night.

We did not know what was in the package. He told us, said "well, we will go in and get our breakfast and feed up everything and tend to everything, and we will bring our well tools back over here. And if we can't find another well, we will have to clean this well out, it may be done caved."

So we taken the well tools back, ropes and keg and everything. That was on Thursday, the next morning. It was 8 a.m. we went back in Mr. Mozart's truck. We got on the hill about a half a mile from where we was at that night; he told us to take the rope and things on down where we was that night and he was going by a colored fellow's house down there named Wilson Woodward and ask him, find out from him was there another well over there and we taken the rope and went back where we was and it was not but a few minutes he come where we was and he said "yes, there is another well, Will said down through this way, and he went down through there, and we went on behind, and finally he found the well and when he found it he called us and said "here is the place, and I walked up to the well and I looked over in it.

q. What did you see on top of the well there?

a. I seen some blood around the well there. (Note: blood but how much?)

q. Did you see a pole across that well?

a. Yes sir

q. Did the pole have blood on it?

a. Yes sir, the pole had some blood on it. He told us all right, said "you go get the rope and the well drags and let's get the package out of here.

q. Does this look like the grabs that was used?

a. Yes sir. I don't know who furnished the grabs. He carried the grabs over there that night.

q. Who carried them?

a. I carried them on the horse. I carried them over there Wednesday night and could not find the well. We left them over there, left everything we had over there that night. We had the drags, and a sheet, cotton sheet, an old bag, sacks swerved together and we had two ropes. and I went and got the ropes and come back, and let the rope down in there, let the drag down in there, and I hung the drag on his shoe. On the man's shoe that was in the well. Mr. Wallace taken the rope and throwed it around like that until he got it around his leg, and said "let's pull it out" and we pulled it out and when he got it on top of the ground he says "wrap the package up, and we taken it and wrapped it up.

It was a man. It was Wilson Turner. I've known him around two years. It was daytime and I know it was Wilson Turner. The back of his head was looked like it might have been knocked off.

q. Crushed in?

a. Well, looked like it might have been knocked off. It was not -- I would not say it was crushed in. I didn't look back there hard. I just seen it was knocked off.

q. After you got Mr. Turner out of the well then what did you do?

a. Mr. Wallace wrapped it, told us to wrap it. We wrapped it. He said "tie it up" and he said "you cut a pole, Robert, and run it through and bring it back over where we can get to it." We cut that pole with Mr. Wallace's axe. I know the axe by the battered on the handle and I know the name of it.

q. The name of it?

a. A plump. The first pole cut was a pine pole about that big around, I reckon. I cut it to tote the package with. It was fastened to Turner's body by tying it up with a rope and run the pole between the rope and him. We wrapped him up in a sheet, tied ropes around the body and run the pole through the rope between him and the rope. We toted him on our shoulders. Albert had one end of the pole and I had one. I walked in front of Albert. We took it I guess -- I reckon a half a mile. It was as near as I can guess at it.

He told us to lay it out there and cut some brush and put over it and told me to take the truck and carry it back to the house and bring Nell and his saddle horse back. Albert cut the brush with a knife. Mr. Wallace said so and I did what he told me. That was round 10am. Wallace told me to take the truck and carry it home to his house and catch his saddle horse and catch old Nell and come back. I got back around 11am. It might have been a little after. Then Wallace told us, said "all right, put the package up on the horse on Nell and tie it up good where it won't turn or fall off, and we put it on and tied it up. He had an old thing called a saddle. We worked it on a dusting machine, what mules pull to poison cotton with. It fits on each side of the vat, and it has a belly band on it and we buckle it tight on the horse and took the ropes and tied it to the saddle on the horse. Crossways. The body was stiff. We went on then and got near to the place where we carried the wood.

We didn't go to the place then. We got about half a mile from where we put the wood, and we could not get across there on the horses and he told us to take the package over and cut us another pole aid "it is not far across here to the saw dust pile over there, you want to leave your pack somewhere around below that sawdust pile, and if I ain't there when you get there don't put it down to the branch put it somewhere on this side of the branch on the hill and cut some more brush and put over it if I am not there, and I will take the horses and go around and be on down there,   and we went on across there and put it down like he said and cut some brush and put over it.

q. How close was that to the pit?

a. Around 50 yards I reckon. Then we turned around then and started back home and met him, and he asked us had we got over there, and we said "yes.   He said "you didn't carry it to the branch,   and we said "no sir, we didn't get to the branch.

He said "all right, you can go back now and get ready to try to fix the tractor and get ready to go to planting cotton" and I spoke and told him. I said, "Mr. Wallace, I am broke down and tired." I said, "I was up all night last night and I am simply sick, I simply don't feel like doing nothing this evening.   He said "all right, you can go and rest up a little while this evening and about an hour of sun I will be back up to your house" and told Albert to meet him back up to my house about an hour to sun, somewhere along there, and around that time he was there. Albert was already there when he got there.

q. Albert was at your house?

a. Yes sir. They (unknown as to who they represent) told us to get in the truck and we got in the truck and went on down near to the place where we carried the wood and walked on down there. Left the truck up there in the old road and walked on down there and got where the wood was and he said, "all right, go to toting your wood there."   There was a pit in the swamp down there. I guess Mr. Wilson dug it.

q. Who?

a. Mr. Wilson Turner. We carried the wood from where we throwed it off that Wednesday night, carried the wood right there to the pit. We carried the wood, and Mr. Wallace stacked the wood in the pit, crossed it up like that and when we got mighty near all of it but about three or four turns of it, he asked us how much more was out there. I told him three or four turns, and he said "all right, go get the package and bring it, and we went and got the package and brought it and he told us to lay it straight up and down the pile, and we laid it on there and he said "get the rest of the wood, and we got the rest of the wood, and he taken the wood and sort of piled -- what we had left -- and piled it around and poured ten gallons of gas on him and he said "stand back.

q. Who poured the gas?

a. Mr. Wallace

q. Did you see any milk cans?

a. I don't know. I didn't pay any attention to any milk cans. Then Wallace threw a match and set the package on fire. A big blaze went up. It went way up in the top of some high trees there, way up in the air. We stayed there about thirty minutes looking at it. We went on home then and he told us all right in the morning first thing he said "I want you to go down there and take the shovel and them sacks and go down there and clean the pit out good."

This would be Friday morning. He didn't go with us but he come behind us. He come there before we got through cleaning it out. We taken a shovel and scooped up all the ashes down to the dirt and put in the sacks. We used three bagging sacks. We taken the ashes, me and Albert and Mr. Wallace taken the ashes down there to the creek and poured them in the creek. It was around sixty or seventy yards I reckon, or might have been a hundred.

q. Was there any part of the body there when you sacked them up?

a. No sir. Was not nothing but ashes.

q. What did you do then?

a. We went on back, started to finish putting the planter on the tractor. He said "well, you can go back now and fix your tractor up and get ready to plant cotton; Mr. Myhand will be up to help you get started at dinner, and I have got to go to Newnan."

q. And you have not seen him since?

a. No sir, before I come up here.

q. What went with the hooks that you pulled the man out of the well with?

a. They give me the hooks when I taken the truck back to get the horses the last time, give me the hooks and he told me to leave them there at Albert's house. Albert said, "don't leave them here" so I throwed them down at the gap below Albert's. I told the officers where I put them.

q. What did you carry down to the pit the next morning to tote the ashes in besides sacks?

a. Not anything but --

q. Did you have any tin buckets down there?

a. Let's see -- it looks like to me we had some sort of little bucket or something, some sort of tin bucket.

q. Robert Lee, were you not frightened to handle that dead man like that? Why did you do it?

a. Yes sir, I was scared to do it, of course. I had never did anything like that, but --

q. Why did you?

a. I was scared not to do it.

q. Did the dead man have anything in his pocket?

a. Yes sir he had a Prince Albert box.

q. Tobacco can?

a. Yes sir. He had it in his pocket when we wrapped him up. I didn't see the can when we cleaned out the pit. We just got all the ashes out of it and then there was sawdust and stuff in there and we taken it out and piled it up on the side, on the side of the pit. Mr. Wallace said "we will clean it out like somebody might be fixing to make liquor or something and won't anybody think anything about it."

No Cross Examination

(Jury returns to the box after recess

John Wesley Ellison (is another sharecropper on Wallace's land)

q. Where do you live?

a. I live on Mr. Wallace's place.

q. Do you know John Wallace?

a. Yes sir, no more than - no more than when he come down there and requested me on Friday afternoon, asked me --

By the Court: He asked you did you know him? Do you know him?

a. No sir. I knowed him this year. I have been living with him.
I know him when I see him.   I have been living with him all this year.

q. All this year?

a. About all this year.

q. During the time you have been down there have you seen him with a gun?

a. I seen him with a gun when he first moved up there about the middle of January.

q. What kind of gun?

a. I took it to be a sawed off pump gun.

q. Sawed off pump gun?

a. Yes sir, I was in the milk dairy.

q. What was he doing with it when you saw him?

a. He come out of his house to get in his car.

Cross Examination
By Mr. Henson
q. Wallace has a lot of cattle roaming around those woods doesn't he?

a. He has a lot of cattle.

q. And all cattle men carry shot guns with them when they are looking after their cattle?

a. Yes sir.

q. Do you know how many cattle Mr. Wallace has or had?

a. No sir. He has a right smart of them.

q. How big is his barn?

a. It is a large barn. He has put fifty cattle in there at one time.

q. What's in the barn now?

a. Nothing but dairy feed.

q. What is it?

a. Cow feed in bagging sacks.

q. What's the barn built out of, wood?

a. Yes sir, timber and shingles all but the walls. The walls are cement up about that high and then board and then a tin top. It has a loft in the feed proposition. It would not be so very easy to burn up. He had two cows stolen after I was there. That is the only thing I knew anything about.

the witness is excused.

We will take a recess until nine thirty tomorrow morning.

(Recess at 4:30 p.m. Tuesday)

Day Three

June 16, 1948   9:30 a.m. Wednesday, June 16, 1948

Albert Brooks: lived on John Wallace's place. He saw Strickland, Mobley and Sivell arrive the exact same time as to when they arrived as Gates gave.

They stayed at Mr. Wallace's house a few minutes and we were up to his barn. Mr. Wallace was not there. I guess he was over in the cotton field where they were planting cotton. He arrived about 15 or 20 minutes later. they stayed about 20 minutes after Mr. Wallace come then they all left. I saw Mr. Sivell again around 2pm that afternoon. He come back and he called me to the car and asked me could I go have a tire fixed for him, and I told him yes, sir and he taken the tire out and give it to me. He handed me two guns. One was a double-barreled breach loader and the other a pump gun. I put the guns in the gear room and then took the tire to Chipley and had it fixed.

I saw Henry Mobley about 3pm. He was by himself. Mr. Wallace got back about 4 or 5 that day.

q. Tell us in your own words about that night.

a. Well, on Wednesday we was working on the tractor and he come where we was and we got through with it. He told us -- well, he said about night, "you go feed up the stock". We goes out and feeds up the stock and he asked me said "I have a job I want you to help me do. I told him "yes, sir.

He taken me -- I went out to his house with him, and in the little car was ten gallons of gas, and I went up the road toward my house and got there and I got out of the car and he went up the road on up the road to Mr. Mozart's. Then he stayed a few minutes and come back and got me and I goes back up the road with him, get back up to Mr. Mozart's, he gets his truck and we goes off in the woods and gets a load of wood.

After we get the load of wood he comes back to Mr. Mozart's and gets the gas and puts it on the truck and comes back to Robert Lee Gates' and gets him and goes in the swamp and throws the wood off in the edge of the swamp and after we throwed it off, come back below my house and got out some drags and rope throwed out beside the road, and he gets Robert Lee to get under the steering wheel and drive the car on to the house, and told him to catch the saddle horse and put the saddle on it and another old horse named Nell, and he gets on the saddle horse and Robert Lee gets on Nell and goes to the Gates place and I walked and he told me "if I got there before he did to wait there.

The Gates place had a pasture gap, and if they got there first they would wait for me and I beat them a little bit and waited and when I got there he told me to open the gap and I opened the gap, and he went in and I walked behind them, and we got up in the swamp I guess about three-quarters of a mile and tied the horses and got off and gets a flashlight and he goes to looking around in bushes.

He said he had a package over there and it had to be found and we hunted around for the package about twelve o'clock that night, and got tired and then they come up and set down and rested awhile, and he said "we have got to find that package, and gets up and goes to looking for it again. He said, "well, it is in a thick place, and it is in a well, and we commenced looking for it then, and I found an old well.

I called him and said "here a well is" and he come and looked down in it and said "this looks like the place, but that well had a little water in it. Well, we went back looking again, and got tired and come back and sat down and looked at the watch then and it was 3 a.m. in the morning. He said "well, we will go home and feed up everything and get us some buckets and things and come back and clean the well out if we don't find nary other one, and we come back that morning.

He put us out on a hill by Wilson's Wood house, and he goes by Wilson's Wood house and said there was another well over there and he come where we was and said I "it is down through here" and we went down through there looking for it and finally he said "here it is, and he told Robert Lee Gates to go up on the hill where we tied the horses to get the well drag and the rope and when he got back he asked Robert Lee did he go in the well, and he said "no, and Robert Lee takes the drag on the rope and hooked the body in the foot, in his shoe, and he wrapped it around the leg and all three got a hold of it and pulled him out, and when we pulled him up on the bank he said "all right, wrap the package up."

And we wrapped it up and he tied him up with a rope, and then he tells Robert Lee Gates to cut a pole, and he cut a pole about that big around and run it between him and the rope and we fixed it up and bring it away about three quarters of a mile, toted it, and we toted it that far, we laid it in a gully and cut some brush and throwed it off like he told us and then we walked up on across the field where the truck was setting and he tells Robert Lee Gates to take the truck and take it to the house and bring the horses, and he brings back the saddle horse and Nell, and we taken the body and laid it up on the horse, laid it across the horse and tied him on there and after we tied him we taken it across the swamp on through to another farm over there and taken him off, I reckon about a half a mile from this pit and toted him through the swamp and he said "well, if you get over there before I do said "don't lay it down next to the ditch; lay it up on the hill and cover it up so nobody won't see it if they happen to go through there,   and we did that and come on out and met him, and he asked if we put it away like he told me and we said "yes sir,   and he said "you go in and get your dinner and start planting cotton and Robert Lee Gates said "well, Mr. Wallace, we have been up all night and we're tired and sleepy.

He said "all right, get your dinner and go on and rest and meet me back here in about an hour by sun,   and I goes home and eats my dinner and I could not stay around there and I left. I come on backup to Robert Lee Gates' house, and a few minutes after I got there Robert Lee was not there and he come and in a few minutes Mr. Wallace come and he said "well, let's go,   and we went on down where we throwed the wood off and toted it to the pit and he fixed a rack down in the pit and I said "how much more wood you got out there,   and he said three or four arms full and he said "get the package and bring it and the gas,   get it and bring it to him, and he said "lay it up on the wood,   and we laid it up there and he poured the gas on the wood. Then I guess I didn't see him pour it and he said "get back out of the way,   and we got back and he struck a match and throwed it on it and it come up in a big blaze and we didn't see the package anymore, and we stayed I guess around about a half an hour and he said "well, let's go,   and we came back here about twelve (midnight) and didn't go back, I didn't.

He didn't call me and the next morning I go up to feed the stock and he asked me, said "well, I want you to go to Robert Lee's and help him throw up, terrace," and he said "go get some sacks and clean that pit out good" and we get up there and start to cleaning it out, and about the time we got it half way cleaned out he come up and cleaned it up and we had three sacks of ashes that come out of the pit, and he said "clean it out good about like it was so anybody would think they had been making liquor, and we cleaned it out good, and after we cleaned it out he said "take the ashes down to the creek and empty them and I taken a sack and Robert Lee taken one, and we taken the other one in our hands and taken it on, and after we got through with that he come back and said "well, go ahead and go to planting cotton.   He said "I have got to go to Newnan.

q. What day of the week was he going to Newnan?

a. That was on Friday morning.

q. Have you seen him anymore since then?

a. Not until I come up here.

q. Who was the man you pulled out of the well?

a. It was Mr. Wilson Turner. I had been knowing him about two years.

q. Who cut the bushes which covered the body?

a. Me and Robert Lee.

q. Did you cut them or Robert Lee cut them?

a. Robert Lee and I toted them.

q. Where were the first bushes you cut with reference to the well?

a. The bushes was across the ditch after we put him down.

q. Did you cut any bushes and cover him near the well where you toted him out and went to get the horses?

a Yes sir. We, cut bushes there with an axe about three quarters of a mile from the well. I would say it was around 10:30 when we left to go get the horses when he got back with them it was around right at 12.

q. And then you put him on the horses?

a Yes sir. We carried him about two miles and a half through the swamp the way we went. The pit was just an old still place.

q. What did you do at Mr. Mozart's house?

a. We went there and got Mr. Mozart's truck, told him he wanted his truck to unload wood.

q. You got the gas and the load of wood at the same time?

a. No sir. He got the gas first and carried it up to Mr. Mozart's in the little model A car and after he got there he told him he wanted his truck and a load of wood on it and he told the hands he had and me to go in the woods and get a load of cord wood.

q. Where was the gas?

a. It was sitting in the little model A car until we got the wood. He come back from the swamp with the wood and got the gas, back to his house and got the gas on there then.

q. You went up to Mozart Strickland's to get the wood. Where was the wood with reference to Mozart's house?

a. It was sort of north of Mr. Mozart's house over in the swamp.

q. You went over in the swamp and got the load of wood and come back to Mr. Mozart's house?

a. Yes sir.

q. Albert, when the body was taken out of that well, what injuries, if any, were on the body?

a. Well, all I seen was just about his head. It was knocked off back here.

q. The back of his head?

a. Yes sir.

q. Did you later show the officers where the sacks were that you used to carry the ashes in?

a. Yes sir.

q. And they got them?

a. Yes sir.

(Albert saw the can of tobacco after it had been burnt but not before. He threw what was left of the tin up on the bank in the process of cleaning the pit out. He identified a pole that was laid over the well that he states had

253

blood on it.)

Cross Examination

By Mr. Hinson:

q. When did you clean out the pit?

a. Friday morning

q. What day was it that you first saw Mr. Wallace?

a. About the first of the killing.

q. You cleaned out the pit and put the ashes in the creek and the ashes floated down the run of the creek with the water didn't it?

a. Yes sir

q. You didn't leave any ashes at all in the pit?

a. No sir, we didn't leave no ashes. After we got all the ashes out, we come back and cleaned it out again.

q. Cleaned it again?

a. Yes sir

q. Albert, you were arrested pretty soon after that weren't you?

a Yes sir

q. And they indicted you and Robert Lee for murder?

a Yes sir

q. And you have been in jail ever since?

a. Yes sir, been in jail ever since.

q. You have not been tried?

a. No sir

q. Where have you been all this time?

a. I have been down in Columbus and up here.

q. What?

a. Down in Columbus.

q. All the time?

a. Yes sir, and been up here a little better than a week.

q. I beg your pardon?

a. We have been up here a little better than a week.

q. You have been in Newnan since a week ago.

a. Yes sir

q. Have you seen anybody since you got in jail?

a. No sir

q. Anybody at all?

a. Well, we seen -- we ain't seen but one fellow one man been down there, one lawyer.

q. Who was he?

a. I don't know his name.

q. Did you send for him?

a. No sir

q. Now you didn't see him until you got to Newnan did you?

a. No sir

q. Did you see anybody down at Columbus?

a. No sir, nobody but the Sheriff.

q. The Sheriff?

a. Yes sir

q. You didn't get any lawyer until you got up here to Newnan?

a. No sir

q. Where is he?

a. There he is right over there.

witness excused

W. E. Irvin a Justice of the Peace at Greenville, Georgia

Direct Examination

q. Did you ever issue any warrant for anyone for Wilson Turner for stealing a cow?

a. No sir

Cross Examination

By Mr. Henson:

q. You don't know who else might have issued the warrant do you?

a. No sir I do not.

q. How many committing magistrates do you have down there in your county?

a. I didn't understand.

q. How many Justices of the Peace with authority to issue warrants do you have down there?

a. Well, there are eighteen districts in the county. Some two or three don't have a Justice of the Peace but they have N.P. ex officious.

q. You have at least eighteen?

a. Eighteen in Meriwether County.

q. Just about twice that many, lacking two or three having that many committing magistrates authorized to issue warrants?

a. Yes sir

q. Judge, you have disability with respect to your vision, don't you?

a. Yes sir. My eyes are atrophied.

q. That makes it necessary for you to have someone else to do your writing?

a. Absolutely. Others have to do my reading and writing for me.

q. And any paper that might come for you. You have to depend on somebody else to tell you what is in it?

a. Yes sir. But there are only two person who are authorized to sign my name when I am away. That is a lady in the courthouse and the Clerk of the Superior Court.

q. What are their names?

a. I would not care to call the girl's name. She is rather timid.

q. That is all right. You need not call her name.

a. My office is in the courthouse, and she works there.

q. And she is authorized to sign your name to a warrant?

a. In my absence she did. That Monday when I was here she issued a warrant.

q. She frequently does that?

a. Yes sir

q. You would not know what warrants might be out with your name on them unless she told you?

a. Well, she tells me. It is very seldom I am away, very seldom?

q. I know. But it is entirely possible for her to sign a warrant without you knowing about it?

a. No I would know about it as soon as I see her.

q. You mean you would know about it later?

a. Yes sir

q. You would not know about it unless they tell you?

a. No. This past Monday she issued two warrants for murder while I was here.

q. And you didn't know about it until you got back home?

a. That is true.

q. The only way you would ever know about it would be for her to tell you?

a. Yes sir

q. And if she didn't tell you, you would not know.

a. That is true.

Redirect Examination

q. Has she ever told you she issued a warrant for Wilson Turner for cow theft?

a. She didn't. I don't believe she did. She did say that she issued it at night -- Sunday night -- no --

q. How is that?

a. What is your question?

q. You are not certain whether she did or not?

a. No sir

q. And she might have?

a. She might have.

q. Might have issued a cow stealing warrant?

a. Yes sir

witness is excused

Charles H. Hixon works at Silver Motor company now. Was working at Ray Smith's service station on April 23rd, 1948.

Direct Examination:

q. Did Mr. Sivell bring a car in on that day?

a. Yes sir, a green 1947 two-door sedan Ford, I washed it out, cleaned it out inside and outside. I seen a puddle of blood on the right hand side on the seat cover on the floor board. It was on the floor mat. It was in the center.

q. How big a puddle of blood was it?

q. Something like about like that. (Indicating circle)

q. How did you get it out?

a. I just taken a wet soapy rag and rubbed it.

q. Did you see anymore blood stains anywhere else?

a. Well, I seen some more spots, but I could not say whether it was blood stains or not. Somewhere on the seat cover. I seen some spots on the outside of the car but it was dusty. I could not tell whether it was blood stains.

q. Did Herring Sivell do anything after you cleaned it?

a. Well, after I got through cleaning it up, he came down there and he taken a rag and dusted the seat off, wiped it off on the side.

Cross Examination

By Mr. Henson:
q. That was fresh blood was it not?

a. I couldn't tell you whether it was fresh blood or not.

q. Could you tell whether it was blood or not?

a. Yes sir. I know it was blood. It was nothing else but blood. All blood looks alike.

q. Do you know anything about what happens to blood when it stays on a fabric from Tuesday to Friday?

a. No sir, I could not tell when it was put on there.

q. Don't you know blood that long would lose its red color? This was real red, was it?

a. Yes sir

q. Sticky?

a   I could not tell whether it was sticky or not. I didn't put my hand in it.

q. It looked sticky?

a. Yes sir

q. Looked fresh?

a. Yes sir

q. Looked right fresh?

a. Yes sir

q. And that was Friday. Now you have seen blood where people killed hogs and things haven't you?

a. Yes sir

q. Don't you know in a couple of hours? It becomes dry and pale?

a. Yes sir

q. Now this was not that kind of blood was it?

a. It didn't exactly look like it was dry.

q. This was red, bright red and fresh?

a. Yes sir

Redirect by Solicitor Wyatt

q. Was the blood soft or dry?

a. I just could not exactly tell you, but it came off, came off the floor mat.

witness excused

Mr. J. H. Turner: father of William Turner

He identifies the picture of William H. aka Wilson Turner

Cross Examination

By Mr. Henson:
q. Do you know that William took that (his brother, Wilson's registration) card to evade the army?

a. No, I don't know that . . . let me tell you what I know about that card. My son Wilson was put in 4-F because his mind ain't good, and he was put there on that account. And me and my son Wilson we done the hardest of farm work and tending to cattle and hogs, and put his 4-H card in the room where he stayed in a dresser drawer. When my son William left the army, he stayed at my house one day before he left, and we didn't know where he went. Well now, he went in that room whenever he got ready --

q. And he got this card?

a. And he was at home, his sister was at school, and his mother was there. and if he got that card, his mother didn't know it. Sometime after that my son Wilson wanted his card for something and looked for it, and it was gone. We didn't know that William had it. My son Wilson didn't know it, and I didn't know it, and my wife didn't know it.

q. Now this boy here didn't want to go to the army?

a. Well now, he went to the army without any trouble.

q. What?

a. He went to the army. He went to the army and trained nicely. And made an expert marksman, and they gave him the badge. He was the best marksman of three thousand men. He made an expert marksman. He trained at Little Rock, Arkansas -

Judge stops him from answering any more questions regarding Turner's military service or why he deserted.

witness excused

Recess called at 10:45 a.m.

after recess

Mr. A. L. Potts

By Solicitor Wyatt:

q. Mr. Potts, you investigated this case in which Wilson Turner was killed?

a. Yes sir

q. First I will ask you did you arrest Sivell, Herring Sivell, and Henry Mobley about this case, about the murder?

a. Yes sir I did.

q. Did you receive a car from either Henry Mobley or Herring Sivell?

a. I got one from both of them. I got Sivell car on Friday, April 23rd this year and sent it to Dr. Herman Jones in Atlanta. Pete Redenbaugh, one of the State Revenue officers drove it up. I got a car from Henry Mobley later and sent it to Dr. Jones also.

q. I hand you this Super Western -- Western Super match box and ask you what that contains?

a. It is not a match box. This is a cartridge box -- Super Cartridge box.

q. All right -- what does that contain?

a. Contains material we found at a pit down in Meriwether County.

q. Contains material you found at the pit?

a. Yes sir

q. What pit was that?

a. It was a pit located immediately behind Robert Lee Gates' house in a swamp, down in Meriwether County.

q. Is that the pit where the body was burned?

a. Pit where the body was burned.

q. Who told you about the pit?

a. Mr. Hancock is the first man that told me about it and then Robert Lee Gates told me and went with me down there.

q. What did you find down at the pit that he pointed out to you?

a. Well, I found a pit there thirteen feet long, about six or seven feet wide, two feet deep, some trees around it, and evidence of a fire having been there, evidence that it had been.

By Solicitor Wyatt:
q. State what you saw there with reference to whether ashes or burned places --

By Mr. Henson: I object to leading him and putting in his mouth exactly what he wants him to swear.

By The Court: Don't lead the witness. Go ahead

a. I saw some ashes. I saw a big pile of saw dust. I saw some white chips that I thought were bones.

By Mr. Henson: I move to strike that.

By the Court: I sustain the objection to that, what he thought.

By Solicitor Wyatt
q. Tell me what you found around the pit?

a. Well, I saw two trees standing on the edge of the pit, trees about sixty feet high. the foliage was burned on them on one side completely to the top, the foliage on either side of the branch, both sides of the branch, for a distance of about sixty feet down the branch all the foliage had been burned off all the bushes and briars going down the branch, and up the branch the foliage had been burned for a distance of approximately twenty feet up the branch. An area of probably forty feet in a radius of forty feet all the foliage was burned on all the growth there. I also saw some ashes and saw this pile of saw dust, apparently had been thrown out of the pit. I saw these white chips.

q. Did you get anything there and put in this box that I handed you?

a. I did, yes sir

q. What was that?

a. Well, the ashes and those white chips.

q. Ashes and white chips you found at this pit?

a. Yes sir

q. Were they down in the pit or where were they?

a. No sir, up on the edge of the pit up on the bank of the pit. Some of it came out of that pile of saw dust. We sifted that.

q. I hand you a handkerchief here and ask you what that contains?

a. It contains some ashes that were picked up down -- I know they are ashes. I picked them up myself. It contains some ashes I picked up down at the edge of the creek and in the edge of the water down about 100 yards below the pit where the little branch runs into the creek. Robert Lee Gates and Albert Brooks spotted the place out to me.

q. How far did you say that was from the pit?

a. I am guessing, but about 100 yards I think

q. Where did you pick up those ashes?

a. Down there on the edge of the creek bank and in the edge of the water.

(He then states that he got an axe from Robert Gates place, a pocket knife from Albert Brooks that was used to cut bushes to cover the body with and poles used in carrying the body. They took many samples of bush that were near the area in which the body was laid. He got two five-gallon cans down at John Wallace's house. One had the smell of gas in it. He got the cans on Tuesday, two weeks after April 20th.)

By Solicitor Wyatt:
q. Who directed you to the well?

a. Robert Lee Gates and Albert Brooks.

q. Go ahead and describe to the jury what you found at the well when you went there.

a. When I went there I didn't find anything but a well. That is all. I saw evidence there where a pole had been cut. Well, I saw a stump where a pole had been cut.

q. All right, did you see anything else? Describe what you saw.

a. No sir, when I went there it was the day after the other officers had been there and cleaned the thing out. I didn't see anything except the well.

q. Were you present when some photographs were made of this well?

a. Yes sir. That is a picture of this same pit that we discussed and foliage and trees around it. This other picture is one that shows the bottom and side of the well taken at the top of the well looking down toward the bottom.

q. Mr. Potts, is there any other thing that you can identify that I have not asked you about?

a. I don't believe so, except that red can there and that bolt tied around it.

Cross Examination

By Mr. Henson: He asks the sheriff for a description that is estimated at 22 yards. Then he asked if the material described here (I think he's referring to the box) whether it had been in the Sheriffs' custody at all times since he picked it up at a well. Then he brings up the point that the Sheriff does not know what was done with the box once it left his custody. The sheriff agrees that he does not know.

q. There is no way for you to tell that these are the same chips that were in the box when it left your custody is there?

a. Well, they look like them. It is the same box.

q. I know you said it looks like them but I say you can't say it was the same ones can you, nothing but little white chips and nothing distinctive about them is there?

a. Well, they look unusual, yes.

q. They look like other little white chips like them?

a. No, I don't think so.

q. Now you say there was some saw dust in the pit you saw?

a. No sir. I didn't say that.

q. You say there was some ashes in it?

a. No sir. I didn't say that.

q. You say there was some saw dust laying up on the bank?

a. That is right.

q. Well, had there been a fire in that pit?

a. Yes sir

q. It was not hot enough though to burn the saw dust was it?

a. It was not burned.

q. Well, if it had been hot enough to burn up saw dust, that saw dust would have burned wouldn't it?

a. If the saw dust had been in the fire, I don't presume you would have found it.

q. That is right. Now when you saw this pit, was there anything in the bottom except freshly scraped earth?

a. Yes sir, there was. There was signs of decayed sawdust. Let me finish the answer. I said there was decayed sawdust in the bottom.

q. And the fire that was in that pit was not hot enough to burn that decayed sawdust?

a. I don't know how hot it was. That in the pit was not burned, in the bottom of the pit.

q. Well, it was there?

a. Sir

q. There had not been a fire in that particular pit hot enough to burn decayed sawdust had there?

a. Yes sir. There had been a fire in that pit hot enough to burn anything.

q. There was?

a. Yes sir

q. Yet it didn't burn that decayed saw dust.

a. No sir, because it was under the fire and covered with other substance.

q. I thought you said that there was some saw dust up on the side.

a. There was quite a lot.

q. And the fire was not hot enough to burn that?

a. That was not burned, neither was the dirt burned. No.

q. Yet you say there was a place there where the trees had been burned sixty feet high?

a. That is right, it burned the foliage. Burned the foliage up the branch, not the bank.

q. Yet the fire in the pit was hot enough to burn green foliage forty feet away and left some dry sawdust undisturbed; is that your testimony?

a. It left a heap of things undisturbed. It left the ground undisturbed. It burned everything in the pit.

q. It burned everything but what you boys brought down here as evidence?
a. No, it didn't burn everything else.

q. Well, did you leave anything at the pit?

a. The banks of the pit were there. It didn't burn them.

q. And the banks of the pit were freshly removed dirt?

a. No sir

q. The bottom. Now these boys --

a. Wait a minute. You asked a question. Let me answer. No, it was not fresh. The banks were not fresh.

q. Now the pit these boys were talking about, that pit did have freshly removed dirt?

a. So did this one, but it was --

q. I thought you said just now it --. Are you sure you and the boys are talking about the same pit?

a. Yes sir. I am sure of that.

q. Well, you described a totally different pit.

a. No. You describe a totally different pit. I am not.

q. It was fresh, this little branch --

By Solicitor Wyatt: Wait a minute.

By the Court: Answer the question.

a. It was an old pit. The pit had been re-cleaned, been cleaned out a second time. There was still evidence there of an old pit all banks, part freshly scraped and part of them were not. The pit had been there probably several years.

q. An old pit?

a. That is right, an old still sight.

q. It was one they remodeled?

a. That is right. You might call it remodeling.

q. How big a branch was that?

a. It was a small branch, but it had a deep bank to it. It was not very wide, but it was a deep bank.

q. Forty feet away the shrubbery was burned to a crisp?

a. No sir, more than that.

q. More than that?

a. Yes sir

q. Now these cans you found, these are the cans that people use that have their own gas tank?

a. They were there in Mr. Wallace's house in what I would say a tool house or something like that.

q. You could find dozens of these in your good county could you not?

a. Oh yes. He had several others there, yes sir.

q. Now these little twigs here -- they were not burned were they.

a. They weren't around the pit, no sir.

q. Where did you find these little twigs?

a. Up on the hill across the branch about sixty yards from the branch.

q. You could have got a couple of truck loads of them could you not, around on the Gates farm, just like them?

a. More than that I guess.

q. What do you know about the well?

a. I know there is a well there, and I know how deep it is. I know where there are three wells in that area.

q. Sheriff, you paid a reward in this case didn't you?

a. Yes sir, I did.

q. Out of your own pocket?

a. That is right.

q. Who did you pay it to?

a. E. J. Hancock

q. Who is he? What is his official -

a. Well, he is a State Revenue Officer, as far as I know.

q. Is he a State Revenue officer now?

a. Yes sir

q. And he was at the time you paid him the reward?

a. To the best of my knowledge that is his position, yes sir.

q. You know what the Revenue Department's job is don't you?

a. Yes sir

q. It is not to investigate homicides is it?

a. They assist, when we ask them.

Redirect Examination

q. How many deputies do you have?

a. One

q. Did you call in additional officers to help you in the investigation?

a. Quite a number of them.

q. Mr. Hancock was one of them?

a. I asked specifically that Mr. Hancock be allowed to help me.

witness excused

Mr. Pete Bedenbaugh

By Solicitor Wyatt:
q. Mr. Bedenbaugh what are your initials?

a. L . L.

Q. Did you deliver an auto to Dr. Herman Jones this year?

a. I did

q. Did you go to a well down in Meriwether?

a. I did

q. Who directed you to this well?

a. Well, there didn't anybody direct us to the well. We went under what this Negro told us where to go.

q. What Negro was that?

a. Gates

q. Robert Lee Gates?

a. Yes

q. What did you find there?

a. I found that pole there about -- as far as from here to the back end of the court room from the well.

q. What's on the pole?

271

a. Blood

recess called at 11:45 a.m. until 1pm

after lunch

J. H. Potts, deputy sheriff of Coweta County

Basically his statement consist of the fact that he went to the well. He got a bucket with some ashes in it from the creek. They cut a lot of stems and gave those to Dr. Jones as well. He found the shirt and pants at John Wallace's house on April 23rd.

q. Did you give the pants and shirt to Dr. Jones?

a. No sir, they were turned over the Sheriff.

q. Turned over to your brother?

a. Yes sir. I got the pants and shirt nearly two weeks before I got this other stuff. The pants and shirt were in John Wallace's house, what I call a storage room in his house. It was in a clothes hamper. The shirt was in the hamper and some clothes on top of it, and a pair of blue pants were hanging up on a hook in the same room right above the hamper.

q. Could you see any coloring or stains on those pants and shirt?

a. Yes sir, I could on the shirt very distinctly.

q. What was it?

a. It looked like blood.

The rest of his statement consist mainly of the fact that he was present when a bucket was taken from the well.

Witness Excused

Sergeant J. C. Otwell Georgia State Patrol

q. Did you help investigate this case?

a. Yes sir. I went to the well. Did you go down in the well?

a. Yes sir

q. What did you find down in the well, who went down there first?

a. We had a prisoner with us that went down in the well, and he says "I have found" --

q. Just tell us what you found when you went down in the well.

a. I got a letter out of the well. It was wrote on these three backs of Prince Albert leaf papers and was folded up something like this.

q. Whose name was signed to the letter?

a. Wilson Turner

q. What else did you find down in the well?

a. I found some blood in the well, two large places of blood like about as much as you could hold in your hand like that? It was coagulated blood. Found some blood on a stick. And found something like that many brains. (Holding up cupped hands)

The trip to the well where he found all these things occurred on May 4th.

(It is interesting to note that nothing else is said about the letter, other than it be stricken from the record. We don't know what it says, with the exception of what is written in the book, but it would stand to reason that it must have been written after the chase scene and he was taken to this area. Thereby reenforcing the conclusion that he did not die at the Sunset Tourist Camp in Coweta county.)

witness excused

Dr. Herman Jones is the Director of Fulton county scientific crime laboratory. He states the following: I took my undergraduate college training at Auburn, Alabama Polytechnic Institute in 1924, I took my master -- that was in chemistry -- then in 1928 I took my master's degree from Columbia University in New York City in chemistry and bio chemistry. In 1939 I took my PHD degree from the School of Medicine, Vanderbilt University in anatomy, the study of the normal tissues of the body, the study of abnormal tissues of the body, blood of identification, typing, that phase of the work. Then in 1938 -- well, I started back in 1930. I began to get into this type of criminal investigative work through the Dean of the School of Chemistry at Auburn, and in 1935 the State of Alabama set up this State Laboratory, and we had to qualify under the State Merit System Law in Alabama through written and oral examinations, the toxicologists, as junior toxicologist and senior toxicologists. I worked in that laboratory until I came to Atlanta in 1942. Then in 1942, from 1942 until the present time I have been doing either part time or full time in this same type of work.

Direct Examination

By Solicitor Wyatt:

q. Have you had any experience in blood analysis, doctor?

a. I have; yes sir

q. This is, Exhibit 20, Dr. Jones. Will you look at that exhibit and tell us what you found?

a. Starting with the shirt?

q. All right.

a. On the right sleeve one small spot of blood on the right corner of cuff underneath, then adjacent to the placket and on the left side was a circle of blood about the size of the area which I have cut out. I cut that out in order to get the blood from the material where our analysis could be made. I left some of the blood adjacent here so it could still be seen. That was tested for blood and proven to be blood, and also proven to be human blood.

Now on the elbow of that same right sleeve is a circle of blood which is heavier on the lower part than it is on the upper part of that circle area. On the left front just under the pocket four small streaks of blood, they are not spots, but looked as though they have been kind of smeared across. One was removed for analysis. Just opposite the lower button hole, another spot of blood. On the right side of the shirt under the pocket was one smear, and then below that area two other small smeared areas. On the right shoulder was just a small clot of blood dried and sticking up, and that little spot was removed and tested for blood and shown to be blood, and human blood, and there is the little speck where it was adherent to the shirt when I removed it.

All the blood was proven to be human blood. The trouser on the front of the right leg also showed to be human blood.

(Mr. Henson objected as the clothes had not been proven to belong to Mr. Wallace only that they were found in his house.)

Witness dismissed and Lamar Potts retakes the stand.

q. Do you know who these clothes belong to?

a. I know who identified them.

q. Who?

a. John Wallace.

q. Why?

a. I told John we found the clothing in his house that had blood on them, probably he would like to explain how they got bloody and he suggested I get the clothing and let him see them, and I did and he said, "I can tell you how they got bloody; I had some scratches on my hands and I got it off my hands, this very shirt, when I was riding my horse through the pasture, and I scratched my hand" and at that time he did have some scratches on his hand and he told me that were his. He had some scratches that appeared to have been made by briers on his hand, and his legs were badly scratched. I had a photograph made of it.

By Mr. Henson: I renew my objection to the testimony because it appears this was Mr. Wallace's blood and therefore --

By The Court: Dr. Jones does not say whose blood it is. He just says it was human blood.

**note; this is a point the jury seems to have ignored.

Dr. Jones is recalled

He looks at the panel of Sivell car and attests that a streak of blood that extended from a point about the middle of a red circle which he placed there too about the middle of the lower circle which he placed, with a red pencil. His testimony is as follows:

You can see where I removed the blood. This was tested just for blood only and proven to be blood but there was not sufficient quantity to test for human blood. Three stains were found on a different panel. One just under the arm rest, one below that one and one below and slightly to the left the way I have it to me now. Those areas were tested for blood and shown to be blood only. Again, there was not sufficient blood there for further analysis.

This is the floor mat from the back seat of the green two door Ford sedan. This is the left side as it fits in the car. An area of that was removed and tested for blood and was shown to be blood by chemical analysis. Just over the portion of the foot of the car where the drive shaft comes, another area which I have inscribed with this red pencil, which showed up with the fluorescent light; it showed to be blood but could not be checked for human blood.

Floor mat had been washed or cleaned because the blood had diffused into it. There was no visual evidence of the blood to the eyes. It only showed up with the aid of the fluorescent light.

The black two door Ford sedan also showed traces of blood on the floor mat.

The seat cover of the green car showed four spots which tested to be human blood.

The box contents was found to contain fragments of bone, charcoal, some silica and, clay type of material. The little paper contained largely small fragments of bone. The box contained three fragments of bone, one about the size of my thumb, and two about the size of my finger. Those three fragments of bone were used for chemical analysis. The box contained human bone fragments. The handkerchief did not.

(There was quite a bit of discussion about the foliage and sawdust that was turned in but didn't give any insight into the death. He discovered that most of it seemed to be largely pine, etc.)

q. Doctor, I hand you "State Exhibit No. 15" and ask you to describe that and tell me where you got it and what you found with reference to your examination of it.

a. We received this from Sheriff Potts. It is a tin metal box of the ordinary shape of a tobacco box. The contents of that revealed the presence of ready rolled -- as machine made cigarettes, and two wood matches.

q. How did you determine whether or not they were ready rolled cigarettes?

a. From the crimping and gluing of the cigarette leaves around the cigarettes.

q. What condition were the cigarettes in, Doctor?
a. Well, they were still intact.

q. Well, were they burned or not burned?

a. They were in a complete charcoal state, yes sir.

q. What about these guano sacks?

a. This was three guano sacks which we received from Sheriff Potts. Two of the sacks showed evidence of having been well filled with the same type of sand clay silica material. Our microscopic examination with all these were made, that is this type material, examined by the microscope, and I say our conclusion, the result of my examination either chemically or microscopically, or either fluorescent lights, the microscopic examination showed two of these sacks from pretty much near the top to be infiltrated with the same sand clay silica material, fine pulverized ashes, charcoal ash and small clumps of charcoal. The third sack didn't show that as high up the sack as the other two.

(Then there was much discussion regarding the pole that was found and the axe and the knife used to cut with.

q. I hand you a dead pine pole marked "State Exhibit No. 13" and ask you what your examination of that pole revealed, and where you got it.

a. We received this from Sheriff Potts. Just on gross examination of this you see the presence of a dark-brown material which on chemical examination showed it to be blood, then on further chemical examination showed it to be human blood.

q. Doctor, I hand you a rock marked Exhibit no. 21

a. We received this rock from Sheriff Potts. On one side examination, microscopical examination, showed a whitish gray material, which was brain, brain tissue. Now imbedded in one section, one area of that tissue, which was also intermingled with blood, I found a very dark brown or black hair intermingled with that brain tissue and blood.

q. Was the hair and brain sticking to the rock?

a. It was; yes sir

q. Please tell us what you found in this bucket.

a. We received this from Sheriff Potts also, and in the examination of the contents of this bucket we found the presence of charcoal from large pieces like that down to small clumps, and a number of twigs and leaves, some of that same type of sand silica.

q. What kind of wood was used in the burning of that ash?

a. Some of this appears to be pine, pine charcoal. Other fragments of it seem to be of a heavier type of wood. The weight of the two types of charcoal seem to be a little different.

q. What about the bucket which contained fragments of brain? Could you tell whether or not that was human brain?

a. I could not chemically, no sir.

q. Could you any other way?

a. Only the judging of the size of the quantity of brain that we had present, knowing by a conclusion that based on our knowledge of the size of a cow brain, hog, dog, squirrel, coon all of that common type of animal and this quantity was about what you could hold in your hand like that, appeared to be too much of a fragment, mental part of the brain to have been the brain of some other smaller animals.

　　　　　　　　recess called at 2:15pm
after recess

By Mr. Henson: we want to ask you to let us ask Mr. New to cross examine this witness on the ground Mr. New is the technical expert on this same line.

By The Court: All right. Proceed.

Cross Examination

q. How much blood can be found in an average human body?

a. The average body usually carries about five quarts or ten pints.

q. Dr. Jones all the blood that you found in the green auto upholstery would amount to approximately what in weight or in volume?

a. Oh it was only spots of it, probably was not -- it might not have been more than a tablespoon full if it all was collected and in the wet state.

q. Do you know the blood type?

q. I did not run test for that and do not know. They only asked me to test for blood and human blood. They said if they could get the type from the army of the deceased, then in that case they would ask me to see if it could be typed. Well, I was never suppled with that and therefore I never tried to test it.

q. I will ask you to state whether or not in your opinion a man with normal blood content, who received a violent and fatal blow which removed the back of his head, and who was laid supine in the back of the automobile from which you took the upholstery you showed here, if it would be possible for there to have been no more blood than you discovered in your investigation or examination of this upholstery.

a. If he was laid flat on there with nothing protecting him, that is nothing protecting the floor mat or any other part, there should have been more blood than I found, yes, but if that was protected in any way, I still might not have found anymore than the circle on the two sides of the floor mat where it would have oozed through, and not have accumulated in the form of a clot.

q. Now if blood in great quantity had accumulated on the floor mat, it would have permeated -- if in the liquid state, it would have permeated the mat throughout?

a. Apparently it did that, because I dug it out of the mat. The mat is about an eighth of an inch thick.

q. Doctor, I will ask you to state whether or not in your opinion, a man freshly dead from a wound which knocked off the back of his skull, leaving the brain exposed, could be carried by another for a distance of three quarters of a mile without leaving trace of blood?

a. Again, it would depend on how he was carried. He may have been wrapped. I don't know the condition under which he was carried.

q. Now in order to prevent him from bleeding, it would almost be necessary to carry him upright?

a. He might have even bled then.   It depends on how they had him protected.

q. Doctor, how long after exposure to air does liquid blood lose the ability to flow?

a. That again is variable, some people it coagulates in about two minutes, some four, some six.

q. As an expert, what does the fact that blood is spattered on the pole mean?

a. Means it was dropped on there.

q. No evidence of any clotting prior to its getting on there.

a. No, because this seems to be spattered as it went on.

Witness Excused

Sheriff A. L. Potts recalled
stated he got Mr. Sivell's pistol out of his glove box Friday morning April 23rd. "Sheriff Collier, Herring Sivell, John Wallace and Gus Huddleston all rode up here in it.

witness is excused.

George Cornett   Fulton county police, scientific crime lab made a plaster of the tire track for Mozart Strickland's truck.

Cross Examination

q. All you did was just to find the track in the field that somebody pointed out to you?

a Yes sir

q. And you didn't know what truck made it?

q. No sir

q. You didn't know when it made it?

a. No sir

q. There are a lot of tires that would match up, isn't there?

a. Yes sir

witness excused

Sheriff A. L. Potts recalled for further questioning, testifies as follows:

DIRECT EXAMINATION

By Solicitor Wyatt:

q. Mr. Potts, I hand you an object marked as "State Exhibit No. 41", and ask you where you found that. Where did you get it?

a. I got it out of the back of Henry Mobley's automobile.

q. When did you do that?

a. After I brought Mobley and his car from Chipley to Newnan. I looked through it here.

q. And you found that in the back of the car?

a. In the foot of the car, yes, sir.

(A black jack is marked "State Exhibit No. 41"
(The witness is excused.)

They begin going through each item marked for evidence and the Judge throws out the black jack as it was never proven that Turner was ever in Mobley's vehicle. The State then offers to retract the door panel and floor mat obtained from Mobley's vehicle but Mr. Henson wanted that left in.

The State Rest.
Recess until 9am Thursday morning.

281

John Wallace, right, sits next to co-defendant Herring Sivell in the Coweta County Courthouse in 1948.

At left are defense attorneys, Fred New, standing, and Jack Allen.

Photo provided by a fellow researcher.

Notice how crowded the courthouse is.

Day Four

June 17, 1948 Thursday morning

The jury enters the box

By Mr. Huddleston: At this time I will take up the examination myself due to reasons personal to me.

By The Court: Anything further for the State?

By Mr. Huddleston: We will let Mr. New conduct the rest of the direct examination.

By The Court: All right, go ahead, who will you have, Mr. New

By Mr. New: I have a motion at this time to strike from the record all the testimony of Sergeant Otwell relating to the writing which he found in the well. The exhibit had been withdrawn from the jury, and the testimony remains in the record, and I move to strike it.

By Solicitor Wyatt: We have no objection.

By The Court: It is stricken then.

The State recalls Dr. Herman Jones and discusses the axe, knife and foliage and pole in great detail.

The State Rest (again)

By The Court; Go ahead for the defendant.

By Mr. New: We would like to call Henry Mobley and we want to call Mr. Herring Sivell as the next witness.

By The Court: They are not here

By Sheriff Potts: They are not up here.

By The Court: Get them up here.

By Mr. Huddleston: I will ask that the jury be excluded.

By The Court: Take the jury to their room. What is it Mr. Huddleston?

By Mr. Huddleston: It will be necessary, if Your Honor please, to have these now, to let the objection that is going to be made be interposed and passed on by Your Honor before.

By Mr. Howard: I represent Mr. Mobley, and I also represent Mr. Sivell, and it is our intention that Mr. Sivell and Mr. Mobley both do not desire to testify in this case, and any evidence that they might give might tend to incriminate them and as their counsel, I notified them, and they do not ` care to testify and I notified counsel for the defendant to that effect and I don't see what they expect to gain by putting them on the stand and have them say they will not testify. Because that is what they will do. I understand they have the right under the constitution, and I know your honor will so rule.

By Mr. New: If your honor please, the privilege of self incrimination is purely a personal privilege, and the only way we can determine that is to ask the defendant if he cares to testify after he has been advised of his right under the Constitution.

By Mr. Howard: That is a layman. He knows nothing about his right. and he employed me to advise him, and I have advised him, and he will follow my advice.

By Mr. New: We don't know that until we determine it. It is still one of personal privilege and not one to be exercised by counsel.

Henry Mobley is called to the stand.

By the Court: Mr. Mobley, the Constitution of this State does not require you to give any evidence that would in any wise incriminate you and by the word incriminate, the law means that would in any way connect you with the crime or anything in connection with the crime. Consequently, you do not have to testify unless you wish to. Now what is the desire in the matter -- or give any testimony that might tend to incriminate you. Now what do you wish to do in the case?

a. I refuse to testify. It might incriminate myself.

By The Court: All right. Go down. Do you want to call the next one?

By Mr. Huddleston: If Your Honor please, if the same thing applies to Mr. Sivell, it might be just as well to let Mr. Howard so state in his place.

By Mr. Howard: I state in my place I talked to Mr. Sivell, and Mr. Sivell takes the same attitude Mr. Mobley takes in the matter, and does not desire to testify.

By The Court: Gentlemen, do you wish to place Mr. Sivell on the stand and let him make the statement himself, or is Mr. Howard's statement sufficient?

By Mr. Huddleston; I don't think that will be necessary if he will follow his counsel's advice.

By The Court: I will put him up if you want that done. Counsel states they do not care to place the witness Sivell on the stand. The statement made by his counsel is sufficient and accepted.

By Mr. Huddleston: I don't know whether counsel for Mr. Sivell makes the statement for --

By The Court: He said the same statement applied. That is the reason I asked that question.

By Mr. Huddleston: All right.

By The Court: Information has come to me that some young boys have been holding seats for people and selling them to them. I wish you would notify all the bailiffs and patrolmen that if that comes to their attention to bring both the seller and the purchaser down here and take them back to my office and keep them until court adjourns. Now as long as there are seats available, they are for any person who may get to them and use them without paying any price or premium for them, so if anybody can find any evidence of that, please just take charge of both persons, the seller and the purchaser, and bring them down here and I will take care of them later. All right.

By Mr. Henson: We are ready.

(a short recess is called)

After recess

By The Court: Bring the jury in. Proceed

The jury returns to the box

Coweta Sheriff Lamar Potts meets defendants arriving for court on July 14, 1948.

From left are Potts, Herring Sivell, Henry Mobley and John Wallace.

Photo provided by a fellow researcher.

John Wallace's statement to the jury

John Wallace, the defendant, makes the following unsworn statement:

By Mr. Huddleston: Mr. Wallace, you are not under oath, you have not been sworn. I will not ask you any questions. The Solicitor here will not ask you any questions. You are permitted to make any statement to the jury in your behalf that you wish to make, and I would like to ask that you speak out so these gentlemen can hear you. Take your time and make whatever statement you wish to make in your behalf. Any instructions you would like to add?

By The Court: Only this. Mr. Wallace, speak loud and distinctly, and you have whatever time that you want to make your statement. Don't get in a hurry, just whatever time you think is necessary, but speak loud and distinctly so each of those men can hear you.

Coweta county court room where Wallace took the stand.

Section One

By Mr. John Wallace:

Thank you Mr. Court, and Gentlemen of the Jury. I am fully aware of the serious charge that I am now charged with. I think in all fairness to myself that I should make some statement about the early part of my life.

I was born on a farm ten miles from Old West Point, Georgia in Chambers County, Alabama. I received my first schooling in a small country school in that community. Later I attended school at West Point, Georgia, Columbus Georgia. I went to Gordon Institute at Barnesville, which was a military academy. I later went to Young Harris College, left there in 1914.

I then went to my present home in that community, took up farming as my occupation. I worked hard; I tried to accumulate. In 1918 I went to the Army. I have an Honorable Discharge from the Army, and after leaving the Army I went back to my home community and farmed again. That was in -- after 1918.

In 1928 I became involved in the liquor traffic. In September, of 1928 I was sentenced to the Atlanta Penitentiary, two years. In 1929 I began to serve that sentence. I served thirteen months, was discharged. I got back home in the early 30s.

The economic situation was very adverse at that time. Everybody practically was broke. I had just about lost what holdings I had. I struggled along there for five years.

In 1935 I again fell from grace. I was tried in Columbus before Judge Bascomb Deaver. I received a three-year sentence. I was given sixty days in which to prepare myself to leave what business interests I did have at that time.

At the expiration of that sixty-day period I went to Macon and had a conversation with Judge Deaver. I convinced him at that time that I was through with the liquor business. On the strength of that conversation, Judge Deaver gave me thirty more days leave or respite, and reduced my sentence to one year. I served that time, which was nine months and eighteen days.

I got home in 36, in the spring of 1936. I again took up the fragments of what I had, my family had been able to hold together since I had been away from home, and went back into the farming business.

During the war period I tried to produce as much food for the war effort as I possibly could. I engaged in the dairy business. I had produced from 250 to 300 gallons of milk daily. Normally my operations cover around 600 acres of land. (excuse me just a minute.) Your Honor, I have notes in my pocket.

By The Court: All right, use them.

By Mr. Wallace:
Gentleman, this period of time covers quite some time, and I have just a few notes that I want to refresh my mind along as I go, please. I would like to state that since 1936 of this time that I served, that I violated no laws that I am aware of, and that I have in my possession a complete and unconditional pardon signed by the President of the United States in connection with these violations. That was twelve years ago. I have tried to make a good citizen. I have worked hard for what I have.

In 1945 I found myself with 300 head of cattle. I had more cattle than I could winter. I sold those cattle down to about 100 head. At that time I had become interested in raising some pure bred cattle, improved my herd. I had possibly fifteen mature registered Guernsey cows. I kept eight-five grade heifers at this time. I gradually grew back into the dairy business, more or less pure bred, and high breds.

Possibly in November of 1945 -- I will go back -- In 1944 possibly I had sold a good many hogs, and a Mr. Rigsby, Millard Rigsby from Carrollton, Georgia, came there and purchased these hogs from me, and somebody I didn't know -- truck drivers -- came and hauled these hogs away. At that time I didn't know who was driving the trucks, and paid not much attention, special attention, to who was operating the truck. But on this November of 1948, a young man walked in my yard one morning and introduced himself as Wilson Turner.

I didn't know at that time that Wilson Turner was William H. Turner. I had no way of knowing that he had deserted the Army and taken the name of a brother who later turned up at Macon, Georgia. I asked him what his business was, and he said he wanted a job.

Now, Gentlemen, whoever among you are farmers can appreciate my position. I was hesitant to mix any white people on my farm with the colored labor. I had previous experience working white people and colored people together, and I didn't want to do it, and I told Turner that I didn't want to mix white people with my colored people on the farm. My experience had shown me unless a white man was the boss man, or some administrative situation on the farm, mixed with colored people, that the process of intermingling, and eventual basis of social equality, come to mix, and sometimes serious problems arise. But he advised me at that time that he was not a bum. He took out ninety dollars out of his pocket and counted it in my presence, and told me that his wife had thirty more dollars at home that they had saved working in the cotton mill, that he wanted to leave the cotton mill because he didn't like to be inside, and he had farmed before, and on this trip to my place in hauling the hogs that he had become impressed with my farming operation and just decided he would come down there and see if he could not work for me. I told Mr. Turner he could come and we would try him out. He said -- that was two months before Christmas -- he said, "if I work for you two months and you are satisfied, will you give me a crop on shares, and I said, "yes, if you can satisfy me for two months I will give you a crop on shares."

I let this man come there over my better judgment. I didn't approve of the set up to begin with, but I was interested in any young man that might want to get a start and of help, appreciated the fact that when I begun my career that help was hard to get, and you had to fight it out pretty much straight from the shoulder; I let him begin work there.

He proved very satisfactory for those two months. I had given him the best living quarters that I had in my tenant set up. I gave him a house that I had formerly lived in myself. I had lost my home by fire in 1940 and I lived in this particular house that I gave him. It was equipped with electric lights, running water. I allotted him this first year about fifteen acres of the best land that I had for cotton. I let him plant possibly ten or fifteen acres in corn. I furthermore gave him a hog. Now he cultivated this land with a tractor. He could cultivate this cotton land and corn crop with two days operation or less after the stuff increased in size. He could increase the speed of his equipment. That gave Turner quite a good little bit of extra time, and this time I gave him employment on my operation, thereby enabling him to make extra money and when he got this crop possibly laid by, I learned that he was a fugitive from Carroll County.

Mr. Lambert, and Mr. Collier, the sheriff of my county, came to my house one night sometime about the time when the summer term of court is over at Carrollton, I don't know exactly the month just now, asked me if there was a man on my farm named Wilson Turner, and I of course told him yes. Mr. Lambert said he had a warrant for this man. I went with them to Turner's house. They took Turner in custody and carried him back to Carrollton. At the request of Mrs. Turner, I went over to Carrollton and was there when he was tried. He was tried for some connection with the whiskey business in that county and he received a fine of $150.00. At the noon recess of court that day I went to see Mr. Wyatt and asked him if he would try and help get Turner's fine reduced, as he had no funds at that time that I knew about to pay a fine.

Mr. Wyatt told me at that time, said, "if you want to ask the Judge about it, it is all right with me. I approached His Honor here, and asked him if he would take under consideration the reduction of Turner's fine, that he was down there on my farm at this time. I knew nothing about any violation of the law that he was pursuing at that time and I earnestly pled with him to reduce his fine so that it would work no hardship on raising the money with which to pay the fine.

His Honor at that time informed me that he would take under consideration this request and let him think it over during the noon hour and on his return to the courthouse in the afternoon he informed me that Mr. Turner could pay a $100.00 fine. I advanced Mr. Turner fifty dollars of that money and Mr. Millard Rigsby of Carrollton advanced or paid the remaining fifty dollars.

Turner then returned to my home and resumed his operation of his farm, and sometime later -- I don't recall the date -- the first brush in that I ever had with Turner was on a very personal situation.

One day during the noon hour at my home our colored house servant came in while my wife and I were eating dinner and told -- Mr. Turner lived just 200 yards from my home in clear view of my house. In fact the two houses were built for tenant houses in a row. I occupy one of them, or did before I came here, and Turner occupied the other one. This servant came in and informed my wife and I that there was a terrible racket going on up at Turner's house and that Mrs. Turner was running around and around this house with Mr. Turner in pursuit. I started up there. Before I reached the house, I didn't see them. I did not see these facts that I have just stated. I was told them by this servant.

Before I reached this house, I heard no commotion, so I deemed it about the best policy to go back home and not get entangled in this domestic affair. I later learned from observation and other sources that while Mr. Turner was in this rage that he absolutely demolished all of his household furnishings, tore them up.

I talked to Mr. Turner after this occurrence. I advised him. I said, "now Wilson, you want to be very careful in these fits or tantrums that you have gone into; your wife is pregnant, not so far from time, and this destroying of your furniture is a most foolish and wasteful thing. Well, Turner resented that advice, or whatever you might deem it, that I had given him about his domestic set up, but with this conversation, I never referred to it again and neither did he.

Some time elapsed. Mr. Williams, Mr. Robert Williams who operates a country store over on the Chipley-Greenville highway from my home, came to my house and told me that he had seen Turner's brother-in-law, Tom Windham, and Windham's wife, go by his store headed toward North, toward Greenville we might say, and they were actually in a trot. Well, I could not explain this occurrence. I thought I would go over and investigate. On my way over to Mr. William's store I stopped at one of my tenant houses. This tenant was standing on the roadside. He told me, "Mr. Wallace, Mr. Tom and his wife just come out in this road a little while ago, and pitched an axe in the rose vines that my mother had planted along this road back in her lifetime."

I proceeded on over to Williams Store. Mr. Williams and I had some conversation about what had occurred, and I then proceeded to attempt to follow Mr. Windham and his wife up this highway. I figured after they had thrown this axe in this brush and concealed it, something possibly dreadful had happened. I drove ten miles up this highway and I never saw these two people. I returned home and went immediately to Mr. Turner's house. Mrs. Turner was at home. I inquired as to where Mr. Turner was.

Now Gentlemen, I want to make this reference at this time. I made reference to Turner as; Wilson Turner, Turner and Mr. Turner. Now on a lot of my dealings with Turner I did address him in those three different titles, no special reason, but it still remains to be a fact.

Mrs. Turner at that time, after I had told her about the actions of these relatives of hers, she could not explain this situation. I asked her then, I said "well, where is Turner now?" She said, "I hate to tell you, Mr. Wallace, but he is over in the pecan grove in a deep ditch making whiskey. This pecan grove was right out in front of their house possibly sixty feet from their front porch. I went on under her directions and found Turner in this ditch with a little possibly sixty-gallon drum set up. I told him about the actions of his brother-in-law and sister-in-law, and I found him unharmed, and he gave me no explanation as to what their actions were based on. After finding Mr. Turner unharmed, I let it drop at that.

I heard no further evidence of any other connection that these in-laws had with anybody else in the community so it stopped there.

I told Turner at this time, I said, "Wilson, I can't have you making whiskey on my premises. I have been in the penitentiary twice for this kind of business. I am not going to have you here. I don't want to get back into trouble." He at that instance said he had completed his operation that he was engaged in at that time, that was the last run that he would make on this little outfit, and pushed this little old tank over with his foot and this whatever was in it drained down the run of this ditch. That was all the equipment that was there at the time except possibly some empty syrup cans and maybe a jug with something in it.

Then I knew nothing further after that time about any violation that Turner might have been engaged in for several months. His crop had matured, and he harvested fourteen bales of cotton off of this acreage, very good yield. I had given him the preference of the place for his farm. I was farming then on shares with all of the operators of my farm who did raise cotton. The only operation I had on my farm at that time independent of my sharecroppers was the growing of feed for my dairy herd. Turner gathered this crop, and we sold it. He grossed a little better than $2400.00 worth of cotton and seed. That gave him around $1200.00 for his share. That was in the fall of the year. I advised Turner at that time to put this money away. He had worked for me between times in the growing of these feed crops that I had on my operation and had made wages and had practically lived on that money, and I paid him somewhat above the average of common day labor, because he was operating this power equipment and could do the work of possibly six or eight men with this one machine.

I told him at that time if he would save this money if the prices would hold up in a very short time he would be a home owner, that he would have enough money to buy him his own home and he would not have to work for the other fellow. I did that through my interest in a young man that was trying to get ahead. I advised him against law violations because I knew where that would lead to better than possibly any of you gentlemen know. He in turn went against this advice I had told him about saving this money that he had accumulated, bought him a used Ford automobile.

 I understood at that time that he promised to pay $1400.00 for this car. A new car, if it could have been obtained at that time, was quite a little bit less than that. Now gentlemen, this automobile really was his undoing. I guess possibly you gentlemen have observed this same situation in your operations. The average salaried man and farm laborer is not financially able to operate an automobile. It takes them away from their work. In other words, it has a very demoralizing effect on the man that has it and does not use it in his business operations, if he has to work for a living.

Now I at this time was displeased about Turner using this money for that purpose. However, I had no control over it, but I did tell him that his money was gone, and when his car wore out that he would possibly be right back after another year where he was when he first begun; that all the money he would make after that he would spend on that automobile. I was undecided as to whether I would let him stay on my farm for another crop. He was a good tractor operator. He knew the equipment and the operation of the equipment, and was really a very desirable man to have on your farm as long as he would behave himself and didn't get in trouble himself and endanger my security.

We had some conversation about a farm for another year. He had at that time become familiar with all of my land holdings, at that time in this community. I had a farm possibly four or five miles from my home, several farms I will add, three to be exact. One of these farms was vacant and had been vacant during 1947. Turner asked me if he could have this farm to cultivate in 1947. I told him that if he would go over there and behave himself and not get into the liquor business anymore that I would let him have equipment to cultivate this whole 100 acres that was in this particular farm, in cultivation and open at that time. He promised me faithfully that he would do the things that I had asked him to do. I equipped him with a tractor, let him use all the equipment used on my farm to plant his crop with. He put approximately fifteen tons of guano under this fifty acres of cotton. He planted fifty acres of corn.

At the time his cotton should have come up, it didn't come up to the stand that he wanted, and he was impatient about giving it more time. To keep down an argument with him, he wanted to plant this land in corn -- you gentlemen know that there is not so much money in corn on a sharecropping basis. What I wanted was cotton. I had given him land that had lain idle the year before.

Land of that type does not produce so much obnoxious vegetation as land that has been cultivated clean every year. I felt like that he could work this fifty acres in cotton, but he didn't want to do it. He wanted to get out of the strain and push that he would be in making a cotton crop. I agreed for him to go then and plant this land in corn. Then some time in March, I don't know just what time of the month it was, I was approached by a lady in Chipley who had some resource to know about the operation of some relative who was an officer at that time.

She informed me that Mr. Turner was under scrutiny or observation of the Federal officers in connection with some liquor operations, that these officers at that time were not going ahead with any preventive measures of trying to -- were not trying to capture Turner with this operation, that they were waiting for some other development that they possibly hoped would occur. I don't know for what reason they had, but they had some reason to withhold their action on Turner.

I, a few days later, went to LaGrange, which is about sixteen miles away, in company with Mr. Pope Davis, on a business matter and we were on our return home about five miles out of LaGrange, and Mr. Davis stopped at a store, at that time sugar was hard to obtain and Mr. Davis purchased some sugar at this time, possibly five or ten pounds. I don't recall just exactly, but some small amount of sugar.

As we were preparing to reenter the car and go home Mr. Carter, Mr. R. B. Carter, who was at that time employed by Troup County as County Policeman, drove up in his car, or a car, with several other men companions, and I saw Mr. Carter get out of his car. I spoke to him and asked him if these other gentlemen that were with him were Federal Officers. He informed me that they were. I asked him if I might speak to one of them. He called to Mr. Lucas. I was later to learn. I was introduced to him.

I asked Mr. Lucas if he had any information on a man named Turner down in my community, and he told me that he had. You gentlemen heard this man say on that occasion that he had some conversation with me, but very short and he didn't recall what it was. I recall very distinctly what it was, gentlemen.

I told Mr. Lucas that if he had any information on Turner in connection with the liquor business that to proceed against him, that I had no interest in that operation, and not to wait to catch me, that I would not be there, that I was not involved, and would not be involved. Mr. Lucas thanked me for my frankness. He says, "I am glad you talked to me about it, and I appreciate your frankness in this matter." I left Mr. Lucas on those terms.

A few days, possibly a very short time, I would not say just how many, I went over to Turner's house. I went over there with the specific reason to tell Turner just what I had told Mr. Lucas. I told him to catch him, that I was tired of this thing. Turner was not at home. While I was there, I walked out to my barn on Turner's premises just for the purpose of seeing what might be there, if anything, that should not be there. I went into the wagon shed that run the length of this barn. I walked back into this wagon shed and there was a shelf across this end of the shed. On this shelf there were two or three sixty-pound bundles of sugar, and on the ground beneath this shelf, as if it had toppled off, were two or three bundles of this sugar, and this sugar -- some of it was bursted open. There was evidence there that the milch cow, or a cow, he did have a milch cow at that time, had gone there and eaten up some of this sugar and tracked around over this that was on the ground, droppings scattered around over it.

I called Mrs. Turner from the house. I said, "I would like for you to come out here a minute." She came on to the barn, and I said, "come back here, please." We walked back, and I said, "look at this." I said, "after all this talk, advice, that I have given Wilson about this business, and officers are right on his heels, he is going to get in trouble, he is going to create possibly the opinion that I am involved in this liquor business. I have heard as much myself. What is going to be done about this thing?"

She said, "Mr. Wallace, you know Wilson as well as I do, and I can't tell him a thing." Now on the same afternoon of this day that I have just made reference to, Mr. Miller and Mr. Cook came there to Turner's house. They searched the premises. They found this sugar. They found a gallon of whiskey out in front of Turner's house in some weeds. Mr. Miller gave me this information. Turner at this time during the conversation that he was having with these officers, broke away from this conversation and ran off out in through some woods adjacent to his home there. Mr. Miller told me at that time that had he not made this attempt to escape he would have possibly gotten by with this distillery that they cut up that I am making reference to just a little later.

He said that they had gone there in search of whiskey. They had found the evidence; he possibly would have let his investigation at that time have dropped. I can't explain to you gentlemen why these officers had any reason for or were willing to leave this man's premises with this evidence on one gallon of whiskey and sugar, when they had evidence enough to bring them there to begin with. Surely they had some of the evidence that the Federal Officers had, but that is the facts as stated to me by Mr. Miller.

Now on this escape that Turner made out through these woods they followed him, and they came upon a site of a distillery. Mr. Miller told me that he found eight barrels that had just been possibly two or three minutes overturned, and the stuff was still flowing from them to some extent. Turner at that time was not in evidence. They didn't find Turner. They presumed that he turned this stuff over where they followed him to, he escaped.

The following day I knew nothing about this occurrence having happened, but I was on my way to my field, horse back, and I saw a man walking down through my pasture, and I rode down into that pasture where he was, and when I got there it was Mr. Miller. I knew Mr. Miller. We had some few words of greeting, and I possibly asked him his business. He said, "I am lost." He said, "I am trying to get into the rear of Wilson Turner's house." I said, "Well, Mr. Miller, you are four or five miles from Turner's house." Then he related to me the happening of the day before about this distillery and whiskey and sugar. He told me at this time, he said, "Mr. Collier, the sheriff of Meriwether county told me if I missed Turner on this trip to see you and have you to get in contact with Turner and bring him up here up to Greenville." So I did. I went to see Turner, and after some persuasion I agreed to make his bond if he would go and surrender.

At that time, Gentlemen, he was not in the process of planting a crop. The fertilizer was in the ground, some of it was, all the land was prepared. I had no other motive in the world for making this bond except to protect my interest as well as his, in this farm operation, so I did make his bond. He was later tried, and I might say at this time that he planted this crop of corn and cultivated it, and I heard nothing more about any violations I don't believe until early fall. He was tried, or either entered a plea, I don't know which, in Meriwether County court in this case that Mr. Miller made against him at this time for this that I have mentioned to you a few minutes previous to now. At that time I didn't go to court with him. I didn't want him to ask me to make any plea to the court for him. I had made one, and the Judge had been most kind and helped him, and I didn't want to have him ask me to do that again. I had become thoroughly distressed and worn out with his behavior. I wanted him off of my neck, Gentlemen, so to speak. That is what I wanted. I wanted him to leave.

Mr. Collier sent this man down to my home. I don't know what had happened in court, but when he came there and told me Mr. Collier said for me to come to Greenville, I did. I returned to Greenville with Turner. He came from the court after me. When I reached the courthouse Mr. Collier asked me if Turner had any money. I told him that I knew of $200.00 that he had put up with Mr. Albert Haynes, who operates a store at Durand, Georgia as collateral guarantee on a bond that Mr. Haynes had signed for possibly one or two of these brothers-in-law of Turner. I don't know just what the nature of that case was, but I do know that to be a fact.

Turner had been fined by his Honor $200.00 at this particular time. Turner was in the custody of the Sheriff. Turner asked me if I could find Mr. Haynes. He was present at the court. I went out in town and located him. He went to the bank and drew out the $200.00 that he held of this man's funds. I took that money and took it to Turner, and he paid this fine with it. I didn't furnish him with any funds. He didn't ask me for any personal funds to pay this fine. He paid his fine with his own money.

I asked the Sheriff at this particular time before sentence was passed on this man, I said, "Mr. Collier, is there any way in the world to get the court to make this man leave the county?" Gentlemen, I am stating these facts in the presence of the same judge that was present that day. Mr. Collier told me that he didn't know what could be done about it. Now Gentlemen, when this man received his sentence he got a $200.00 fine. He also was suggested or commanded to move out of that county. I heard this man ask His Honor if he might have time to gather his crop. He was informed by the Court he would be allowed ample time in which to do that. We then returned home. I believe that was in August. I am not certain.

I heard nothing more about Turner's operations until September of last year. On the sixth of September I, in company with seven other people, formed a party of two automobiles and went to Texas, into Mexico. We were gone on this trip eighteen or twenty days.

On my return home about the -- one of the first things that greeted me -- I will say the first unpleasant thing that greeted me was information that Turner was operating this liquor business. I went to the site of this operation, ascertained whether the facts were true as I had received them. I got to this place, and there was signs that something had been done there, but the thing was gone. He, in addition while in my absence, had used his influence to have a colored tenant on my farm, this Robert Lee Gates that has been before you in this trial, take his cow, and his hogs, and $50.00 as I understood Turner supplied, and bought him a pick up truck, a pick up truck, of which he had no apparent need for. I was pretty well stirred up about it; all the means in the world that the Negro had for milk and butter, fall prospects for his meat was gone, the burden on me to feed him, with an automobile, a truck, with no visible need for. He had no funds to operate it with. It was the most disorganizing thing for the Negro to have. It gave him a way to get away from his work, possibly to load up the rest of them as they sometimes do, have them away from their work when they should be at home. On the first Saturday after my return home from this trip to Texas, Turner drove into my yard. That was the first time I had seen him since my return home. I approached him about this situation of Gates and his truck and I explained to him what he had done to the Negro.

I said, "you have used your influence here now and supplied money on this truck; who is going to finish paying for it? I understand there is a balance due on it. How is this Negro here going to live and keep up the payments on a worn out truck to begin with?" It was a pile of junk.

He resented the fact that I was displeased about it, and finally in our conversation I told him, I said, "Wilson, you have become a great menace to this farm. You have done more to demoralize my labor and get my labor where I can't control them than anybody I have ever had any experience with." I said, "you drive around here and park in the yard and associate with them, on a more or less basis of social equality, and it has become most unfair to me to say the least of it. I would like to ask you at this time to get off of my premises."

These Negroes, Gates and Brooks, and other Negroes were present at this time too when I gave him this lecture about his dealings with disorganizing my tenants there and what how.

I said, "you go home, and you stay there and gather your crop. Don't you come back to this place unless I send for you. You stay away from my Negro tenants houses. You cut this liquor traffic out. You are going to get every Negro I have got in the chain gang and me too." Turner didn't appreciate that. He knew I was telling him the truth, but he didn't like it.

He drove out of my yard and told me on leaving, he says, "I will see you later."

I had planned a trip to Atlanta on that particular day. This man had caused me to miss my bus that morning. When he left, I went to Chipley to catch a later bus. I had an appointment in Atlanta on that day. I didn't know whether I was going to make it or not. When I reached Chipley, I bought a ticket, and while waiting for this bus my uncle Mozart Strickland came to me. He says, "what has happened between you and Wilson?" I said, "I don't know, what do you mean?" He said, "I was over at Dr. Ellis' office." -- Dr. Ellis is our community town physician -- "Turner came up to me there and told me that you had hurt his feelings, that you had mistreated him, that he had a forty-five pistol and he was going to settle matters with you." I have a name for my uncle, and it is known all over the country in that section by both white and black as "Cap, I said, "Now Cap, let's let Turner alone. I am going to Atlanta this morning regardless of what Turner has to say. Maybe he will cool off during the day."

I took the bus to LaGrange. After I got to LaGrange, I was called off the bus to the telephone. the bus stopped at the bus station in LaGrange to take up passengers, and vice versa. I went in to the telephone and found it to be my wife who had put in a call. I called her at Chipley. She informed me that Mr. Williams over at this country store that I made reference to before had come to my home after my departure and told her that he had some conversation with Turner, and that Turner was on the warpath, that he was armed and had stated to him that he was going to kill me on sight.

Now I told my wife at this juncture to meet me on this highway between LaGrange and Chipley. I had no means of transportation up there. I went down to the Farmer's Supply Store, who was operated by the Phillips Brothers, one of whom you may know about, that lost his life in the Chattahoochee River just a few weeks ago while fishing.

They handle the Purina line of feed down there that we call the Checkerboard Store. I told Mr. Phillips that I wanted to borrow his truck. I didn't tell him what I wanted with it, but he loaned it to me very readily. It had a complete coverage of these checkerboards, the sign of the mill. It was completely camouflaged, as you might say, with this advertising decoration.

I drove on possibly seven miles down this highway toward Chipley, and met my wife. I assured her that not to worry about Turner, and not to worry about me, I was going to Atlanta and would be back that night on the 9:18 train. I think that is true. After leaving my wife I turned around and started back to LaGrange and returned this truck with the intention of going on to Atlanta, and which I did. I had driven maybe one mile after leaving my wife, and Turner passed me on this highway headed toward LaGrange. I recognized him, and recognized his car. I didn't know whether Turner was going up there in pursuit of the bus I was riding on. I didn't know what he was doing. Of course I had some room to imagine what he was doing from the reports that I had just had. Being in this truck as I just stated, he failed to recognize me, and passed on.

Then, I didn't drive at a terrific rate of speed, possibly a quarter of a mile from the city limits of LaGrange I met this man coming back, headed back toward Chipley. I was, as I said before, camouflaged in this Checkerboard truck, so he passed me up.

I went to Atlanta, and I had developed a headache such as I have never had before or since. I got a taxi, went to the Piedmont Hotel and I missed my business engagement. I lay down that day, all day, from the time I reached Atlanta until time enough to catch a 7:10 train that night. I got up and caught this train back home, and when I reached Greenville Mr. Perkerson, who was at that time a deputy sheriff of that county, came into the train. I was sitting near the end of the coach, and he called me, said "John, you get off." I didn't know for what reason he asked me to get off. I could not imagine for what reason he was asking me to get off of the train. I wondered then. I asked myself the question, "what now?"

I did get off of this train without any question. I followed him out to the automobile, and I found the Sheriff of my county sitting in that car. I was then informed that they had been informed that this man was out gunning for me, had stated that when I reached home this night, that when I alighted from this train that he was going to take my life. They told me that they were going to see me safely to my home. They did this. They carried me home. When the Sheriff and Mr. Perkerson started to drive out of my yard I asked the Sheriff, I said; "Now Sheriff, what recourse have I got? This man is out gunning for me. I can't stay in my house all the time. He has not gathered his crop. Just what am I to do?"

He said, "now John, I can't tell you what to do. The only thing I can do is advice you that when and if the cause arises you will have to use whatever means necessary for your own protection." They left my home at this time.

The following morning was Sunday morning. I drove down to Chipley, which is possibly three miles away, for the morning paper. On my return home between my home and the highway, I have a lake and the dam to this lake is a public road, and this dam is probably eight hundred and better feet long. I drove up on this dam on this roadway, and I recognized Turner's car parked on this road with the rear of his car toward me. Now Gentlemen, I didn't know what to do right at that time. A lot of things ran through my mind. I most assuredly was excited to some extent. There is a man parked in the road that has made the assertion to other people, that I had learned on Saturday night that Robert Williams and my uncle was not the only folks that he had told about this difference that he had with me. I hardly knew what to do, but I drove up alongside of that car. I decided whatever was going to happen it might as well happen then. Sometime it evidently would have to happen, the way he had made his threats.

I had no desire to harm this man. I had no intention of harming him. The only thing that occurred to my mind was to protect my own life. I was not particularly mad with him or for his conduct back before that time. I was displeased with it, with his conduct. He had just about worried me out of my mind, but I don't think that I -- I have never been in a rage with Wilson Turner; at that time or at no other time have I ever been in a rage with him. I was trying to steer this man in a straight and narrow way. I had experience that was most unpleasant which his operations were certainly leading to, and I was capable of telling him what he was headed for.

I pulled up alongside of this man's car. I made no effort to harm Turner. I, of course, was afraid to pass him. When I pulled alongside to his car I found my uncle, Mr. Mozart Strickland, standing on the opposite side of the car. This man was parked on the right hand side, I was driving to pass him on his left. Mr. Strickland was there in conversation with Turner and his wife at this particular moment. When I stopped opposite Turner's car I spoke to him. He had both of his hands on the steering wheel. He was in a very nervous -- apparently -- his hands were trembling on this steering wheel.

Now Gentlemen, I was familiar with this automobile that Mr. Turner owned. I knew that right on the inside of his car just under it on the left hand side, would be opposite his knee nearly, with his foot on the clutch, there was a scabbard compartment with an open end sewed to the upholstery of that panel under there and I had seen Turner with a pistol in this automobile. I didn't know whether he was going to reach down there and get that gun and shoot me or not.

After I greeted him I asked him to -- after he had finished this conversation with Mr. Strickland to please drive by my home, that I wanted to talk to him. At that moment he made like he was going to drive. I passed on. I admit to you gentlemen I was afraid at that minute for my life. I didn't know but what he might shoot me in the back, but I took the chance.

I went to my home, and after a very short time Mr. Turner and Mrs. Turner, and my uncle drove up in my yard. I invited Mr. and Mrs. Turner and Mr. Strickland into the house. They came in the house. Mrs. Turner came in and their small child came in with her and Turner came in, my uncle came in. After they entered the dining room of my home, which opens out on the terrace, a brick terrace, an open top porch to my house, they came in this entrance, and I asked Mr. Turner and my uncle to come out on the front porch, that I wanted to talk to him.

They came out and I asked Turner about this behavior the day before. I said, "what on earth do you mean, Turner" -- I actually said Wilson to the best of my memory --"you have gone around all over the community and told numerous people that you were going to kill me on sight. What have I done to merit that treatment? I have never abused you in my life. I always tried to be kind and considerate. I have helped you in every way under the sun to try to be somebody and have something. You demoralize my labor, and you made liquor all over the community and you lay me liable for trouble as well as yourself. How much better treatment would you ask a man to give you than I have given you? I never offered to do you any harm, and here you come riding the roads and spreading the news that you are going to take my life."

Turner said, "Mr. John, you made me so mad yesterday that I don't know what I did do." Now sometime along about this same hour -- we use electricity in my home to cook with -- something had happened to the wiring of this stove. Wilson was a sort of a mechanic, jack of all trades. I asked him if he would see about this stove. He went in, and we got up some other wiring, and he wired the defective part of this stove, at the same time that I have mentioned.

We made no further reference to that situation after we left the porch. Turner and his wife went home. I then -- I knew though when Turner left my home that day that he was not satisfied about this situation. He resented me calling him on the carpet. He didn't want me to make suggestions to him about his policies of how he wanted to conduct his own affairs. He resented it and showed it the day that I mentioned on this Saturday morning. I knew that Turner was not in any good humor about this situation. I was not in any specially good humor about it either. I was not mad or enraged with him, but I was very much displeased. I then took up this angle of his liquor traffic that had been carried on while I was away form home, and I had already found it moved. I didn't know where it was moved to, but I wanted to know.

I had never before that time been able to find Turner with an operating still but one time, and that was the first time. He just stayed one jump ahead it looked like to me, every time I would get right on the trail of him. He found out possibly I was on his trail and would get him a new location.

Some little time elapsed. I don't know just what date. Mr. Lucas recited to you gentlemen about destroying a still, and I believe he said in October of this same year. A few days after this occurrence of the stove and these happenings, we had a little rain about noon time. Sometimes you gentlemen possibly know who are farmers a rain in the middle of the day disorganizes what you are doing. You have labor scattered around over the farm at different places working. You possibly will call them all together and do some other job, a rainy job. That was the situation with me on this particular day that I intend to discuss with you.

After this rain at noontime I went to Albert Brooks' home and asked for him. He was away. I went to this Gates man's home and asked for him, and he was away. I asked where they were, or where he was, the Gates Negro, and his wife informed me that he had left there in this truck that I mentioned to you that he had no business with. I got on this track. After I reached the point in the road near the Brooks Negro's, it was the only traffic that led away from that community right at that time off of this particular road. I got on the track of this truck, and followed it. I followed it three or four miles. I asked some darkeys along the road if they had seen this particular red truck come by.

I was tired of this truck riding and the demoralizing of the labor, and running up and down the road when they ought to have been at home at work, with this conveyance that they had gotten in there and didn't know how to use.

When I reached a point possibly four miles from my place this truck left the road, the main road. However, it followed a pretty well traveled road. I didn't know where these Negroes had gone. I turned off of this road. It appeared to me possibly as a sawmill road. There is a lot of pulp wood hauling down in my community. I didn't know just where this road was going to lead me where these Negroes turned off into this road, but I followed these tracks.

This road and these tracks led me to this Gates Negro's truck. It was parked down near a swamp. I went into this swamp and found this Gates

Negro, and Brooks Negro, and Turner's brother-in-law, Tom Windham, and a Negro that was known as Rube McGruder. I understood later possibly his name was Charlie McGruder. They were there at a distillery.

Now, gentlemen, you heard before from a witness from this chair that this distillery was not such a large distillery. I am going to tell you gentlemen that it was a large distillery. It was as big a one as I have ever seen, and I have seen some big ones. These men were operating two small stills down near the branch. Those two stills were in actual operation at that time. Up near this still was another still.

It was -- I will not say the exact dimensions, but I will say they would be nearer the figures that I give you than they are any other figure. This still was eight feet in diameter and eight feet deep or tall, whichever way you might want to determine it. That tank was full of fermenting mash. To my knowledge of the turn out of whiskey and mash by ration, that mash properly fermented and sweetened would have made one to ten, one gallon of whiskey to ten gallons of mash.

That tank would have possibly held more than 1500 gallons. I would not say it might. I will say that it would have held 1500 or 2000 gallons.

Now Gentlemen, if that was not a right nice little honey I never saw one. That is the distillery that I reported to the Atlanta office, these three stills. There was not two; there was three, two in actual operation and another one full of mash set up for operation.

I had these Negroes to leave the site of this still. I also told them at the time, "I have told you Negroes time and time again this man was going to get you in trouble, you hanging around this still. If the officers were to come up here now, what would happen? You would be caught, and I would be caught at a still in operation." I left this distillery with these Negroes, went back to my home and put them back to duties that I first intended them to do when I started out in search of them.

I had some conversation with Mr. Lucas. He had told me back in March, and this was October, that he had some information about Turner's operations. I didn't know why this man was allowed to just flagrantly violate the law around over that community and make liquor apparently unmolested. Most certainly they were getting paid to ascertain those facts and bring people to trial for those violations.

I was engaged in my farming operations down there. I didn't have time to police the country and walk every branch in the community trying to ascertain who and where the liquor law violators were. I will venture to state they are in each one of you gentlemen's community. They have been there, you know they are there, and you don't know it, and they will always be there. I don't know that I have ever heard of a community that didn't have some liquor law violation. You can even violate the law and still have legal liquor. You get more than one quart and come into town and be locked up for it. You have liquor law violations all over this country. I didn't know why these officers could not stop this man. He was demoralizing my labor, he was giving the community a reputation of which I was ashamed of. I had done enough to it back in the days when I was fooling with the stuff. I had lived twelve years trying to outlive that very reputation that I made during that time. I am sorry that I ever saw a drop of liquor. It is the beginning and the ending of the saddest part of my life that has ever existed, the fooling with that liquor.

I got out of it. I meant to stay out of it and I did stay out of it. I promised that Judge when he cut that sentence from three years to one year that I would never come before him. I have lived in my county thirty-five years. I have never been hauled into my county court on any charge. I have never been into that court except in the interest of helping somebody else that was in trouble that ought to have help. The man in trouble is the man that needs help. That is the only time I have ever been in these courts. I have lived right there thirty-five years, and there has never been a case. I have never been sued or prosecuted for any offense in my county, and I am proud of it, but I am ashamed of the conduct that sent me to that penitentiary, but I have tried to live it down.

Now when I left this distillery, I didn't know hardly how to proceed. The officers weren't destroying the stills around there, and why weren't they? I asked myself that question, Gentlemen. I could not answer that question. I went down to Chipley and went into the bank. The cashier of my bank was there present. He is right in the hearing of my voice now, because I spoke to him today. I told him this situation. I said, "Mr. Askew, I don't know what to do about this situation out there." I said, "this Turner is making liquor all over the community. I am certain that the officers know something about it. I have discussed it with one of them, and there has been no apparent action taken."

He said -- at that time and at the present time I had a little old nineteen-year-old automobile down there, my only means of transportation today. I possibly could have had better, but that is all I have got. It is paid for. If I had any better, it would have had to be bought on credit, so I feel better riding in that 1928 model Ford and it being mine than I do riding in somebody elses automobile that I should put the money on my debts. Mr.

Askew was aware of the fact of my method of transportation. He said, "John, don't you lose any time. You notify the proper authorities about this thing. You can have my automobile out there if you want it, and go wherever you want to go."

I didn't use his automobile. I took this little old Ford, and I went to Greenville. Now Gentlemen, my purpose for going to Greenville was to call the Atlanta office, the headquarters of the State Alcoholic -- I mean the Federal Alcoholic Control Unit, or whatever it is termed. You gentlemen are familiar with this, with the revenuers I will say. We all know who the revenuers are. My purpose in doing that was to contact the headquarters so that we could, or they could, have a large enough force at hand, or marital enough, bring enough officers together to get this outfit, operators and all.

Now I went to my attorney. He had been in the service of the O.P.A. setup there, setup in Atlanta, and I knew he knew just who to call. I told Mr. Huddleston this situation. I said, "now Gus, I want this thing stopped. It has reached a point until my safety is at stake, my liberty is at stake. This thing is getting too big. It is getting too magnanimous. It is just too much." He called the Atlanta office, I don't know who he had his conversation with, I was present, and advised them or requested them to send somebody to see him.

On this same night Mr. Lucas and Mr. Bedenbaugh I believe is correct, his partner that travels with him, came to my home. I got in the car with these two gentlemen, and we drove near this -- I say near -- we drove within two miles of it I will say; this particular distillery was at least four miles by the roadway to my home. Of course if you take it as the beeline, why it would reduce that distance possibly better than two miles. We concealed this car and walked through the swamps.

I took these gentlemen to this distillery. We counted the equipment. There were fifty-one 50-gallon barrels of beer and mash there. That is 2,550 gallons approximately. There were fifty gallon containers. There was this eight-foot tank and eight feet in diameter which was another 1500 or 2000 gallons.

Now Gentlemen, I am going to tell you Mr. Lucas on this stand told you gentlemen that they destroyed this distillery. He later, Lucas, had booked me on it, or charged me with some connection with this distillery. At the time I notified these officers there was no apparent danger of it being destroyed. It was in full operation. It was set up for further operation. Nobody seemed to be disturbed or distressed about the thing ever being destroyed.

(Holds conversation with the Court.)

By Mr. Huddleston: If Your Honor please, I believe due to the fact that the defendant is tired at this particular time and it is now the usual time, it would be well enough if Your Honor cares to take a recess at this particular time and allow him to resume the stand when we come back without any other interruption.

By The Court: All right.

(The Defendant leaves the stand.)

Gentlemen of the Jury, you will observe the instructions which I have given you prior to this time in connection with discussing the case. We will take a recess until one o'clock.

AFTER RECESS

By The Court: Proceed, Gentlemen.

John Wallace resumes the Stand, and continues his statement as follows:

By Mr. Huddleston: will you permit the reporter to pick up and refresh him on where he left off?

By The Court: Mr. Wallace, if you get tired, or if you want to stop and rest at any time just tell me, or if you want some water, or if you want to be excused, say so. Don't push yourself. If you want to rest a few minutes it is all right.

By Mr. Wallace: Now Gentlemen, as I had stated, there was no apparent uneasiness of the operators of this distillery that it was going to be destroyed. Now Gentlemen, I stated that there was no apparent uneasiness on the part of the operators of this outfit. I just want to state here that Mr. Lucas stated on this stand that he had charged me with some connection with this particular still. Now I want to state to you Gentlemen that had I had any connection with that distillery with Turner, for what reason would I have reported it at that time, fully loaded so to speak? That thing would have turned out a good little bit of finished product, and that stuff properly marketed would have meant some considerable money to somebody.

If I had been involved in the operation of this thing, the most reasonable

309

thing that I could have done even though I wanted to have it destroyed at any time, would have certainly been at the time after the material had been manufactured into a finished product. It would have still been just as much still empty as it would have been full and ready to go.

I can see no reason why that Mr. Lucas would sit up here and under oath tell you gentlemen that he had charged me with any complicity in this setup. It certainly is no evidence that I had any financial interest in it. It certainly showed the opposite. When the thing was destroyed it was destroyed in full readiness for operation.

Now when I took these gentlemen over there, I took them over there in my car in the middle of the night and put them out near this distillery after they had concealed their car, and I provided them with a thermos jug filled with water and a blanket so if they got cold during the night while watching this distillery that they would be more comfortable and would not have to leave the scene of concealment to get even a drink of water. That certainly showed my full cooperation with them.

The next thing I learned about the thing, that they left the scene at sometime after I left them. I don't know whether they even stopped long enough to take a drink of water out of that thermos jug or not. I learned on the following afternoon that Mr. Lucas and Mr. Bedenbaugh, and Mr. Miller -- I learned from Mr. Miller at a much later date, but I was discussing this situation with them, asked them why they didn't catch somebody before they destroyed it, and he said Mr. Lucas called him, and that was the first he knew about it. They drove down there in the afternoon of this following day after the midnight trip that I made with them and put them in concealment, and showed them where to go and how they could watch the approach to the outfit. I knew the roads in that section of the country better than they did, and they boldly drove down there in the afternoon with no apparent concern after they had the thing located, to try to catch anybody, drove down there in the afternoon and quietly destroyed the outfit and drove away.

I learned from my tenant after the thing was destroyed, the same Robert Lee Gates that I had driven away from there or commanded to leave or insisted that he leave the place before I notified these officers, this same Negro told me that Mr. Turner came by his home and picked him up in his car and they went over to this distillery site to ascertain as to whether the fermentation had completed itself, functioned enough for the stuff to be distilled, and when they reached the site of this distillery Mr. Turner walked up on this big high tank. It was down in the ground and the top of it nearly possibly one foot elevated from the top of the ground, a big hole dug out in the bank of this swamp, and Mr. Turner walked up on this still and looked in it, and he said, "good gracious alive, he said "this thing has got a leak in it, and they had cut the sides of it and the contents had run out. Some further investigation Mr. Turner had this darky make they discovered that somebody had destroyed it, demolished the outfit, so they immediately left with all haste for fear that maybe the officers were in hiding in the vicinity.

Now I can't see where I come in as aiding and abetting having been a partner in Mr. Turner's operations of his law violations there. That is just something that I can't understand, why their apparent indifference about stopping this man's operation of that unlawful operation that he was carrying on in that community there. He was a menace to the whole settlement.

I was most concerned about my future. I didn't want to get involved in his illegal operation there, and I just could not explain that. I can't explain it. Mr. Miller testified here before you gentlemen that on the following day that he and Mr. Cook proceeded over to Mr. Turner's home. After all, Gentlemen, as long as Mr. Turner occupied that place, that was just as much his private home as any of you gentlemen's homes happen to be whether you rent it, or own it, or however you live in it. It was his home. He had a right so far as his own actions are concerned, as long as they were within the law that he wanted to do, he most certainly had the right to carry on my farm operations. That is the only reason he had my permission to live there.

Now these gentlemen went over there and discovered two brother-in-law's of Mr. Turner in the yard in the act of manufacturing two tanks. They evidently considered them stills. They testified here they destroyed them. If they had been water tanks or some other, meant for some other use there on the premises, I certainly would not think the officers would have been authorized to have destroyed them, so they evidently destroyed them on the presumption they were satisfied in their mind that they were illegal property and constructed for the use of violating the law, and they destroyed these two tanks they said they found them manufacturing.

Now I don't know, I have never heard of these two men that were manufacturing these tanks having ever been tried in any court. I would not say they had not, but I think I would know it if they had. I think I am safe in saying they have not.

Now you gentlemen can readily see my helpless feeling. I had endeavored on occasions, had volunteered to the officers about these transactions, and had no apparent relief, and apparent utter disregard for the information that I had given them, but I determined then that if he did make liquor in that community that he would not have any peace doing it. I was going to see that some way or other they were destroyed.

We had a Sheriff in my county that could have destroyed some of those stills had he been physically able -- Mr. Collier. It is a known fact too. I will say Mr. Wyatt knows it to be a fact. Mr. Collier has been in very ill health for several years. He has had trouble with his heart. When he came to my place on the visit to first serve the warrant on Turner back there in the summer of 1946, I went with him to Turner's house, and when we reached Turner's house Mr. Collier was so exerted at that time that he had to sit down in Turner's house and rest a few minutes before he had breath enough in his body to read the warrant to Mr. Turner. I knew my sheriff was not physically able to make these raids.

I followed up Turner from this setup that I have mentioned to you gentlemen, and I had a farm over across the railroad from where Turner lived, east of the railroad a mile from his, had a tenant that lived a mile from him. There was an overhead bridge that crossed the A B & C Railroad in going to this darkey's house. I went to this darkey and asked him, I said, "do you know anything about Mr. Turner's whiskey operation now?" I said, "if we don't get this thing stopped here every one of you Negroes are going to wind up in jail. You all drink all the liquor you can get your hands on, and Mr. Turner had just so much influence over those Negroes' he could take a pint of liquor and lead them around like you would a pet pig with a slop bucket. He would just take a little liquor and they were ready to go with him and help him do anything in the world he wanted to do in his operations, and I knew these Negroes were in that racket with him. I heard it. Between my labor I learned these facts.

I didn't get into any specific case of them being directly engaged with him, but I knew it, and I didn't know it. I told this Negro, I said, "this thing has got to be stopped." "Mr. Turner won't listen to me. I can't understand why the officers won't catch him, but he just keeps on having this liquor and he makes it all over the community unmolested. I just can't see through it. So I told this darkey, I said, "do you know anything about any of his operations?" I could not get him to gather his crop. He would not gather his corn crop. He would not stay at home long enough. I venture to say, gentlemen, he had already then swapped off that old sorry $1400.00 Ford he had and got him another one, and he told me that he paid $700.00 difference between this car and this $1400.00 car he had. He had $2100.00 tied up in an $1100.00 automobile. He was really running loose, so I told this darkey, I said, "you take this money" -- I gave him $1.00 out of my pocket -- I said, "you go up above here" -- This darkey told me he had seen some beer and mash spilled out on this overhead bridge where it went over this railroad, and he had seen him come by his house on a Sunday night after this big distillery was destroyed and slackened up some when Mr. Lucas destroyed it, and some of this mash and beer had been -- I don't know where it came from, but this Negro apparently knew something about it. He knew more about it than I did. He informed me about it. It spilled on this bridge. He said, "they have gone up this road somewhere above here. Well, I didn't know how far he had gone, but I gave this Negro one dollar. I said, "you go up above here in this community somewhere above here, visit among your neighbors up there, Negroes, and buy a little liquor with this dollar if you can find any, and sit around and listen at them talk and take a few drinks of that liquor with them and see if you can find out if there is any liquor being manufactured up there around this community."

Well, he did as I told him. He came to me and told me that he had been in about two miles above his place there which was a pretty -- possibly three miles from Turner's house -- and had found out that there was some whiskey being manufactured up in that community somewhere, but he was unable to find out the exact location or the source.

Well, I wrote Mr. Miller a letter asking him to come to my place, that I had a matter I wanted to discuss with him, and I told him to come alone. I told him to come alone for the reason I didn't want anybody except the officers that I actually contacted to know what I was doing. I didn't want any chance of any leak anywhere. I didn't know but what it might be discussed somewhere, and somebody might overhear the conversation, and then it would get back of my activity about ridding this community of this menace.

Mr. Miller did come to my place, and I went with him and I actually drove within 500 yards of that distillery that night and didn't know it myself. Mr. Miller informed me on this trip, he said, "Mr. Cook and I, and some other of the county officers, Meriwether County deputies have searched every branch in that locality." He said, "we have walked every branch in this community, Mr. Wallace, and we have not been able to find any still in here." He said, "I have had some information that somebody saw some whiskey right down within 1,000 yards of this distillery in some kudzu vines." I said, "well, Mr. Miller, it certainly must be in this vicinity somewhere if there is whiskey being stored alongside of this road right here."

We rode out and we saw a car that night pull off from just about the position, the actual location that Mr. Miller testified to you that when he finally raided this distillery that he saw Turner and some other parties drive away from, but he was behind the car walking in the road and was not close enough to catch them. I noticed that car that night and called Mr. Miller's attention to it, but of course we didn't know who was in the car and why it was stopped on the road.

We went on to Durand, headed toward my home. We were just about two miles north of Durand at that particular time. When we drove into Durand, we saw Mr. Turner's car. I recognized it. It was headed toward Warm Springs. I mentioned the fact to Mr. Miller, and it was rather late at night, and a little unusual I thought, knowing where Turner lived, and what reasonable business he might have for his car to be out headed for Warm Springs at that time of the night.

Mr. Miller said, "we will just stop and see who is in it and what is in it. Well, I didn't want to have him expose me there riding around with him in the middle of the night. I didn't want Turner to know that I was in company with Mr. Miller and was searching his car, and I asked Mr. Miller before he searched the car, I said "put me out and then pick me up. We passed the car, and we saw that there was a man driving it, we didn't know who, and we were driving rather fast, and he went on ahead of this car far enough to get out of sight. I got out of the car. Mr. Miller blocked the road. He searched this car, and now gentlemen, he testified to you that he found a can, a five-gallon can in that car with some whiskey in it. If there was a pint or half a pint of whiskey or whatever amount he said it was, either a pint or a half a pint of whiskey in the can, it was still whiskey. It was not water. It was whiskey. Mr. Miller told you that it was not enough whiskey for him to make a case against the driver of that car.

Under the law, gentlemen -- I am not a lawyer and I don't profess to be but I understand the law there -- an officer has the right to confiscate an automobile transporting a half a pint of whiskey as easy as he could if it was transporting a gallon if it was illegal whiskey. He didn't do that. He turned him loose. I can't tell you for what reason. He didn't arrest that man with this illegal whiskey or make an effort to ascertain whether it was legal whiskey or un-tax paid whiskey.

Now imagine my feeling, gentlemen. You place yourself in my position, trying to get the law enforced in your community and get that kind of cooperation. I just felt like I didn't know where to turn. I didn't know who to turn to.

Now Mr. Miller, after making the search, picked me up, took me back to my home, he then started on his return to his home. He lives at Woodland. He goes through ordinarily from my home he would go through Warm Springs and Manchester going on his return to his home.

When he got back in the vicinity of Durand why he encountered this car again. Mr. Turner was in the car. I don't know whether his brother-in-law was in it at that time or not, but Mr. Turner stopped him, halted the officer of the law on the highway in the middle of the night, and reprimanded him, upbraided him, or gave him --demanded some explanation as to why he would stop his car and search it on the highway, and from what Mr. Miller told me at the following conversation I had on the following morning, Mr. Turner evidently was abusive to him.

On the following morning I was over at Mr. Turner's farm assisting in the harvesting of that corn crop that I had been unable to get him to gather. He had 100 acres in corn, and he pulled down possibly two or three hundred bushels of it, and it began to rain and corn was sprouting in the shucks on the ground, he just let it keep laying there one rain after another, so I told him, I said, "Wilson, if you are not going to gather this crop I will get up labor at home and come and gather it myself and you can pay for the labor. That was his share of the deal. I really had no reason to be required to even go into that field and help gather that crop, but I did do it. I took this labor that I had and went over to this farm, and was hauling in this crop, and Turner had gathered some of his corn before I started. I don't know just how much, and he had shucked it up and sold the corn. I didn't question his honesty about the division of the crop. I asked him how much he had gathered, and he told me how much, and so I began my operation with the division of the corn as he said it should be divided. I put a truck load of corn in his crib, put a truck load in my crib.

Now on this following morning after this occurrence with Mr. Cook -- Mr. Miller, pardon me -- while I was there having his corn unloaded in Mr. Turner's barn with Mr. Turner assisting at that time, Mr. Miller and Mr. Cook drove up on the scene. They called to Mr. Turner and he went out, and they had a conversation in my presence, and Mr. Miller advised Mr. Turner that he was not going to put up with that treatment that he had given him the night before, and he was going to search his car whenever he wanted to and wherever he wanted to, that he had tried to act fairly with him, and he wanted the same treatment, that he was not going to have him stopping him on the road at night or any other time, abusing him for performing his duty.

Now gentlemen, at this time I don't believe that I know of any further liquor violations that Mr. Turner had. We were in the process of gathering that crop. I could not keep him on the premises to gather it. He would not provide the labor.

He had four hogs on his premises at that time. He deliberately turned those hogs out into that crop in the process of harvesting. I told Mr. Turner, I said, "your hogs are going to destroy the corn pulled down here in the field and some of it too wet to haul up." We started to pull some of the corn that was on the stalk that had been protected from the rain and haul that in first and give the corn that was on the ground a chance to dry out. We spread it out and let the air hit it, and the hogs just ate up places I won't exaggerate, gentlemen, when I say more than half as large as that jury stand there, where he had pulled his corn in sacks and made piles out of it, and we opened it up for the air to hit it, and these hogs absolutely destroyed this corn.

I prevailed on Mr. Turner to put the hogs up out of my crop. I told him they were going to eat my crop up. He refused to do it. He just turned a deaf ear and told me that my cows at sometime or other had accidentally -- he told me that they -- I didn't mean, gentlemen, that Mr. Turner told me anything accidentally. Mr. Turner told me that at some time the past year that my cows had gotten in his cotton and that there was nothing done about that, so he didn't see any reason to worry about his hogs.

Now gentlemen, my cows had never been turned willfully in Mr. Turner's cotton. They had never done his crop any amount of damage so to speak. I could not understand Mr. Turner's attitude except that he was mad with me because I would not let him make his whiskey and carry on his law violations in my community unmolested. I would not give him that permission. I tried to correct his actions. I tried to prevail on him to behave himself as any law abiding citizen should, and he resented that fact, and then he wanted to sell his crop at this time, said "what will you give me for my part of it.

I told him, I said, "now Wilson, that was not our trade. You are supposed to make this crop and harvest it. Then you receive your half of it." I asked him what he would take for it. I thought if I could not get it gathered, maybe I could buy it at a price and gather it myself. He made me a proposition. Before I could get the corn, get back to gathering the corn, he changed his mind.

I went down to Chipley while these tenants were hauling some of the corn. I was not present at the time, for Mr. Kimbrough who is in the livestock business down there, approached me and said, "what about this corn up there on Turner's farm, said "he wants to sell it to me. He said, "will it be all right with you for me to buy it?" I said, "yes, he has already sold it to me. If you want to buy it, go ahead and buy it. I don't know why he should want to sell it to you when he is supposed to have already sold it to me, so he said, "well, I just don't want any dealings with him. He said, "you certainly need the corn. You have a lot of cows to feed, and you go ahead and buy it from him and use it on your own farm, which I knew to be a fact that I did need it and could use it.

But when I went back to see Mr. Turner he had changed his mind. He didn't want to sell the crop then to me. I weighed some of the corn thinking that I was going to buy it before I had time to be informed that he had changed his mind. He was off riding up and down the road, and my labor was gathering the corn and hauling it to Chipley, three miles, or a four-mile drive to be exact, to get to weigh it so I could pay him for his share.

I then went to Mr. Myhand, Mr. Broughton Myhand who had formerly worked for me, and in the capacity of overseer for several years, had charge of my dairy. He was a good friend of mine, and he knew Turner. I asked him, I said, "I wish you would go to Turner and see if you can straighten him out on the corn. He sells it to me one day and wants to sell it to somebody else the next day, and I don't know how to gather the crop."

He went to Turner and bought the crop from him, finally bought it. I proceeded to gather it on that basis, where I had the crop gathered, and I paid Turner before the crop was gathered. We bought it on a lump sum basis. Mr. Myhand bought it. I in turn furnished the money.

I told Mr. Myhand, I said, "now Broughton, I don't know whether Wilson owes this bank anything over here or not. We had better find out before this money is paid, about whether there is any liens against his part of the crop." So I went over to the bank and asked the cashier of the bank. I asked him if Mr. Turner owed him any money, and he told me he owed him a note of $200.00 and interest that amounted to about $4.00 I believe. I told him that I bought this corn and a yearling from Mr. Turner, and Mr. Myhand was going to handle the transaction, and when he came in to get the money I told Mr. Askew to supply the funds to make the deal. I gave Mr. askew a note for the $200.

Mr. Myhand took Mr. Turner over to the bank to settle with him for the corn in the presence of the bank. The bank in turn demanded pay for his note. the banker was settled with.

Now Mr. Turner some time, very short time later moved away from my farm. I didn't know where Mr. Turner moved. I was not there when he -- on the premises of his home when he left it, and I didn't know where he had gone to. It was sometime in -- that was around the first of November I believe -- sometime in January I was traveling on the public road from here near Robert Gates' home. He and Mr. Turner were pretty good friends. I saw Turner's car parked in this darkey's yard. That was since he had moved away, completely away from my farm. I had an idea of approaching him. I drove out to the darkey's house and saw it was him. I was tempted at that time to ask him to leave this Negro's house. I had an experience with him before that had been most unpleasant about practically the same situation, and I just didn't do it. I spoke to him and asked him where he lived. He told me that he lived somewhere near Carrollton.

Sometime in February, possibly a month after that or six weeks, I would not be definite, there was a distillery destroyed near this Gates Negro's home. This Negro was captured on the site, and a King darkey that lived with me was also captured. These Negroes were brought up here by the officers to Newnan and placed in jail. I was notified by their families about this occurrence, and I came up here and stood there Negroes' bond for the reason that they lived on my farm and they had share crops there. I had nothing to do with their liquor operation. I don't know whether they were operating this distillery or why they were there, but they were there, evidently.

When I came up to make this bond, I had some conversation with Mr. Thompson who lives here in this town, a deputy marshal. I told him at that time about some of these experiences that I had down here at my farm with this man Turner, and that I was confident that this distillery sprung from his efforts. I had no way to prove it. I had seen him there on the premises. He was the only man that I had seen at this Negro's house that joined the land to where the still was that was destroyed just a few hundred yards away. He was the only person I had seen at this Negro's house that I had any experience with in having violated the liquor laws to that community. I felt like that Turner was implicated with these darkeys.

I had some conversation with Mr. Potts here on that day. I don't remember just what it was. We discussed this illicit liquor business to some extent. I told Mr. Potts on this occasion that the liquor laws had been violated down there, and I had a lot of trouble in my community with it, and I had no connection with it personally, casting a shadow over my reputation, and possibly was either commented or advised, officers at that time possibly had some idea that I was implicated in these operations.

Section Two

Later, I heard no more from Turner until about the 10th of March, I believe it was, but during the winter months on this farm that lay back in this section there where Turner had lived I had placed about seventy-five head of cattle to graze on wild honeysuckle vines that were in the low lands and creek swamps and the branch bottoms, and there was quite an acreage there that didn't belong to me, but was lying out, nonresident property, and I turned these cows back there on open range, and they pastured and grazed there during the winter months. I would go over possibly every week or ever so often and salt these cows and round them up and count them, and see if they were all there.

In March they began to scatter and some trouble to keep together, and I rounded them up and when I finally succeeded in getting them rounded up I was about eighteen or twenty head short.

I rode the country high and low horse back, all through those swamps for several miles radius, followed those creek swamps on down for several miles, went every place I knew to go and inquired of all the adjoining land owners as to whether they had seen any stray cows, and I never found about twenty of these cows, and I have never found them up to now. I don't know where they went. I didn't see them take them, but for some reason people in the community that knew the character of Wilson Turner, my neighbors told me that "Wilson Turner has gotten your cows".

Now Gentlemen, I took the remaining fifty some odd head and drove them home, which was as I said, four or five miles distance, and put them in a pasture near my residence, and of course had to begin feeding them some added feed.

I think around March 10th Mr. Berry, a white man lived with me there, had charge of my diary operation, he was supervisor and assisted in the milking of my cows. He came in on this morning and told me that "one of our pure bred Guernsey Milch cows was gone. I didn't know where the cow had gone. Mr. Berry told me she was gone. He says, "I don't believe this cow broke out of that lot; she has never broken out before. She is one of the heavy milkers. I believe somebody has driven this cow away."

That morning I took Mr. Berry, a colored man that worked in the dairy with him, and a little colored boy there on the place, and we searched the swamp land below this dam at my pond. We tried to search every foot of it for fear this cow had been in the mire some place. Mr. Berry told me she had been in the barn the night before. I didn't know whether she had been in the barn or not. I didn't know whether the cow had come from the pasture the afternoon before. I went down into this pasture and we searched as best we could to see whether this cow happened to be in them or not. I rode all over the adjacent pasture land near my barn, and never found this cow.

On the following afternoon I was on the road passing the farm that joins the farm that Robert Lee Gates lived on. There is a road that came out of it through this farm into the public road. This particular farm belonged to a Mr. Chambers. This road came from the direction of this destroyed distillery that King and Gates had been captured at.

When I got nearly even with this road Wilson Turner and a man that he introduced to me as being a Mr. Adamson came out of this road in an old model Ford car that had been cut off behind the front seat and converted into a little pickup truck, a homemade pick up truck.

I stopped my car and got out before they drove into the main road, and approached this car. I asked Turner, I said, "what are you fellows looking for?" I had not seen Turner since I saw him in this Gates' Negro's yard in January. That is the last time I had seen him. He said, "I have been over here to show this man how to make a gas still." Now that certainly convinced me that he knew something about the still. I had not seen him since January. There he was in March showing a man he said that lived over around Carrollton, seventy miles away from this particular spot, a distillery. Now I certainly figured that he must know something about it.

I didn't mention to him about the loss of these cattle. I didn't try to harm this man on that day. If I had wanted to, or ever intended to, or ever had any desire to have done this man bodily harm I could have done it that day. He was down there on my premises so to speak. He was a lot nearer my home than he was his. It is certainly human nature for a dog to bark louder in his own yard than he would in somebody elses. I most certainly if I had any idea of trying to harm him, I would have taken advantage of the situation of him that far away form home and me right in my front door.

I didn't mention to him the missing of any cattle. I didn't mention anything to him other than greeted him and asked him the question I have made reference to. I didn't want to harm the man. I wanted to find out where my cows where that were missing.

The liquor business looked liked it was just about subsided with this last situation. I didn't know of any further liquor operation, but I did know my cows were gone, and gentlemen, I had worked hard to own a herd of cattle. They don't come just with the free request. It takes years to build up a herd of cattle and to breed a herd of cattle. It is a life time job, the dairy business is. The only thing I wanted to do was find my cattle. I had not accused Wilson Turner of stealing those cows. I had people suggest to me that he had done it. That was certainly not evidence enough to proceed on.

So Wilson Turner drove away from my premises after he had moved away, and my cattle had been missing, more than twenty head, just as unharmed as any of you gentlemen are right this minute so far as I know. He certainly was not harmed by me, or neither was he abused by me in anyway, shape, form or fashion.

Now on the following Sunday night or Monday morning I will add, the same Mr. Berry came in and informed me that we were two more pure bred cows short. Now gentlemen, these were registered cows. One of them was the best bred cow that I owned. I bought her in South Carolina at public auction. I paid $750.00 for her. She had a 517 pound butter fat record. That is 517 pounds of butter fat produced in a year out of approximately 11,000 pounds of milk. This other cow was also a cow with an established record that I bought at the same time, paying $525.00 for this cow. That was $1,275.00 in those two cows.

The first cow that I lost of the pure bred line just previous to my seeing Mr. Turner up there in this road which was possibly thirteen or fifteen days back, cost me $330.00 at public auction at Ben Hill. Mr. W. B. Crawford sold out a pure bred herd there in 1941 I believe, and I bought this cow there. Now I had lost $1,605.00 worth of pure bred cows. I had lost better than $2,000.00 worth of grade cows. That made my total losses in the cows that had been lost, strayed or stolen better than $3,000.00.

Now gentlemen, I could not stand many losses like that. I owe a lot of money. I think it is a lot. My obligations run into possibly better than $25,000. These cows that have been stolen from me are collateral for some of this money. Many licks like this and I would have been bankrupt. My collateral was being taken away from me and being done while I was asleep. I just was in the most terribly distressed situation.

When Mr. Berry told me about these last two pure breds being gone, of course my mind went back to Turner being on the premises on Thursday before this thing happened on Sunday night or sometime before milking time on Monday morning. I went down to this lot. I said, "let's go see if we can find where they got out. Well, we found some tracks where somebody had evidently had some difficulty with an animal in a trench silo that was in my night lot, and we followed these signs from this silo, and they led down to the fence of this pasture, lot fence, and we saw where that fence had been broken down and that cow had, or a cow had been taken across this fence, and there was the cow tracks and the man's track.

Now we further located another place close to where this broken down part to this fence was that showed signs of some scuffle with an animal there, cow's tracks and a person's track there, so we followed these tracks from this place and they led out over this same break in the fence where the wire had been mashed down. We followed these tracks on, the cow track and some person's tracks, and came across a little wash in the land. In this wash was where sand had been gathered and made smooth surface, and we saw them distinctly the tracks along with the cow tracks.

Mr. Turner was a small man in statue. He was tall but he possibly weighed 150 pounds. I don't say that he didn't weigh 120. I don't say that he didn't weigh 150. My idea was the man weighed around 150 pounds. He had a comparatively small foot. I saw this track there. I had no way to identify that as being anybody's track. It had no name on it, but it brought to my mind that it was not a very -- such a big man that was driving or leading that cow, because it was right fresh and right alongside of each other.

We followed these tracks over across this dam in the public road, and found where a cow had been tied in some little pines for some period of time. I don't know how long, but there was droppings there that signified the tracks around this little tree, and the bark was rubbed off of the tree. I guess the rope had been used on this tree. I figured that one of these cows had been tied there.

We went out into the road and found the prints as if a truck body had been let down in the middle of the road. There was the imprint of the edge of a tractor. It appeared to be that, across the road. At this same spot there was some sawdust and some small particles of manure as if it dropped out of this truck possibly.

We saw these cow tracks in the center of this road, saw where they were led back, or one cow. I don't know whether there was two tied out there or not, but two cows were missing on this particular morning. We of course believed that these cows were loaded there in that road and hauled away from there. I didn't know where they had gone. I had no way to know. I didn't know when they disappeared except that they had disappeared sometime between sundown and milking time before that previous afternoon and the time they were discovered as missing on this morning.

I went and called the sheriff of our county and reported this theft, this last theft of these cows. That was the only direct evidence that I had that they had been hauled away by anybody. It was the only evidence that I had to show that my cows had ever been actually carried away from my premises, and that was following the tracks directly to a place that showed signs as if they had been loaded.

Mr. Collier and Mr. Biggers came to my place. Mr. Biggers, Willis Biggers from Greenville, Georgia drove him down there, chauffeured his car down there. Mr. Smith of the Georgia G. B. I. was called by Mr. Collier, and he drove into my yard at the same time Mr. Collier was present.

I asked Mr. Collier -- I stated what facts we had to go on and Mr. Collier says, "well, what would you suggest I can do for you?" I said, "Well, sheriff, I want to cover every sale that I possibly can today, every sale barn. These cows that have been stolen are going to be marketed somewhere." He says, "where would you have me to go?" I said, "I would like for you to cover the sale barn in Montgomery, Alabama." He said, "all right, that is where I will go."

I got Mr. Tom Strickland, who was my cousin, to take one of my tenants that had dealings with this herd of cattle and help me to drive them, corral them over there on this operation that they had been running on my farm several years and knew my pure bred cattle, to go along with Mr. Strickland to Macon to cover every sale barn in Macon, every livestock dealer in Macon. I got Mr. Herring Sivell, who is jointly charged here with me, to go to Carrollton with this Mr. Berry, who was in my employ.

Mr. Sivell was my neighbor. I assisted him in arranging his finances when he entered the dairy business. I have been into Illinois, Wisconsin and Minneapolis with Mr. Sivell buying dairy cattle for Mr. Sivell. I charged him nothing for my services. He possibly paid the greater part of my actual traveling expenses. Mr. Sivell was ready to help me try to locate my lost cattle. We certainly had a business that was mutually intermingled with each other. All of us have kind of a fraternal feeling because we have the same operating difficulties to overcome. We have diseases among our cows, and ailments, and what not that come up, and we get together and discuss those things, and we go to the dairy meetings together, and I have been instrumental in several of my friends down there getting into the diary business, and we most certainly face a time of agricultural diversification. They tell us that our cotton is a thing of the past. We have got to get into some other kind of business. This dairy business is the next best bet that I know of. It most certainly brings you in cash daily, or monthly, or however you may market your milk. It is a ready cash market. Well, I have been interested in all these boys down here that have gone in the dairy business. I was about the first one, maybe Mr. McGruder in my section. We were the first two men engaged in the diary business in that section of the country. It was not so expensive as I have had at later times.

May I be permitted to ask a few minutes? I am getting a little tired.

BY THE COURT: Yes, Let the jury go to their room. We will take a recess of about ten minutes.

(A 10 minute recess called at 2:15.)

By The Court: Proceed. Bring the jury in.

(The Jury returns to the box at 2:30 pm)

By Mr. John Wallace: Gentlemen, I believe I stated to you that Mr. Sivell and Mr. Berry, my dairyman who was in charge of the handling of these cows in this barn, went to Carrollton on this Monday to cover the auction sale that is conducted there on Monday, livestock auction. Mr. Smith of the Georgia -- G. B. I. -- that is the Georgia Bureau of Investigation, if you gentlemen are not all familiar with that arm of our law in Georgia -- went to Newnan here and promised to call into Atlanta to some of the other agents to have them notify the different sale barns up there to be on the lookout for these cattle in question.

I had the Carrollton sale covered by Mr. Berry and Mr. Sivell. I had the

Newnan and Atlanta barns covered by the G. B. I. I had the Macon barns covered by Mr. Tom Strickland and this George O'Nell, who was a tenant farmer of mine and familiar with these cattle. The sheriff and Mr. Biggers covered Montgomery, Alabama, those sale barns and livestock dealers. I went to Columbus and visited two auction sales that morning and contacted the men in charge of these sale barns and described these last two cows that had disappeared.

I told these sales barn operators that these cows would certainly stand out above any other cows they would possibly, have in their sale for the fact of their marking and their breeding, and they would certainly show themselves that they were not ordinary beef cattle.

I went to Americus. I went to Buena Vista. I went to Sylvester. I came back by Albany and contacted the livestock dealers and the operators and the barns in those different places. Some of them were having sales that day. Mr. Sutton was having his sale at Sylvester, who was our former State Veterinarian at one time.

I came back home, arriving late that night. That was Monday night. Tuesday was Ragsdale-Lawhorn auction day in Atlanta. These parties that made these different inspections on the day before reported that they didn't find any trace of the cattle. However, Mr. Sivell told me that he drove into the Carrollton auction, arrived on the scene, that he saw Mr. Wilson Turner present at that sale barn. He parked his car and went in to observe in company of Mr. Berry, to observe the cattle that had been placed there for sale that day. When he went in he never saw Mr. Turner anymore that day after him first seeing him as he drove up. He said he was certain that Mr. Turner saw him.

On this Tuesday that I mentioned of the sale in Atlanta Mr. Sivell and I went there. Mr. Sivell had better means of transportation than I had. He was kind enough to take me up there. He was interested in me recovering my cattle. I would have been just as interested in his cattle had he lost any.

We went to this barn and inspected the pens, and looked at the cattle, and stayed until the sale was practically over, at least until all the cattle had stopped coming in to the sale. I came home on this Tuesday afternoon or night and on the following Wednesday I had found that there would be an auction sale at Rome, on Wednesday.

I, on this day, Wednesday, went to Rome, and my wife, Mr. Otis Cornett, Mr. Chipley and his wife, Mr. Broughton Myhand's wife of Chipley, Mr.

Louis Morgan of near Chipley who is the husband of my wife's sister, went along in the same automobile, six of us. I will mention at this time that Mr. Morgan's wife, who is my wife's sister, is confined in Battey Hospital at Rome. These ladies in the party went along with Mr. Morgan to visit his wife, while I and Mr. Cornett were going to this sale to observe what cattle were sold there that day.

We went to this sale and observed all the cattle possible at this sale. We failed to find my lost cattle. We returned home possibly around -- arriving in Chipley at ten o'clock on Wednesday night following this Monday morning disappearance of these last cattle. When I reached Chipley Mr. Myhand told me that the Sheriff of Harris County had been to my place on this afternoon during my absence, in Rome, and had left word with him at this store and filling station at Chipley. Mr. Hadley knew about Mr. Myhand's former connection with me on my farm and my dairy operation so he left this word there. Mr. Hadley told me the reason he didn't tell anybody on my premises that he didn't want any information to get out before it reached me about the cattle.

Mr. Hadley didn't know where these cattle had gone. He had received a telephone call through the efforts of Mr. Sivell on the previous Monday. Mr. Sivell had talked to the police in Carrollton and advised them about these cattle being from my place, and gave them my name and address, and I was informed that Mr. Threadgill, who was the chief of police, provided Mr. Sivell with an officer to go out to the cattle barn and show him the way out there as a courtesy.

On this information I got from Mr. Myhand, Mr. Hadley the Sheriff of Harris County wanted to see me, I didn't wait until the next morning. I went down there then in the middle of the night to see what the Sheriff wanted. Mr. Myhand told me that the Sheriff had told him it was in some connection with my lost cattle. Mr. Hadley told me that he had a telephone call from the Chief of Police at Carrollton. In giving the Chief of Police or this officer my name and address, he had made it Chipley, Georgia which is my post office address. That was the reason that the Police of Carrollton called the Sheriff of Harris County. He didn't know that I lived in another county and received my mail in Harris County.

Mr. Hadley told me that the Chief of Police asked him to deliver a message to me, I did not have a telephone and tell me that he thought he had one of my cattle, one of my cows located.

I drove back to Chipley with Mr. Cornett. He had accompanied me to Hamilton, and Mr. Myhand volunteered to go along and help me identify this cow. I had the registration papers and I got them and Mr. Myhand was familiar with the cow. Mr. Myhand was present when I bought the cow at auction in South Carolina, so we, Mr. Cornett, Mr. Myhand and I went back to Rome that night.

We got back to Rome. We found the police. We were taken down to a small pasture that I understood belonged to a Mr. Shirley who operates a general store over there right in the city limits of Carrollton. The police told me on my arrival in Carrollton that he had been advised by Mr. Shirley, or Mr. Shackleford, who I believe is a livestock dealer in Carrollton, that there was a stray cow in his pasture or in this grazing lot inside the city limits of Carrollton.

We went down to this grazing lot in the night time, and the moon was shining. We very readily recognized this cow as being one of my pure bred and registered milch cows. Nobody seemed to be able to explain why or how this cow got into this lot. The owner of this property has assured Mr. Threadgill, who was Chief of Police of Carrollton, of his full cooperation in anyway that he wanted to handle this cow after she had been located.

Mr. Threadgill and I together decided that if we should watch this cow -- she was placed there by somebody, she was placed there for some purpose. I figured that the cow would bring $175.00 in beef. That is a lot of money for a beef cow. It cost me $525.00. So Mr. Cornett took Mr. Myhand home, back to Chipley and left me there. I stayed with the cow to watch and see if anybody came to get her. I watched that cow all night. Mr. Threadgill said he didn't have the force to have her watched and police the town at night, but he, with the aid of Mrs. Shirley --Mrs. Shirley seemed to be afraid when whoever came to get this cow of mine would possibly steal her cow. She had a milch cow in the same pasture, so she was most anxious to keep her eyes on the cows too. She didn't want to lose her cow in the deal.

I watched this cow until day the next morning. Mr. Cornett came back after taking Mr. Myhand back home, so he could operate his business during that day, came back for me up in the morning, possibly eight or eight-thirty. I was at the Chief of Police's office at that time, having spent the remainder of that night there in a little small cow barn with this cow, lying within fifteen or twenty feet away in this lot, pasture.

When Mr. Cornett came back for me that morning -- Mr. Cornett knew Mr. Turner. I am a little ahead of my story, Gentlemen. I am going to back up a little bit. On my way to this sale -- A lot of details in this statement. I have just got an ordinary mind like you Gentlemen. I forget some of these things. However, I know them. I know the facts. I know the truth, the whole truth. I am going to give it to you that way. Whatever I state to you is going to be the truth, is going to be the whole truth, whatever way it might sound. It is going to be the truth.

Mr. Cornett told me, said, "coming in this morning I met Wilson Turner on the road inside the city limit of this town." I said, "well, Hoke, did he recognize you?" He said, "I don't know whether he did or not. Well, we started away from Carrollton that morning. On the outskirts near the city limit of Carrollton Mr. Cornett and I both saw Mr. Turner parked on this road, the highway, the paved road leading from Carrollton to LaGrange. I don't know why Mr. Turner was parked out there on that road. I don't know why he was on that road that morning. He didn't live on that road. He lived several miles in a westerly direction from Carrollton and on this day, on this Wednesday that I went to Carrollton after passing Franklin, Georgia which is possibly twenty-eight or thirty miles from Carrollton, I passed Wilson Turner. In passing this man my wife recognized him. She said, "we passed Wilson Turner awhile ago."

I didn't want Wilson Turner to know I was going to the Rome sale that day if I could prevent it. Mr. Sivell had just told me that he saw him on Monday at the Carrollton sale, and he vanished as soon as he saw him. It appeared to me that Turner had some reason for Sivell not seeing him at that barn, that sale barn. I tried to get away from Turner. I drove faster than the speed limits to get away from him. He stayed right on my trail. Just before we drove into Carrollton, he became involved in what you would term as a traffic jam.

Some other people were between he and I after we got in the city limits. That cut him off from me. He was meeting traffic coming on the left. I took advantage of this traffic as it passed me, and passed the traffic in front of me, that had him cut off. Turner saw that he was losing sight of me there at this particular point, which was within a block or two of the post office where the Newnan road goes into Carrollton, at the intersection of the Newnan road and the LaGrange highway.

When I reached this intersection I turned to my right as if I were coming back to Newnan. I didn't know where Turner was. I knew he was somewhere in the rear. I thought that if I was out of sight and that he was following me, that he would probably turn toward Carrollton at the corner of this post office, thereby I would lose him. I pulled down this street headed out toward Newnan for a block. I turned around then and headed back toward the city. Before I got back to this point where I had turned off of my main route, I met Turner headed - coming out from toward Carrollton.

He had met me face to face. When he got in this traffic jam he turned off to the left and made a cut and went into the square of Carrollton by another road to try and ascertain my movement. At least I had good reason to believe that, because he had really exerted some effort to keep me within his observation.

I proceeded on to this sale, as I told you. After going back to Carrollton on this night, identifying this cow, and going home the following day, I had been up all night Wednesday night, I had not slept any. I went home, and on Thursday, we were late in our preparation of our farms this year --you farmers whoever you might be on this jury, know that to be true. You other men who are not engaged in farming possibly know it to be true. We were at the rush season. I was trying to get my power equipment assembled to start my planting operation. From one season to another, Gentlemen, your equipment gets scattered. Your operators forget how to assemble it. It required my attention and presence to get this work done. I worked all day that day, that being Thursday.

I had told the Chief of Police at Carrollton that I would be back Thursday night. I was going to watch that cow until somebody moved her, if he would watch her by day, I would watch her by night. I called the G. B. I., Mr. Smith. He came over there and met me at the Chief of Police's office. I told him the situation, got one of these cows located now that we had in question several days ago, and I was going to watch her. Mr. Smith told me, "well all right, he said, "if I can help you any, just call on me.

Now Gentlemen, I had already called him. He was there on the scene and we had a cow under observation. We had a cow, watching her, that had been properly identified as being my cow. We had a chance -- the G. B. I. had a chance to assist me in capturing whoever placed that cow there. I figured from a reasonable standpoint. That is all I have got to figure from. I am not no super mind. My mind is a mind of just an ordinary country man. I figured that man would come back there and get that cow, and I certainly felt in a helpless condition or situation when the G. B. I. told me that if they could do me any good just give them a call. I had just given them a call.

I had called the State patrol and they had referred me to this G. B. I. department and I had called the Sheriff and he had brought the same man to my place. I had gotten no extra help about this cattle a stealing business. I called the office in Atlanta and they informed me on this occasion that I called them that I would find their agent of that section or that district at Buchanan, Georgia.

I called the Sheriff's office at Buchanan and asked for Mr. King, and he told me that I would find him in the Chief of police office at this particular time at Bremen, Georgia. Mr. Gray I believe was his name. I called him there and located him. I asked him to meet me in Carrollton on this night, and as I stated, he did. Now that is all the help I got out of the G. B. I., was the man's presence there and telling me that if I needed him to give him a call, and he left me there, Gentlemen, with that cow in this pasture and me there watching her alone except for the fact that Mr. Threadgill let one of his night officers go with me on Thursday night and watch this cow.

Mr. Threadgill told me, he said, "Mr. Wallace, I don't believe you are going to catch anybody with this cow." I had told him who I believed had something to do with the stealing of these cattle. He informed me that they were having a lot of cattle stealing in that community and vicinity at that time, that it was a real menace. He told me at that time that Wilson Turner had a new pick up truck, and that Mr. Millard Rigsby had a new pick up truck, and they were watching the operation of these two men, possibly from some other missing cattle or some information they had most certainly that caused them to watch these two men.

They informed me that on Tuesday that one of these trucks that had a cattle body on it had changed color, that it was red on Monday of that week, and on Tuesday it was an aluminum color. It had been - was a new truck and a newly painted red truck, then over night changed its color. I don't know who changed the color of that truck. I had no way to know, but I certainly had some imagination about it. Most any man would have had under the same circumstances that I was now placed in, would have had some wonder in your mind as to why these men had disguised the truck or changed its appearance so soon after it had been newly painted in a color that was certainly not objectionable.

Now Gentlemen, I watched these cows, this cow, on Thursday night after having been up Wednesday night and all day Thursday. I had not taken my shoes off. I want you Gentlemen to take note of what I am saying with all the mind that you have got.

I realize that my life is in the hollow of you Gentlemen's hands. I realize the crime that I am here charged with. I am endeavoring to tell you the truth, the whole truth. I have got nobody to bring here to substantiate these facts. I have been denied the testimony of anybody else that might have been involved in this. Whoever might have been or was indicted in this case with me, I have been deprived of their testimony. I am just here in a strange county by myself. I have got nobody to help me. All the help I have got is what God is going to give me to help me tell you the truth. That is all the witness that I can bring before you.

Now Gentlemen, when I left this place on Thursday morning I came again on Thursday night. On this night Mr. Otis Cornett, who is the same person that made this Texas trip with me, he is my friend, my neighbor, he was the man that went up there on this Wednesday with me, he went back with me on Thursday night.

We took turns about. One officer went with Mr. Cornett and watched this cow from possibly eight o'clock at night for two hours. They came back and I went and watched the cow two hours with another officer who was a member of Mr. Threadgill's night force in Carrollton. The only sleep that I got on Thursday night was a little sleep that I got between these shifts, which possibly amounted to two shifts for me, rest periods I might say. I pulled three chairs together in Mr. Threadgill's office in the city hall and lay down on those chairs to try to get a little rest. That was on Thursday night. We watched this cow Thursday night. Mr. Cornett and myself went home Friday morning and when I got home all the sleep that I had was these little naps that I caught between these watch shifts.

Friday I was busy on my farm. I didn't have time to go in there in the house and go to bed, right at the peek of planting time. I had no overseer at that time. I had to get out there with these colored people and keep the work planned for them and get my farm operations under way.

On Friday night I went back to Carrollton. I believe on this Friday night I went alone. I went by and asked Mr. Myhand to go with me, and he said he could not stay up all night and operate his business in the daytime. I drove back there Friday night, and I watched this cow alone that night. For some reason, Mr. Threadgill didn't have a man to go with me.

Now Gentlemen, I was placed in a disadvantage. I was seventy miles from home. I didn't know many people in Carrollton, a very few if any. I knew His Honor lived in Carrollton. I knew a Mr. Lambert in Carrollton who had come down to my place after Mr. Turner at one time, but I had nobody that I could ask to go and help me watch that cow.

Now I told Mr. Threadgill on Saturday morning, I said, "Mr. Threadgill, you are allowing me - this is in the city limit of your town, I am being exposed to a very serious situation." I said, "suppose whoever comes for this cow, I see them start away with this cow, I try to prevent them from going away with this cow, what am I to do? If I get killed, why I will be dead. If I should happen to hurt somebody else, I will be in a strange county with possibly the appearance of taking the law in my hands."

I know, Gentlemen, that I have got the right to prevent a man stealing my property. The law gives me that right. The law gives any private citizen -- I am not making a speech as a lawyer, but I am trying to tell you that I know these facts. I know my right to some extent. I knew that I had the right to prevent anybody from taking that cow, because she was my property, but I didn't want to be exposed to that danger of getting hurt or having trouble in that community and having anybody have the idea that I had taken the law in my hands and was trying to do anything that I should not do.

Mr. Threadgill told me at that time, he said, "now Mr. Wallace, he said "I admit I felt kind of bad about not giving you a man last night." He said, "that thing occurred to me too." He says, "I am going to give you somebody else on your next night that you watch this cow," but said, "I don't believe you are going to catch anybody with this cow." He says, "I believe the parties, whoever put this cow in this lot knows just about as much about your watch here as you do yourself."

I said, "Mr. Threadgill, if Wilson Turner put that cow in that lot, he is going to come back and get her just to show me and show you that he will do it. I know him. He has the daring, and he has gone to show us that he is going to have that cow." I said, "I venture to say he will come back and get her if he knew he was going to be caught while in the act."

He said, "well, as long as you are willing to stay up and lose the sleep and watch her," he said. "I will help you." Now on Saturday night I asked Mr. Cornett to go back with me. Mr. Cornett advised me that he had an invitation somewhere for dinner that night, he and his family, and he would go but he hated to break this engagement. I took my wife along. She did the driving. I never slept a wink on Thursday. I never slept a wink Wednesday night. All the sleep I got Thursday night was these little naps I took between the watch shift on that cow. Friday I never went to bed. I never took my shoes off. I caught a little nap possibly on the way from Carrollton to Chipley. Saturday I was up all day. My shoes had never been off.

Saturday night my wife drove me back to Carrollton. I got a little nap on the backseat of that car going to Carrollton Saturday night. I went down there, and Saturday night was a bad night for the town police. They have a lot of activity on these Saturday night brawls, and Mr. Threadgill didn't have an available man on Saturday night.

Sunday night I went down to Mr. Sivell's and asked him if he would go with me. I was worn down to a frazzle, Gentlemen. I had been up since Wednesday night, every night, all night and every day all day except that little time on Sunday afternoon.

Mr. Sivell went to Carrollton with me on Sunday night. I was a little bit late getting away to come home. I reached Carrollton about I will say nine o'clock. It possibly was nine o'clock when I reached Carrollton.

I drove directly to the Chief of Police office as I did every time I went there, to find out if any developments and what. When I reached the Chief of Police's office that night, I could not find him. I went up on the square and inquired if he had come in any offices there. They said they didn't know where he was at that time. I parked there. They said, "wait around here a few minutes and he will show up."

While parked there possibly five or ten minutes a car drove up. I didn't know who was in that car. I didn't pay it any special attention. Cars were passing around and around this square and the traffic was proceeding back and forth. The first thing that I realized that was out of order was the running of some of these officers that were standing nearby down toward a street that led off to the south from this square. I didn't know what had happened. A car pulled off in front of where I was parked, and somebody said, "run around that way and head him off." I didn't know who they were talking about heading off, but I asked this, somebody, I don't know just who, I said: "Who is this? What has happened?" He said, "the Chief is after a fellow."

Well, I pulled off behind him. I wanted to see what was happening too, so I pulled right in as quick as I could in the same direction that this car had gone. They said it was the Chief in his car. He pulled down the first block heading out, or the first alley way, I didn't know whether it was a street or alley, I believe though it was a small alley, that turned to the right headed toward Newnan. He turned into this alley. I saw him when he turned in and I followed him.

Just as I came up to the rear of this car that had stopped in front of me down in this alley, I heard a shot fired. I hopped out of the car out of curiosity to see what was going on. There I saw Mr. Threadgill, two or three other officers that had come down the main street leading from this square and come into another alley that made an intersection. These two alleys meet together, back into the back of these buildings.

Mr. Threadgill, was on the ground near his car. These officers were there, and Wilson Turner was standing there, and Mr. Threadgill had a hold of him holding him. That is the first time on Sunday night that I had seen Wilson Turner, or had heard anything about him since the time that I had seen him parked on the highway on Monday morning, on Thursday morning, when Mr. Cornett took me from Carrollton home after the first night watch of this cow.

Mr. Threadgill told me at that time, says "well, I got your cattle thief." I said, "well, I am glad you have." He said, "Wilson Turner has told me that he and Rigsby, Millard Rigsby, stole your cows." He said, "I am going to put him in jail, then we will go and see if we can locate the cow." He said, "I have not found the cow, but I have the cattle thief. He has admitted that he stole your cows and that a man named Adamson has now got this cow out at Shirleys in custody and is leading her down a swamp, down a creek to an old mill site about a mile or more from where she was located in this pasture."

We went by the jail. Mr. Threadgill placed Turner in jail. Mr. Sivell, and Mr. Threadgill and I got in Turner's truck. Mr. Threadgill told me that Turner told him that this man was going to lead this cow down to this old mill site and he was going to meet him there, they then were going to get another truck and load her up and take her some place.

Mr. Threadgill and Mr. Sivell and I got in this truck, Turner's truck. Mr. Threadgill had charge of this truck, took charge of it, and I didn't take any possession of his truck. I went along at Mr. Threadgill's suggestion to see if we could find the cow where Turner had directed him she would be.

We drove down this road down into the south of Carrollton to this old mill site. Mr. Threadgill said that Turner told him that he would find Adamson sitting on the side of the road waiting for him, waiting for Turner when he came for him. We drove down there and didn't see Mr. Adamson.

Neither did we see the cow. Mr. Threadgill gave a few little light touches on the horn as if he were signaling for somebody in that vicinity. Nobody showed up.

I told Mr. Threadgill, I said, "Mr. Threadgill, that fellow has told you a lie about this man." I said, "he has sent you off down there to get rid of you." I said, "I don't believe that man is coming down here with that cow. If he was coming, he would have already been here. He has had time enough to come a mile."

Mr. Threadgill told me at the beginning of this night -- If your Honor please, could I have a drink of water? -- at the early part of the night, that he had drove down to check on this cow, he had his day men at different times. There was a road that went around the south part of this pasture, and you could see all over it. It had no vegetation, just a few shade trees in it. You could see from this road an old pasture, from this, if you were traveling around in a car where the police made their rounds, so they were checking on this cow along through the day, and on this Sunday night Mr. Threadgill said he went down the early part of the night to give a checkup -- to get a checkup on this cow -- and when he came near to Mr. Shirley's residence, whose premises this cow was on or had been on, he saw Wilson Turner parked on the street near the driveway of Mr. Shirley. He headed into Mr. Turner's truck and when Turner saw that it was the police, he put his truck in reverse and tried to get away from him, tried to back away from him.

Mr. Threadgill said he crowded him too closely with his car, that he lost control of the back end of the truck, and it started to sway with him. He started to jump out of the truck. Mr. Threadgill caught him as he alighted. Then was when Mr. Threadgill said he admitted to him about the cattle and that Adamson had one down this road with the cow.

Now after leaving this mill, we started back to town. We met an officer, who was a city officer, and I understood the man with him was the Sheriff. We went back to town. I said to the Sheriff, I said, "Sheriff, what time will you be in your office tomorrow morning?" he said, "eight-thirty or nine o'clock." I said, "well, I will be back here tomorrow morning. I want to take up with you about Turner and this cow case." We didn't know where the cow was at that time. She had disappeared out of that lot.

Mr. Pike, who is an officer of that city, Mr. Sivell and I went back to the pasture where this cow had been. Mr. Sivell had a spine operation. He had something - a disc removed out of his spine, the lower part of his spine. He had a truck accident, been broken up. He had another accident in a truck and was broken up. He is not good at walking. He stopped in this pasture and Mr. Pike and I walked all the way around the fence to try and see if we could find where this cow had been taken out of this pasture in the night time. We found the wire loose in the pasture fence, but we saw no tracks.

I told Mr. Pike, I said, "let's go up to this piece of wood back of this pasture and see if we can see anything of that cow up that way." That was twelve o'clock in the night. We walked up to this wood and struck a road, a wee defined road. It seemed to lead through this wood. We followed this road back out to an opening. It was a field. When we reached that field we went around the edge of this wood back toward this pasture. We had gotten inside of the wood, and when we reached the corner of this wood, nearly to the corner, I heard this cow belch. You gentlemen who are farmers know when a cow belches there is what is known as the cud usually goes up into the throat and they chew. It makes a fuss. I noticed that fuss before I saw the cow.

Mr. Pike and I found this cow tied in the corner of this wood at one o'clock, twelve or one o'clock at night. We took the cow back and put her in the barn down there. Turner was in jail, so we put the cow in the barn and fastened the door.

On our return from this old mill I overlooked one thing that happened. Mr. Threadgill, Mr. Sivell and myself were in this truck. We met a car, and Mr. Threadgill recognized Mr. Millard Rigsby driving this car. We stopped. Mr. Millard Rigsby asked whoever was in that car -- I don't think he even waited to find out -- but whoever was in the truck said, "where is Wilson?" in a very excited tone of voice. So Mr. Threadgill told Mr. Rigsby, says, "he is in jail." He says, "he has told all about the cow business," he says, " and you might as well come on and admit your part of it." Mr. Rigsby in the middle of the night was on that old mill road. I told you about. He traveled with his own wife, and Turner's wife and child in the car with him, just after Turner had been captured, up there near that cow.

Now after fastening this cow up in this barn, I talked to the Sheriff, as I told you, and at that time that I had this conversation with him he told me when I asked him what time he would be in his office the next morning, he said, "I don't see much that I can do for you." He said, "Turner is not going to talk anymore; I am surprised that he said as much as he did."

Now, Gentlemen, why was I placed where I was placed then? Mr. Threadgill had caught the man there right near the cow. The man had confessed that he had stolen the cow. The Sheriff told me that he was surprised that he had said what he had said, that there was no need to come back there the next morning and try to make any further investigation.

You Gentlemen possibly can imagine my feeling at that time. I had stayed up Wednesday, Thursday, Friday, Saturday and Sunday night, trying to locate and find any of those cows, and after I had found the cow, had the man in jail, the Sheriff of the County told me that he didn't see much that he could do about it. I was helpless again but I had this to travel on. He told Mr. Threadgill that he had stolen my cows. He admitted it. I thought at that time, I possibly might think so now, the best of my judgment though -- he stole my cows. He didn't steal my cow in Carrollton. He stole my cow out of my lot in Meriwether County.

After the Sheriff gave me this encouragement about not being able to do me any good about my cattle being stolen - I had lost three thousand dollars worth of cows, and finally trailed one down and left hanging on a limb. I called the Sheriff of Meriwether county. I told Mr. Collier, I said, "I have located one of my cows. I have located the man that has confessed getting the cow. Get a warrant and come over here and get him and put him in Meriwether county jail."

Now Gentlemen, I have got a right to the function of my own mind. It is a thing that I can't control. You can't control your thoughts. I saw that it appeared to me that if I was going to ever get any further information out of Wilson Turner that he had better be in Meriwether county. I certainly was not going to get any co-operation out of the Sheriff of that County. Because he had assured me he was surprised the man had talked to him at all, or talked to Mr. Threadgill at all.

Now Gentlemen, Mr. Collier came to Carrollton. Mr. Threadgill said on this stand that he didn't know of his own knowledge whether Mr. Collier had a warrant for this man. Now Mr. Collier told me that he had a warrant for him. I have got no reason to tell you this except Mr. Collier told me that. I am not trying to defend anybody. I am trying to tell you though that so far as my knowledge is concerned, that we took this man back to Meriwether County with full authority of the law.

Now when we went down to the jail to get Turner after Mr. Collier came over there, Turner asked me if I would sign his bond myself, if I would sign his bond and release him from jail after stealing this cow most certainly from me. I told him, "no, Wilson, I can't sign your bond. You have admitted stealing my cows. Where are the rest of them? I have lost twenty some odd head. I believe you got them all. You got this one. You said you did." I said, "where are the other two pure breds? Where is the cow that disappeared with the one we have got here?" I said, "we found her tied up over here in the wood. She is here. She has absolutely been found."

He denied at this time that he knew anything about any cows to me, but he had admitted it to the Chief of Police. We took this man back and put him in the Meriwether County jail.

Now gentlemen, since I have been here in this jail locked up myself as a prisoner, there has been a cow that answered the description of one of my missing cows found over near Whitesburg dead in the creek. I didn't see that cow. I have not had the privilege of seeing her. Somebody has seen her, I don't know who that is, but the information that has come to me that was one of my cows. There has been some investigation made about it. I just don't now what.

Now another cow has been located and identified down near Macon, Georgia this $750.00 cow. I have here the photograph taken at the scene of where this cow was found dead down near Macon with the head cut off. I have the registration papers of this cow showing the same markings. These registration papers don't show a photograph of the cow. They show the white and the colored portions on a diagram. They are drawn here. Now these diagrams of these cows are somewhat the same as a man's fingerprints. I don't guess that you ever find any two cows that carry the same kind of markings. This dead cow carried the same markings as compared on the -- on the scene. I didn't compare it. I don't know for a fact whether it was ever compared or not. My information is that it was.

This photograph that I see here shows this cow's head and the course with this registration certificate, the markings do. The people that went down there and viewed the cow -- the Sheriff of Crawford County called and located this cow. The real Wilson Turner near Macon, Georgia whose name this William H. Turner was using on my farm, admitted that the real Wilson Turner brought this cow to his home and told him that he had taken her on a debt and she was worth $1,000.00. And to keep her until he called for her. That was established by the Sheriff of Crawford County.

The brother-in-law of Wilson Turner, Tom Windham, called Mr. Potts here since I have been in this jail, or called some representative of Mr. Potts office and asked to be allowed to surrender and be put in jail, that he wanted to tell what he knew about the stealing of cattle, that he and his brother-in-law, who was Wilson Turner, were involved.

Mr. Potts told me while I was in jail that Windham, Tom Windham, told him that Millard Rigsby had this cow in custody and led her out to a truck and he, Tom Windham, Wilson Turner and Rigsby loaded her on this truck and Windham went with Turner to this brother, farmer, down near Macon when the cow was taken down there.

Now Gentlemen, there is no argument in my mind about who stole two of these cows. We have got an admission. I have an admission from Wilson Turner through Mr. Threadgill. I guess maybe under the terms of the legal status that they term it sometimes as hearsay evidence, but I believe Mr. Threadgill told me the truth about what Mr. Turner told him. I believe that just as much as I know what I have been telling you is the truth.

Now when Turner went down to my place he was most certainly guilty of stealing one cow. He had been down there in my community when he was under suspicion of stealing a lot of cows. I had seen him on this occasion. I had not threatened Turner. I never threatened to do him any bodily harm. I never threatened to do Wilson Turner any bodily harm in my life.

Now after Turner was placed in jail, I went home. It was day. Day had come, Wednesday night, Thursday night, Friday night, Saturday night, and Sunday night. Gentlemen, my shoes had not been off of my feet except a little while Sunday afternoon while I lay down in my living room. That is the truth if anything that I have told you is the truth.

Gentlemen, if I tell you one lie in this statement, everything I have told you is a lie. I promised myself and my Maker before I ever came on this stand. I told the Sheriff of this County I never made a statement in this case. This is the first statement I have ever made.

I told Mr. Potts when he asked me for a statement, I said "now Mr. Potts, at the proper time I will make a statement and whenever I do make a statement it is going to be the truth, and don't you worry about that." I said, "I am going to tell the truth about this case." He came to me and told me of some confessions that somebody that is indicted along in this same case with me had made.

Now Gentlemen, I heard Mr. Potts when he told me those things. I was familiar with this case. I am the one of two men in the whole world that does know exactly all of this case, and that is the truth, and the whole truth. If that is not the truth, then nothing I have told you is the truth.

Now I knew these statements Mr. Potts told me that three co-defendants or whatever you might call them, alleged accomplices or whatever I might have had in this situation, I knew whether Mr. Potts was telling the truth or not. I didn't tell him that he was telling me the truth. I didn't make any statement about this situation, but I knew all along through this case, step by step, as Mr. Potts built it up, I knew where he was progressing. I knew when he was on the right track and I knew when he was on the wrong track. He was not giving me any information that I didn't know.

While the trial is going on, Mozart is still stuck in jail.

Application for Bail by Mozart Strickland

The State vs. Mozart Strickland
No. 447 Indictment for Murder   March Adjourned Term, 1948 Superior Court
Coweta County, Georgia

Now comes, Mozart Strickland, the defendant in the above-stated case and makes this his application for bail and alleges as follows:

1. That he is indicted for the offense of murder and held without bail in the common jail of coweta County and it is alleged that he did kill and murder William H. Turner, alias Wilson Turner, by striking and beating him, the said William H. Turner, alias Wilson Turner with a pump shot gun - - - and by striking and beating the said William H. Turner, alias Wilson Turner, with a certain blunt instrument - - - thereby inflicting a mortal wound and wounds upon the said William H. Turner, from which mortal wound and wounds the said William H. Turner, then and there died.

2. That there is no evidence to sustain such an indictment.

3. That the highest offense under the law and the evidence defendant could be guilty of would be that of accessory after the fact, which offense is bailable.

Wherefore, defendant prays that the matter herein presented be inquired into by the Court and that he be discharged from the common jail of Coweta county where he is now held without bail.

That a rule __ be granted requiring the State to show cause on a day certain why bail should not be granted.
signed E. K. Whatley, Jr
G.A. Huddleston, Attorneys for Defendant.

Due and legal service of the within petition is hereby acknowledged and other and further service is waived.
This 22nd day of June, 1948
L. M. Wyatt   Solicitor General Superior Courts Coweta Circuit

I hereby recommend this bond be granted in view of the fact that the evidence against him is that he was accessory after the fact only.
This June 22, 1948
L. M. Wyatt, Sol Gen

The within petition having been read and considered it is ordered that the State show cause before me at 10 o'clock am Friday, June 25th at LaGrange, GA why the ___ of said petition should not be granted.
This June 22 1948
Samuel Boykin, JSCCC   Minute O page 358

Section Three

I am not up here to do but one thing, and that is to tell you gentlemen the truth, the whole truth, about this situation. I realize that I am charged with the worst crime a man can be charged with. I know that you gentlemen hold the breath in my body in the hollow of your hands. I would not attempt -- I want to say further, gentlemen, before any of you gentlemen were qualified for this jury and accepted, my counsel ruled on your selection. Before any one of you gentlemen were ever accepted my counsel asked me "what do you think about that man?" Gentlemen, I passed on you, every one of you, out of my own heart, trusting that every one of you were good men, law-abiding men, fair men, and would give me a fair trial up here.

I know it is a hard case. I have got nobody to call in here and substantiate these statements I have made to you. This counsel here that represents these other men that have been charged with me with being implicated in this thing, evidently have advised their clients not to testify. You gentlemen saw them. You didn't see them -- I beg your pardon. I asked for the other parties, two or three of them, that knew some of the facts, asked one of them knowing all of the facts, to be allowed to come here and testify not especially in my behalf, but in our behalf. That has been denied me.

I don't know why these boys are not here to testify. They promised me they would testify the truth. That is all I ever asked them to do was to tell the honest truth about this case. That is all that I want anybody to tell. That is what I stand before you -- sit before you this afternoon and do, and I am going to do. I have got to do it alone with nobody to help me. I don't see why the law is fixed where a man can't be made to tell what he knows without anything, unless it is on his own wife or child. Maybe that would result in something awful happening to them.

Now after this man was put in this jail in Greenville, I went home. I have told you gentlemen that I had no rest from Wednesday night through the following Sunday night. Gentlemen, I am fifty-two years old. I hope I am not dead with old age, but I am certainly in the afternoon of life. I can't hope to live fifty-two more years. I have got some limit of endurance. You can break iron. You can break anything into or down with enough pressure. I have been through months of it. I have been struggling with this man since the fall of 1945 --the fall of 1946 -- I beg your pardon. I labored with that fellow from the fall of 1946 all through 1947, trying to make him be the kind of citizen that he should be. I tried to help him.

I got into this trouble, Gentlemen, trying to help a young man get a start in life. If it had not been that I became involved with Turner at the first, I would have certainly not been involved with him on the tail end of this thing, and I did it. I didn't need Turner on my farm. From his labor that he could perform, I had plenty of colored people down there on that farm to operate it. I had been operating it for several years without Turner's help or assistance.

I got involved with this man trying to help him just like any of you gentlemen would have wanted to have been helped maybe when you started out, and didn't have it. I didn't have help when I started out as a young man. Had I had this help, I would have gotten over a lot of hurdles that I didn't get over. I possibly never would have gotten in the liquor business if I had the proper financial help with somebody to pick me up when I fell down. I have got no rich relatives. I have got a good credit through, Gentlemen. I will tell you that. I know a lot of people that have got money, and every one of them has got confidence in me. My banker at home has never turned me down for a loan.

I have done business with several banks. I have done business with the banks in the State of Texas. I have done business with the banks in Alabama. I have done business in my home bank at Chipley. I have done business in the banks of LaGrange. I have done business with the bank - the Production Credit Association in Greenville. Every one of those lending agencies are my friends, and they have got confidence in me. When I tell them something, they know that I am telling them the truth. If it takes the top of my head off this afternoon, I am going to tell you the truth. I am not afraid to die.

If it means my death to tell you gentlemen the truth, I will die telling you the truth.

On this morning, Tuesday morning, on the Monday night following the placing of this man in jail. Monday night was the first night that I had been at home since the Wednesday night before. I had just lain down in my bed. I could not sleep. I had lost sleep so long until I could not go to sleep. I had been awake so long until I could not sleep.

Mr. Collier drove up to my place, the Sheriff of my County. He came into my bedroom. He say, "John I have just been over to LaGrange and talked to the Solicitor General, Mr. Wyatt." Mr. Wyatt was present. He knows whether or not I am repeating the facts or not. Now I can't vouch for what Mr. Collier said as being exactly what Mr. Wyatt said, but Mr. Wyatt knows whether I am telling the truth.

He came into my bedroom, and he told me, he said, "John, I have been over to LaGrange and talked to the Solicitor General about this Turner cow business." He said, "Mr. Wyatt told me that we had a weak case, that it did not appear to him that we could place Turner within Meriwether County with these cows." Now the thing to do was prosecute him in Carroll County.

Now Gentlemen, there I was, laying in my bed, having lost night after night sleep to apprehend this man to bring him to the bar of justice, and I had him in jail and my Solicitor sent me word, or informed the Sheriff, that we could not hold him, we would have to prosecute him in another county.

Now Gentlemen, I have told you before of my experience. I don't mean any reflection on anybody. It would be far from me to want to hurt anybody's feelings. I have got the highest regard for Mr. Wyatt. I have known him many years. He has always been my friend. I have always been his. I don't guess he is getting so much glory and pleasure out of having to prosecute me for murder. I am sure that I would hate to have his job and prosecute him, but my previous experience with the Sheriff of Carroll County made me most discouraged to think that I would have to go back there and prosecute this case in that county.

Now I don't mean to reflect on the character of the Sheriff of Carroll County. I never met the man but one time that I know of. I only stated to you exactly what happened between the Sheriff and me. Now I drew my own conclusions. I give you gentlemen the same privilege.

I told the Sheriff in this conversation, I said "Mr. Collier, if you have to go over there and prosecute him" -- I knew nothing about these other cows, never knew that any of the other cows would ever be located, I had no way to know that -- I said, "if that is the way we are going to have to work it, you might as well turn him out."

He said, "well, he can be presented to the Grand Jury and prosecuted over there anytime between now and court time." Now I had a little information before I left Carrollton that night from Mr. Threadgill that I didn't tell the Sheriff about. Mr. Threadgill told me that the party that furnished him this information didn't want it told to anybody, that he was afraid Turner and Rigsby, and whoever else that might have been implicated with them over there might do him harm. I knew that Turner knew more about those cattle than that one cow.

I went the next -- after Mr. Collier left my place I tried to rest a little that night. As I tell you, Gentlemen, I had been up so long until I could not sleep. I am not telling you gentlemen that for any reason except that it is the truth. If any of you gentlemen have ever seen through - some of you gentlemen certainly were in the Army - you know after you go a certain length of time you reach that stage to a certain extent. You get to where you can't sleep when you get the opportunity to sleep. I had reached that stage.

That Tuesday morning -- I told Mr. Collier when he left I would be up there to see him the next morning to decide about what to do about Turner. I went down. I notified Mr. Tom Strickland who was my cousin and kinsman, who had been to Macon on this Monday to make this investigation. He was interested in helping me find my cows. He ad demonstrated on that day he drove two hundred miles to help do it. I went down and asked Mr. Sivell to go and help me do something about the location of these cows, find out something about it. Now Mr. Sivell was under some obligation to me. I had been all over the country helping him buy cows, used for a front man in some of his financial stresses, and I didn't feel like I was imposing on him to ask him to go help me find out about where my cows were.

We had the man in jail and he confessed to stealing some of them, and I wanted to know where the rest of them were. I saw Mr. Mobley, Mr. Henry Mobley. Mr. Henry Mobley is my friend. In fact I don't know anybody much that I don't like. A lot of people possibly don't like me but I don't know of anybody that I don't like. I have not got a grudge against a man in the world. I went to the penitentiary twice, Gentlemen, and the officers that sent me there are still on handshaking terms with me. Mr. Hancock, as I remember, was one of the officers that helped prosecute me the first time I was ever prosecuted.

Since that time, Mr. Hancock has been to my home and enjoyed the hospitality of a meal at my table. Now how many enemies have you got, Gentlemen, that you would invite in to eat dinner with you? I have not got an enemy in the world, so far as I am personally concerned, so I didn't ask these boys to go with me for any reason except they were my friends and they were interested in my welfare just as if I would be interested in their welfare or your welfare if we lived in the same community. If you had come after me under the same conditions, I would have gone with you and tired to help you find your cattle. I am sure any of you gentlemen would do your own next door neighbor the same way. That is all I have done.

I started out to try to find my cattle. This man would have broken me if I had not stopped him somewhere; with three thousand dollar licks I could not last very long at that, and most certainly my creditors would be ruined because the collateral would be all gone.

Now I contacted these men. I also saw Mr. Myhand, Mr. Broughton Myhand. Mr. Myhand failed to go along. I don't know for what reason. All right, I am glad he didn't go, most glad that he didn't go. We four men in two cars drove to Greenville.

Now Gentlemen, I am not going to get up here and try to mislead you. I had a shotgun in that car. I didn't take that gun along to kill anybody with. I guess you gentlemen have had guns in your hands at sometime. You didn't pick it up necessarily to kill a man with. Neither did I. I had no idea of killing anybody. I have never intended or had any desire to kill William H. Turner as he actually proved to be. I never had any desire that morning to kill anybody. I didn't leave my home with murder in my heart. I never have had murder in my heart, that morning or any other morning in my life.

I have never had the desire to take any human life. I am an average church going man. I go to church and Sunday School on Sunday. I love my God just like you love your God. Your God is my God. There is only one. I am no cold-blooded head hunter. I have never wanted to harm any man. I certainly tried to show you gentlemen (of the jury). I have gone in quite a few details. They might not seem so essential to somebody, but they do to me. They are essential to me. It is my statement, and it is the truth. It is all the truth. It is all this case. I can't tell you half of the truth and half of it untold. I am telling you all of the truth and giving you all of the facts to the best of my mind. That is what I am trying to do.

Now when we four men got to Greenville, I was not excited. I was not going out man hunting. I was going out to talk to this man but I didn't mean to talk to him in jail. I meant to talk to him somewhere else.

It was not the first time that a man was ever taken out of jail and talked to. There is evidence that I know about in this particular case. I was never taken out and talked to since I have been placed in jail, but now Mr. Sivell was taken out down to his home after this crime was charged by the Sheriff of this County, and the Sheriff told me out of his own mouth that he took Mr. Sivell down there for the purpose of obtaining a written confession form this man in connection with this crime that has been charged.

Now Mr. Henry Mobley has told me he was taken out of the jail and brought into this courthouse in the middle of the night. I don't mean that with any mean spirit. I am trying to tell you gentlemen that my actions, although I am not an officer of the law, so far as my personal contact with a man that is guilty of a felony, and I believe him to have knowledge of a crime committed, I have got the right according to my information, of an officer of the law up until the time this man can be delivered to the proper authorities in a reasonable length of time.

Now when I reached Greenville, I went into the Production Credit Association office. Mr. Sivell who rode to Greenville with me, went into the same office. He borrows money from those folks, and I do too. I had some stock in this Association that I didn't use this year. I didn't borrow enough money to use this stock. The stock was laying there. I told our Secretary of the Association, I said, "sell this stock for me. Let me have the money out of it. Somebody else is borrowing money, and let them carry the stock." I was carrying my proportion of it according to the money that I am using, so I went in there on this morning to discuss with him the sale of this stock, or if he had sold any of it. He had been instructed previous to that time to dispose of it.

When I walked into this office Mr. Sivell was in there in the act of writing a check. I asked for Mr. Clemmons, who is the Secretary of that Association, and his stenographer advised me that Mr. Clemmons was busy at that time. I saw Mr. Miller sitting over there, who is the State Alcohol Tax Unit. I greeted Mr. Miller. My mind was not completely gone, but it was under the greatest strain that it has ever been since I have known myself.

I went on out and left Mr. Sivell in this office. Mr. Sivell came on to his car. I don't know where Wilson Turner was at that minute. I thought he was in jail. I didn't know that he had been turned out. I told Mr. Sivell to park his car just above this filling station. Mr. Mobley had already parked his car with Mr. Strickland's alongside this courthouse, headed facing in the direction that anybody might take out of Greenville except the

Columbus Road, he was facing every road; he was facing the road that circles the courthouse. He commanded all the avenues of travel right in Greenville, Mr. Mobley did.

I went down to the jail. When I went into the jail I knew Turner's truck had left there. I didn't see that truck parked in front of this jail, neither did I see it anywhere. I could see the Sheriff's garage was open. The yard was open. I didn't see Turner's truck parked anywhere. I walked into the jail, and Mr. Collier was having his noon meal. I asked Mr. Collier, I said, "what has become of Turner?" He says, "I have turned him out this morning." I said, "where did he go?" He said, "I gave him a dollar to buy some gasoline to put in his truck and he said he was going to LaGrange. I sent some word to Mr. Louis McLoggin, who is a salesman at the Ford dealer in LaGrange" -- Mr. Collier stated to me that he sent word by Turner to tell Mr. McLoggin – I knew him. Turner knew him. He traded automobiles with him twice -- that he, Mr. Collier, would not be over to LaGrange that afternoon. If you don't mind, can we have a little recess?

By The Court: Let the jury go to the room. We will take a recess of about ten minutes.

(Recess called at 4:40)

By The Court: Let the jury come in.

(Jury returns to the box at 4:45)

By Mr. John Wallace: Now Gentlemen, when I reached the jail, I entered the jail, I rung the doorbell, Mr. Collier himself answered the door, he invited me in and informed me that he was eating his dinner at that moment. In fact he said he was nearly through with his dinner and he asked me to come in and have a bit of dinner with him.

I asked him where this Turner was. He said he had turned him out that morning. I walked into the dining room of the jail and had some few words of conversation with the Sheriff and I ate a few mouthfuls of food with him. I will tell you in detail, if I may. On that table I ate some mashed potatoes, they had string beans on the table. The reason I remember that so well, I don't like string beans and I didn't eat any of those beans. I had some iced tea and some sliced peaches and small piece of cake that I ate some of.

I didn't tell the Sheriff that I came up there to see Turner. I didn't mention that fact to the Sheriff. I asked him where Turner went when he left there and he told me he didn't know and I have already related to you what his reply was.

I left the jail, I walked back up this road leading out to the highway directly from the jail. Mr. Sivell was parked there. That is where I left him parked while I went down to the jail. When I approached Mr. Sivell's car, I thought at that time that Turner was possibly at home. I glanced to my left, which was back toward Greenville, I saw a truck, a green truck that resembled the truck that Turner owned. I recognized Turner. He slowed down at this filling station. I didn't know where Turner was going from that filling station. I didn't know whether he was coming or going to Newnan or where he was going but he was headed that way.

I got into the car as quickly as I could. I told Mr. Sivell, I said, "pull on over the hill." Before we got over the hill I said, "Turner is right behind us. He is right down there at that filling station." About this time Turner passed Mr. Sivell and I, and when he passed us I don't know whether he recognized us or not but from the speed that he took up at that minute I imagine that he did recognize us. We left in pursuit. My reason for that was that I wanted to talk to Turner about this cattle theft business. I meant to put him back in jail because I had never consented for the Sheriff to turn him out. She Sheriff told me that the reason he turned him out was that Turner told him if he would release him he would tell him who got those cows.

Mr. Collier told me in that conversation that Turner told him that Rigsby, Millard Rigsby of Carrollton, and a Negro named Shine got those cows. Now we left behind him. He was driving just about as fast as that truck would run I imagine. We were possibly 150 or 200 yards behind him. To begin with he gained on his speed, but we, of course, done all in our power to overtake him. I have no reason to tell you gentlemen this except that it is the facts. I have told you that I was going to give you the facts. I am going to give them all to you regardless of what. You are going to get this case just as I promised you when I begun on it. I am going to give you all of it and not half of it. Everything I tell you is going to be the facts so far as I know them.

We kept in pursuit of this truck until we reached Moreland, this Sunset Tourist camp. We had never overtaken him. When we pulled in this filling station, when Turner pulled in this filling station he drove into the north side. That testimony also far as entering into that filling station, has already been given to you, and I admit that much of it was true. We pulled in behind him. Turner got out of his truck and attempted to enter this cafe. I got out in pursuit of Turner with a shotgun in one hand and my other hand empty.

When Turner reached this door I was there. I caught hold of Turner. He, in the confusion gentlemen, I don't know just what the man said. I don't know whether anybody there knows what he said or not. I don't know whether any of you gentlemen had you been present could have sworn to his actual words, but I caught Turner with my left hand.

Now Gentlemen, I ask you in all earnestness to follow me now and from this minute on especially. I caught hold of Turner with my left hand. I took this hand that had the shotgun in it. I didn't have it by the stock. I could not swear to you exactly the location I had it, but I had it somewhere above the trigger guard and the barrel. I attempted to take Turner back to this truck.

Now Gentlemen, I never struck Turner with that gun at that time. I never struck him with anything. I tried to take him back to that car with the strength of this right and shoving him toward the car. Mr. Sivell didn't come over there to that door as a witness testified on this stand. My only reason for telling you this, Gentlemen, is that it is the facts. Mr. Sivell was standing at this car with the right hand front door open just as I had left it, when I left that car.

When I reached the car with Turner I attempted to push him in the car. He never caught hold of that car with both hands and his foot on the fender and pushed back. Now Gentlemen, if I had struck that man with a shotgun over the head with him in that position and he had become limp and given away he would have fell down at my feet on the outside of that car. There would not have been anyway under God's Heaven for him to have fallen in the car with his weight against the car with one foot and both hands propped against that door. Now I know the facts, Gentlemen, I had a hold of the man. I know more about it than anybody else in the whole world knows about it. I am the only person that does know the facts about this case, in regard to this particular incident and circumstances.

When I reached the door of this car I shoved Turner in the car. I had him over-balanced pushing him. He didn't catch hold of that car and just being pushed in. I never struck Turner with that gun at that time. I never struck him. I never struck Turner wilfully with that gun at any time. In pushing Turner in this car the barrel of this gun at some time in shoving him with the hand that had this shotgun in it, struck his ear, and on his ear it broke the skin where it joins into the head, to the best of my knowledge. That place bled. I would not say profusely, but it did bleed. You had an expert witness testify before you yesterday that testified I believe that a tablespoonful of blood properly distributed would have made the spots that showed up on that floor. Now I don't know whether he bled a tablespoonful or how much he bled, but I do know that he didn't bleed much.

Now when I pushed Turner in this car the barrel of this gun was higher than the top of the door of the car, and when it hit the top of this car the gun fired. I didn't hit Turner with the gun when it fired. I hit the top of that car in my effort to shove Turner in that car. He was not standing up with his head higher than that car. He was not standing up erect. I had him pushing him, and he was over-balanced from me behind him with my weight and what force I could command at that time carrying him to that car. He was not injured on the way to that car except as I say, that in the pushing of him with this gun in this hand I could not hold to his body and to the shotgun at the same time. If I had taken both hands, Gentlemen, and taken this gun with all my might and struck Turner over the head with the gun, where was Turner when I removed this hand from his body? He would have been free. He could possibly have escaped.

That testimony, Gentlemen, against me won't bear out. I didn't return this man loose and strike him with this gun with one hand or with two hands. I didn't strike him with the gun at all except more or less - and Gentlemen listen to me. I struck this man more or less accidentally in putting him in this car. I never made any effort to strike this man with this shotgun. If I had released him, what method would I have had to have continued with him on the way to the car?

You heard the testimony of this lady. I have got the greatest respect for any lady. I don't give the lie, but I do say she is mistaken. She was mistaken. She didn't see, Gentlemen what she told you she saw because it did not happen.

Now Mr. Smith swore against me here. I was down there listening at his testimony just like you gentlemen are listening to my statement. I heard him say that I struck this man with all my might. Well now, I don't say the man lied. I am not going to come up here and us a whole lot of vicious language in my defense. I am not mad with anybody. I was not enraged with Turner at that time. I was only trying to apprehend the stealer of my cattle and have him brought before the proper authorities and dealt with as a man guilty of the crime that he was guilty of at that time should be dealt with. I was not in a rage with him. I told you gentlemen I had never been in a rage with him. I have never been in a rage with the man.

I am looking you gentlemen in the face and I am stating the facts - not half of them, but all of them. I am telling you all that happened up to this present moment. Now when I put this man in this car I shoved him in the car. I don't know where I laid that gun when he got in the car. I don't know where I laid that gun. I could not tell you gentlemen whether I laid it on the backseat of the car or whether I laid it in the front seat. I don't know where I laid that gun. It does not make any difference right now where it was laid.

He is in the car. I got in the car with him. I never struck him a blow with any instrument in that car. Mr. Smith swore to you that I had some object in my hand and was beating this man with this object, possibly four or five inches. Now the reaction of my mind to his testimony -- I have just got an average, ordinary mind -- it appeared to me that he was trying to convince you gentlemen that I had a blackjack or some short deadly weapon in my hand beating this man. I didn't strike him, not one blow, in that car.

I held my hand over his mouth to stop his hollering. Now I did that act, Gentlemen. I didn't do it with any effort to injure the man. I placed my hand over his mouth to stop the alarm that he was making. There is nothing unnatural about that. I did the natural thing that a man would have done. I was holding him down in this car with my left hand, and I had my right hand over his mouth.

Now Gentlemen, when he was in this car, his feet were not in that car, but his legs were not limp. He was not in any limp condition, in any lifeless condition. He was just as much alive gentlemen, as you gentlemen are or I am at this minute. That is a fact, just as much of a fact as anything else that I have told you in this statement that I have made. I have not tried to cover up anything. I am not trying to cover up anything now.

Mr. Sivell and I put his feet in the car. I will say I was possibly leaning over and holding him. I don't remember exactly how his feet got in there, but to the best of my knowledge, Mr. Sivell pushed his feet in and closed the door. We drove around this filling station. The man was just as alive as he ever was in his life before. He had no deadly injury. I had struck him with nothing up to that moment with both of my hands, with no shotgun or with any other instrument. The only wound on this man was this cut that I have told you about on his ear which was done more or less in an accidental way.

I am going to tell you gentlemen the truth about how the man lost his life. I am not trying to cover up anything, but he didn't lose his life at this filling station. He didn't have a fatal injury at this filling station. We drove out of this filling station and I was in the foot of the car and Mr. Turner was in the foot of the car. I was not sprawled on top of him trying to smother him to death. He never tried to holler anymore after we started to drive off. I just held him in the foot of the car.

When we had gone practically a mile from Moreland, we met Mr. Mobley and Mr. Strickland approaching, coming North toward Newnan. Mr. Mobley was driving the car, and Mr. Strickland was in the car with Mr. Mobley. They had left Greenville when they saw Mr. Sivell and I pull off. They left in the rear when Turner left. Mr. Mobley didn't know Mr. Turner's truck. He was sitting too far from the filling station when I first noticed the truck to have known that it was Mr. Turner in the truck, but when we pulled out of Greenville Mr. Mobley was sitting there watching our car just as I had instructed him to follow in this car that Mr. Sivell and I was in. Mr. Mobley turned around and started back following Mr. Sivell, Turner and me.

At that time I was sitting on the backseat of this car. Turner was offering no resistance. He was sitting up in the foot of the car just as normal as any man could sit in the foot of any automobile. He didn't complain about this ear. He was talking. I don't remember just what he said, but he was saying something. I don't remember just exactly what my conversation was. Of course at that minute I was excited. I am not an iron man. I had been under a terrible strain for days and nights. I had no sleep. I don't know what I said to the man. What I told Sivell when we reached this road, I said "pull out in this road and let somebody go back and get that truck so Turner will have a way to go home later."

Now Mr. Mobley pulled up to the left of this automobile that we were riding in with Turner. We got out of the car. I got out on the right side, on the side that I was sitting on. Turner was in the rear of the car. Sivell got out on the left side of the car and opened his door and got out. Turner got out of the same side that Sivell got out of. Tom Strickland got out of Mobley's car and opened the right-hand door which was just about opposite the left-hand door of Turner's car. Turner got into Mobley's car. He was not manhandled to put him in there. He got in there under his own power, and sat down in the foot of the car at my instructions. Mr. Tom Strickland got in behind him. Mr. Mobley was already sitting in the car, and I got in the front seat.

We had noticed at this time that Mr. Sivell had a flat tire on his car. Mr. Strickland I believe called his attention to it. Said, "hell, you have got a flat tire." All right, we could not leave Turner there and go back and get his truck and we could not take Turner back to Moreland and get the truck, so we just left Sivell there with his car and his flat tire. We left Turner's truck where it had been left originally at this tourist camp. I didn't see Sivell anymore that day. We left him there with a flat tire. This man got out of Sivell's car under his own power with no apparent serious injury. We drove down the road, before we reached Greenville.

I naturally knew that there was going to be some investigation made of this incident that had happened up there at this Tourist Camp, so we left the paved highway. We drove into the west of Greenville. I didn't know where Sivell was. We had left him up there with his flat tire. I never saw him, I repeat, anymore during that day. We left this highway and on the trip before we reached the time that we stopped that car Turner had lost his tobacco in Sivell's car. I got this information from the Sheriff of this County. He told me that he went to this place with Sivell where he had this flat tire, later, and Sivell told him before he got there that he would find a tobacco - Prince Albert box of smoking tobacco in some weeds close to this car, that after we had left with Mr. Turner in our car that he had found this tobacco box in his car and he threw it out in these weeds.

Now Gentlemen, I knew nothing about that tobacco can at that time except Turner had no tobacco. He didn't have that box of cigarettes in his pocket that the prosecution introduced against me here as evidence, and a letter in it. If he did, why didn't he smoke his own cigarettes? I am not arguing the case. I am not attempting to, but I am trying to show you gentlemen that this man on this trip asked me for a cigarette and I gave it to him. He lighted it under his own power.

Mr. Mobley's left front door was open at the time and it blew the match out. I am not telling you this to establish anything except that it is a fact. Mr. Turner asked Mr. Mobley, said, "will you raise your window? I can't light my cigarette." Mr. Mobley raised that window, and I gave Mr. Turner a match and he did light that cigarette.

Further on down that road I recall Mr. Turner said to Mr. Mobley, said, "these last model cars" -- this was the latest model I believe at that time -- "has given a lot of trouble about the fitting of the door." He said, "a lot of dust comes in around these doors." Now the reason I imagine that Mr. Turner detected that dust as quickly as he did, he was sitting in the foot of that car and that dust was coming in there and attracted his attention. That is exactly what he said to Mr. Mobley. He told Mr. Mobley he had the same trouble with his own car, he had started, he had an intention of making the dealer take his car back if he could not stop it that the dust come in around the door.

353

Now we drove further on down this road, on our way to our final place that we did stop. Turner on another occasion asked me for a cigarette. Mr. Mobley I believe, if I remember correctly, close his window at that time without being requested, until Turner lighted his cigarette. Turner smoked two cigarettes to my certain knowledge. I don't know whether he smoked anymore or not. That is all that I remember supplying him with.

We passed before on the way -- finally went to the farm where Turner had last lived on my place. On this road before we got to this overhead bridge that I have already told you about my tenant living and I supplied the money to get the evidence of this liquor being in this particular community, we passed this Will Truitt's home. Turner said to whoever was in the car, all of us, he remarked, "I wish I could see old Bill Truitt. Truitt, the person that lived at this particular place was named Will Truitt. He had been Turner's neighbor down there before he had moved away from there. We went on past this Negro's house. Turner was not lying down in the car. He was sitting up, and could see out of the doors of the car. He knew where we were. He knew the section of the country we were in. He recognized all of the country that possibly we had been through. He had been living down there and he had been circulating a good little bit around through that country, but most certainly he made a comment at this time about this particular man living at this place and his desire to see him.

We drove on over this overhead bridge that I have mentioned before in this statement. We drove on around this road and we came to a little creek that you had to Ford, you had to drive through it to get across. It had no bridge there. After leaving this creek there was a small hill there. This hill at one time during Turner's residence there at this place, had been very rough, and going up this hill Turner noticed that it had been top soiled and he remarked at this time, he says, "this hill is sure a lot better since it has been top soiled, since it has been worked."

Now Gentlemen, we drove on past the house, the house that Turner formerly lived in was just up beyond this particular hill that I have mentioned that Turner made mention of, and we stopped in the middle of the road.

Now Gentlemen, I took this man back to the scene of the first cows that I had missed out of my herd. These cows were on pasture right on this particular farm, and walked this same road while they were in that community grazing. I stopped this man on the scene of the first cattle that I had lost. Now Gentlemen, my reason for doing that was for the reason possibly -- the same reason that while Mr. Sivell was in this jail charged with this crime Mr. Potts removed him from the jail on some sort of promise of a statement. I don't know at that time whether he had that promise or not, but Mr. Potts took this man Sivell right back into the same location as near the same spot as he had been told by a member of -- another person who was indicted along with me on this charge.

Now I don't know for what reason Mr. Potts took this man down there. He had a prisoner and he wanted a confession from him. He took him on the scene, the only scene that he had any information about up to that time. Mr. Potts told me about the information that Mr. Strickland gave him about where this man was taken down there in his car. Now I took this man down there on the scene of where I thought and had reason to believe was the first scene of his cattle stealing activities.

My other reason for taking Turner down there was to try to gain a confession from him and tell me where my cattle were. I had never done him any bodily harm up that minute except this place that I have mentioned to you. It had no apparent painful effects. I never heard that man mention it at that time up to that time. I had never heard him mention it. When we reached a location in this road I asked Mr. Mobley to stop his car, which he did. Mr. Mobley never left his car. He never placed his hand on Turner that day. My only reason in telling you that fact is that it is a fact.

These gentlemen have not been permitted to come here and recite to you this same testimony in my defense which I need so badly. I need some backing up on this statement I am making to you. My only hope in the world is resting in whether or not you believe this statement. I have not got and have not been allowed the privilege of introducing one eye witness to this occurrence. Now Gentlemen, I have got a very helpless feeling. I have had it ever since I learned that these boys weren't going to testify and establish the facts and swear to them under oath that I am not permitted to do. I am giving you these statements without oath, and I have got no way to make you believe what I am saying. My only hope is that you can see just as far inside of me as I felt like I was seeing inside of you when I agreed for you to sit on this jury.

Now at the time we stopped this car I got out on the ground. I took out of this car when I got out of it a shotgun, Gentlemen. I don't know whose shotgun that was. It was not the same shotgun that I had at the Tourist Camp. It was a double-barreled hammerless shotgun. I do not hunt. I never killed a quail in my life. I have killed very few rabbits. I am just not what you call a hunter. It is a great sport but it is one that I have never had the time to indulge in.

When I alighted from this car, I took this gun out. I saw it there and I picked it up. Turner got out of that car, and Mr. Tom Strickland got out of that car. Mobley left us standing in the road. I was not very far from my home. I was in easy walking distance through what we call a beeline. I could walk from here to my home in not such a long length of time. I let Mobley leave there and had him to leave. I told him to go on home. I didn't know what developments were going to come up. I didn't have any idea of what was going to happen and did happen. There was no way that I knew. I had not planned at that time to harm this man. I had no premeditated determination to take this man's life.

In all my dealing with this man I had never attempted to wilfully harm him, not since I had known him, in a physical way. When Mobley drove away from that place Tom Strickland and myself left that road. I was in front leading the way. At that time I didn't know exactly where I was going. I had not made up my mind. I didn't have any definite plan, but I wanted to bluff out of Turner where those cows had been taken and where they had been disposed of. We walked out across this pine wood. We reached a three-stranded barbed wire fence. It is a new fence. It is not an old rotten wire fence. It is a fence that is in good repair.

When I reached this fence I placed my foot on the bottom strand, after I had crawled through the fence myself and raised up the middle strand, and Turner came through that wire fence. He was not dragged through there, and he was not lifted through there. He went through there the same way that I went through there. He crawled through the fence and Mr. Strickland followed.

We walked on after leaving this fence and it occurred to me I remember that in this wood there was an old well or some wells. I had them wells covered with logs every winter when I would have cattle placed in this pasture to keep the cattle from falling in these wells. It occurred to my mind as we walked through this wood. We came up on one of these wells. I was not particularly hunting for the well, but I had not made up my mind where to stop and talk to Turner but we reached this well, Turner stopped and I stopped and Mr. Strickland stopped. I was still in front of Turner and Mr. Strickland was to the rear. He was not holding Turner to keep him from escaping. Turner had made no effort to escape. In fact his conversation had been along the line that I allow him to move back down there to this former home that he had made a mistake by ever leaving there, he was sorry for his conduct, but he just got in with a bunch of bad folks and he was sorry about it all, that I had given him a good chance down there to make money and he wanted to move back in that same house and be allowed the privilege of starting over again.

Now, I had never abused the man. I had not talked harshly to him either. When we reached this well, I walked around and looked in the well. Mr. Strickland was standing directly at this time in front of Turner, facing Turner. I looked in this well. I didn't say "I am going to throw you in the well." I didn't tell Turner I was going to do anything to him. I didn't make any threat. I looked in the well and looked at Turner.

Turner asked me at this point, he said, "Mr. John," said "put me in that well and let me stay two or three hours." I don't know why Turner asked me that question, but he did ask me that question. He made the request. He said "put me in that well and let me stay two or three hours and let me out of there, and I will go back and move back down here and help you find your cows."

Now Gentlemen, that is this man Turner's statement and request to me. He at that time -- I walked around in the direction of Turner. Strickland was standing facing the man. Now Gentlemen, I am going to show you, if I may, the position of Mr. Turner at that time. Mr. Turner was sitting in this position and I was facing him from this direction toward the well. Mr. Strickland was standing over there in the direction of this juror with his foot on the rail facing Turner. I walked around within possibly five feet of Turner, for what reason I don't know gentlemen why I even walked around in his direction. I reached a point within I will say five feet of Turner. Then I turned to my - heard to my right somebody holler.

Now Gentlemen, down beyond this well not very far away is a railroad. I didn't know who it was that hollered. I didn't know for what reason they had hollered, but somebody did holler and I heard this, somebody's voice over in that direction. I turned my head in the direction of this noise that I had heard. I don't know for what reason I took this gun that was in my right hand and laid it into the bend of my left arm; that instrument, Gentlemen, this gun fired.

I looked back to my left. I didn't see Turner when this gun was fired. I turned my head when the gun did fire. Mr. Tom Strickland was facing this man and saw him, was looking at him when this accident happened. I looked around at this man.

Tom Strickland was facing this man and saw him, was looking at him when this accident happened. I looked around at this man. He was laying full length on the ground with the top of his scalp torn off.

I am not trying to put any flowers on this statement, Gentlemen. It is a horrible thing. I am telling you the facts. I looked at this man there with the top of his head shot off.

Now Gentlemen, I had been under a terrible strain, I had been up for days and nights. I had been under a strain with this man for months. I have been deprived of the only eye witness that can possibly come here and swear to the truth of this thing and help convince you gentlemen that I am telling you the truth. Mr. Strickland saw this thing happen. He had no connection with it. It was no effort of his that this man lost his life. It was no effort of mine. He was just as innocent of this crime as I am. He could have come here and made this statement. I have not had that benefit. I am here without anybody to back up this statement, but it is a fact. I needed this man's testimony. I need it now. I needed all these boys' testimony.

This man Sivell had no more to do with this man's death than any of you gentlemen did. Mr. Mobley is just as innocent of this man's death as any of you gentlemen are. Mr. Tom Strickland is just as innocent of this man's death as any of you gentlemen are. Gentlemen, I am just as innocent of this man's death as any one of you gentlemen. I did not take this man's life wilfully. I had no control of that gun that I knowingly had of that gun when it fired when this man lost his life. I didn't know that he was killed before I looked to my left and saw him laying there full length.

Now Gentlemen, if this gun had one inch more elevation than it did have Turner would have been living this day. It took the top of the scalp off. I didn't shoot him in the breast. I didn't shoot him anywhere in his body. If I had been going to wilfully take the man's life and had taken him to the well with the intention of taking his life, why didn't I shoot him with a hole plum through him with a shotgun, knowing he would have to have been dead when the gun was fired.

Now Gentlemen, I have told you all that I know about this case. I did not know this man was dead until I saw him laying on the ground. I did not fire this gun wilfully. I didn't fire it at all to my knowledge. This is all I have got to bring to you gentlemen. This is the end of this case so far as I know. When I looked at this man on the ground, I had lost so much sleep, the horrible sight of this man, I don't remember a thing that happened for several days after that time. I don't remember this man being put in that well. I don't remember how that gun ever left the scene of this well or this accident. I don't know anything about what became of his body. I don't remember it. It was three days before I could get myself together any sort of way and gentlemen I want to state to you this with the same degree of - coming from my heart and soul. It was ten days after I was locked up in this jail down here before I could convince myself that this man really had lost his life. That is the truth. I could not convince myself that the thing had ever happened. I wonder how it did happen. It is all a bad dream.

I never tried to do this man any bodily harm in all my life When Mr. Turner -- I will go back. I want to say this. When Mr. Turner told me to put him in that well and let him stay two or three hours, he says "I am not mad with anybody." He says, "this little old scratch on my head don't mean nothing." Now Gentlemen, that is the facts. I have told you where the man lost his life. If I had taken his life in Moreland, if I had done that I would have told you so. I have not told you half of anything. I have told you the whole of everything that I know about this case.

I hope when you gentlemen go into reach your verdict - I have prayed with my God over this thing. I have done no crime. The most terrible accident has happened. I am sorry about it. I will tell you gentlemen that there was never anything in my life that come into it that has done what this thing has done to me. I am fifty-two years old. At best I won't live so many more years, taking the natural span of life in consideration. Let me go back home to what little I have got left. I have got no money. I owe a lot of money. This trial has cost me money. You gentlemen know that. I had to raise funds. I want to say this though, gentlemen. I told Mr. Potts when I came to that jail and I had discussions with him along the line, I told Mr. Potts, he asked me for a statement, I said, "Mr. Potts, when I make a statement I will make it to the jury if I am brought to trial." I told Mr. Potts at that time that I was going to tell the facts regardless of what happened. I was going to tell the facts. I have done that.

I did not, and never had any desire to take this man's life. I only wanted to find out where my cattle had been taken to. I had that right, Gentlemen. Any of you farmers would want that right if somebody had stolen your cattle and made way with them. You most certainly would want to know where they went to. You might possibly use some mental persuasion on a man to get a confession out of him. That is all that I did. I never struck Wilson Turner a blow in my life with the intention of harming him. I did not wilfully take his life at this time. It was an accident.

I have told you my story as far as my mind will let me tell you. Now Gentlemen, I have had this awful accident. I am the man. I have got to live with myself. Nobody can live with myself but me. I won't have so much time to live. I have got nobody down there with my family, or with my business set up like it is now. Everything I have got will be lost. I have got no way for my wife to be supported. At this particular time she is -- her health is not such as it should be.

Now Gentlemen, when I leave you, I ask you to take this case as I have told it to you. You know whether I have told you the truth or not. You know just as well as I do. You can see just as far into me as I can you. My face is wide open. You can look at me. I look at most any man and tell when he is telling the truth. I have told you all I know. Let me go home, Gentlemen, to my family and to my home. When you go into the jury room, commune with my God. I have prayed to my God. My God is the same God as your God. Go in there and commune with my God and find out the truth about this thing. I asked my God to allow me and to guide me through the presentation of this statement to you gentlemen and to guide me in telling you the truth. I thank you.

By Mr. Huddleston: May I state what county?

By The Court: You know you can't tell him. You know the rule about that.

By Mr. Hinson: We want to direct the statement and ask him if he wants to make that statement.

By The Court: No

By Mr. Wallace: Can I continue?

By The Court: If you have anything you want to state you can do that, but counsel can't make any suggestion to you.

By Mr. Wallace: Gentlemen, I would like to add at this time that pasture and this well where this accident happened was on the property of the Chattahoochee Valley Lumber company. It is adjacent to the farm, joins the farm of Wilson Turner lived on and is in Meriwether County. I thank you.

(Statement concluded at 5:50 p.m.)

By the Court: Gentlemen of the jury, you will observe the instructions that I have given you on previous occasions during this trial with reference to discussing this case with anybody or with each other. Just do not discuss it. Keep your minds open until it is finally concluded and submitted to you for consideration Just forget it until tomorrow. We will take a recess until nine o'clock tomorrow morning.

Day Five

Friday morning, June 18, 1948

By The Court: Is there anything further for the defendant?

By Mr. Huddleston: We rest, Your Honor.

By The Court: Anything further for the state?

By Solicitor Wyatt: Yes sir.

The following people were called in rebuttal by the State:

Dr. Herman Jones

By Solicitor Wyatt:
q. Dr. Jones, if a person were to strike another with a pump shotgun with full force across the back of his head and this person after being so struck falls limp into a car and does not move etc. would such a blow cause death?
.
By Mr. Huddleston: If Your Honor please that seems to be a very leading question and calls for a conclusion.

By The Court: Question disallowed as it is not in rebuttal to the defendant's statement.
                    witness is excused
~~~~~~~~~~~~~~~~~~~~~

Robert Lee Gates
Robert Lee states he has been in the liquor business with Wallace during the year. I don't know how much we made, but I was making for him. He was paying me $30 a run to make it. Make about forty or fifty gallons a run. Made anywhere from two to three runs a week for say two months. Me and Cleveland King got caught when we were making still for Wallace. He states Turner's back of his head was knocked off.
(Can't tell what he means as he is pointing to his head. Keep in mind that Gates still has a murder charge out on him.)
He states "from right along across here back was off, and right here on down, and the face - "
(We're left wondering as to what part of the face.)

361

Albert Brooks

Albert Brooks recalled in rebuttal, testifies as follows:
I know about the liquor that was found over there. Me and Mr. Wallace put it there, Mr. John Wallace. I forget what date it was. It was before this thing happened and before I was put in jail. As near as I can get it, I imagine around about three weeks I think. There was something over 100 gallons. I don't know whose it was. He come and got me to help put it there. I don't know whether it was his or who. When I saw this body of Turner when they pulled it out of the well, the back part of his head was off. Mr. Hall owned the land that the house was on, that the liquor was put in. James Bray lived in the house. We put it in a little smoke house. I told the officers about it on Thursday. This last Thursday was two weeks. Now they come down to Columbus and got us, and told me they found our liquor, and I asked them whose liquor, and I asked where they found it and they said they had found it in James Bray smoke house, something over 100 gallons, 103 gallons I think it was. I told them it was not mine, and they said well Mr. John Wallace said he and me put it there, and I told them I did help put it there.

Note: (Mr. Brooks still has a murder charge out on him as well.)

Sheriff A. L. Potts

I didn't see any blood around the well. I saw a pole that they told me they had moved from the well.

J. H. Potts

I was the first one to the well and I did not see any blood or brain tissue around the well. The only blood and brain seen came out of the well was on a pole.
Note: (Of course he meant the first law enforcement.)

Earl Lucas was also recalled and gave a long statement in which no new information was obtained.

Note: (His statement just pertained to the moonshine business. In which he stated that Wallace had turned in Turner's still. No one at any time, asked him how the still was missed during April when everyone was searching the three counties for Turner's body. Obviously, the authorities wanted a back up plan in case the murder charge didn't stick. It is totally absurd to think that a moonshine still could have been missed during the massive man hunt that was conducted. These allegations of moonshine only serve to reinforce the notion that someone had it in for Wallace. It is interesting to note that Turner had a problem with blacking out, falling down unconscious and then coming to shortly after.)

By Solicitor Wyatt:

q. Mr. Lucas, this distillery that was reported to you down on the defendant's place in February of this year, what, if anything, did the defendant say to you about the distillery after he reported it?

a. Said -- In February of this year?

q. Yes, Sir.

A. It was not reported to me. Mr. Miller and Cook seized that distillery.

q. Well, did the defendant talk to you about the distillery?

a. Gates and Cleveland King both made statements in my presence.

q. I am not talking about them. I am talking about the defendant on trial, Mr. Wallace. Did he talk to you about it?

a. I went by there and asked him about the land line. That was after they had seized the distillery, asked him if it was on his place, and he said it was not, it was on Mr. Chambers' place.

q. Did you go down to raid the distillery?

a. I went down. Miller and cook arrested them, and I docketed the case. They brought the men here, and I went back down and helped them finish destroying the distillery.

q. Before the distillery was raided, did the defendant say anything to you about raiding it or when to raid it?

a. No, sir. He has never talked to me about any distillery other than the one big distillery he carried me to October 22nd.

q. Well, what about that? Did he say anything about when to raid that distillery?

a. Did he? Yes, sir.

q. What did he say?

a. After they had called me down there, he suggested that I wait ten days, about ten days, before I made any move. He said "let them get it in full blast."

q. Was the distillery going at that time?

a. yes.

q. In operation?

a. It had been operating there a long time. They had worn out one still and put in a new tank there, a large tank. In other words, they had increased the mash capacity just recently. That was just before we seized it.

q. About how much mash and beer was there that had not been run at the time you raided it?

a. Well, there was - the tank still was full. It would hold about two thousand gallons, and possibly forty barrels of mash there.

q. What reason did the defendant give you when he asked you to wait about ten days to raid it?

a. Well, he said so they could get it in full operation.

q. Well, was it in full operation when you did raid it?

a. When we arrived at the distillery that night we promptly ascertained it had been in operating during the day, yes, sir.

q. Was there anybody there when you got there that night?

a. No, sir, there was not.

q. How do you know it had been operated that day?

a. The steam was rising out of one of the stills and the mash was scalding hot.

Cross Examination

By Mr. Huddleston:

q. Mr. Lucas, when did you say you had this conversation with the defendant here?

a. That was on the night of October 22nd.

q. the night of October 22nd. Where were you after that?

a. Well, in the afternoon and night, and morning, in the early morning. it lasted throughout the afternoon and night.

q. Well now, let's get the whole operations that day in the record.

a. All right.

q. First of all, you got instructions from Atlanta to come down?

a. I was in Atlanta on official business, and Mr. Frank Clark, who is acting investigator in charge advised me that you had 'phoned Mr. Tydings.

q. That I had phoned?

a. Yes, sir. I went down to your office and you explained in detail about Mr. Turner causing all this trouble down there, and also explained about getting him a tax pardon I believe it was, and then stated --

q. As a matter of fact, mr. Lucas, let me refresh your recollection. Mr. Wallace had just received a presidential pardon?

a. I don't know. All I know about it is what you told me, and what he told me.

By Mr. Goldberg: I insist he be permitted to answer the question.

By Mr. Huddleston: I will let him answer the question. me and mr. Lucas will get along all right.

q. Mr. Lucas, you came there and we went into all the details of what was going on, as well as I knew them.

a. Yes, Sir.

q. Mr. Bedenbaugh was with you at the time.

a. That is right.

q. And I went in the car with you down to see that you got to Mr. Wallace's.

a. Yes, Sir, at your suggestin we went down to see Mr. Wallace.

q. That is right, and we talked an hour or so.

a. We went to Mr. Wallace's house, and from there we went to a vacant house just in front of Robert lee Gates' house, and drove in the yard, and there we had a lengthy conversation.

q. That is right. We conversed for an hour, or such a matter.

a. Yes, sir.

q. And Mr. Wallace went in great details with you as to why he wanted to break up the liquor business.

a. He talked a lot, yes, sir, he sure did.

q. He went in great details about why he could not afford to have somebody making liquor around there.

a. Yes, sir.

q. He gave you the information then and there, told you where the still was and wanted it raided then.

a. He suggested we wait about ten days I beleive it was at that time, or after you left. I don't recall.

q. He told you that because he said he was very anxious to have the people operating it caught.

a. I wanted to see the distillery, and we made an appointment to meet him back there at eight o'clock.

q. That was after you carried me back home?

a. Yes, sir. he set the date and the time, eight o'clock, and we went bak there and walked from a point not far from his house through the woods to the distillery.

q. Now this distillery, Mr. Wallace's house was on the west side of the

Central of Georgia Railroad and State Highway 41 is it not? Mr. Wallace's house is on the west side of State Highway 41?

a. Northwest I guess, yes, Sir.

q. Something like three-quarters of a mile or a miles across the field from the highway?

a. Yes, Sir.

q. And it is three-quarters to a half a mile or a half a mile to three-quarters to 41 highway over to the Central Railroad isn't it?

a. About right, yes, sir.

q. All right, and this still was then beyond another county road on the east side of the railroad in a swamp was it not?

a. It is on a branch about two miles from his house, maybe two and half.

q. That is what I was trying to establish, the distance. It was some two or two and half miles east of this house?

a. Yes, sir.

q. And a rather large outfit?

a. Yes, sir, it was.

q. And at the same time that afternoon -- to go back to that afternoon, Mr. Wallace told you at that time that this was a big outfit.

a. Yes, sir.

q. And that when he was in the liquor business twelve years before that he operated big outfits didn't he?

a. He did, yes sir.

q. And that when they got to putting up big outfits liek that around him somebody would think it was his.

a. That is right.

q. And he wanted this distillery destroyed.

a. Yes sir. he wanted Wilson Turner caught. I am convinced of that.

q. He wanted the liquor business broken up, and that was the gist of his conversation with you?

a. He wanted Turner caught. he sure did.

q. He knew if you caught Turner you could break up the liquor business. Was not that what he told you?

a. I don't think so.

q. All right. Now he showed you where the still was that night?

a. Yes, he went to the still.

q. Gave you a thermos bottle and blanket to make you comfortable while you watched it?

a. We went to the still and looked it over, and came back and decided we would go in after midnight, so we went in and got lunch, went to LaGrange and got a lunch, and picked up a jacket or two, and when we got back we met Mr. Wallace at the place called Fair View, and he was parked in behind on the side of the place there, and he had --

q. What kind of car was he driving? (This question was never answered)

a. He brought this thermos jug and blanket, one or two blankets.

q. He gave them to you for your comfort?

a. We went on to the still and got out and got in the woods where he said to get, and we remained there until almost light. He had told us that Wilson Turner would be in there at four o'clock in the morning, we would see everything. He said get his car, get the truck, get anything, "they will bring a load of sugar in here about four o'clock, and be in here." Well, just about light I saw we were in the wrong place, so we moved on the opposite side of the still and watched it there until about noon, and it started sprinkling rain. Nobody showed up at the still. We walked back to where we had our car concealed, and I went to Warm Springs and called the State Revenue Agent, Miller, and asked him to come up there and helkp us destroy the distillery, and we destroyed it, and several days later i went to mr. Wallace's house and carried him his jug and blanket back and told him we did not arrest anybody, and he told me then, "well, you cut it too soon; they came in there the next day". And he aid, "that man is off right now, got two of my Negroes building and setting up another still", and he said, "I will know where it is in a few days and I will call you." Well, I never did hear anymore from him.

q. He said he was off with two of his Negroes right then setting up another still?

a. yes sir.

q. And he was talking about Wilson Turner?

a. He was talking about Wilson Turner.

q. You went back down there the next day or so and found some other stills that were being made?

a. No sir, I did not. Mr. Miller destroyed -- I went, I saw them.

q. You saw them?

a. I went up there to question Wilson Turner about the big still, and when I drove in the yard Wilson stuck his head out the door, slammed the door and ran out the back door and ran about 100 years and fell like he was dead, and he was white as a sheet. Well, I didn't run after him. He got up and came up there, and I questioned him.

q. You say he run down across the field and fainted?

a. Yes, sir. He fell. He got up and come up. he could not talk. He pulled up his sleeve and showed me his arm, and I saw where a hypodermic needle had been stuck in his arm.

q. You don't know what he was treated for?

a. No , sir.

q. That is immaterial.

a. And when he gained his breath, I questioned him a little bit, and he said, "you know I could not set up a still of that size." That is all he said. that is all I got out of him. I asked him about two trucks parked there in the yard and about these tank stills that was in the yard and he said "Mr. Miller and them made a case against my brother in law for building these two tanks there."

q. There was a couple of trucks in the yard?

a. Yes, sir.

q. These two cut up tank stills were there in the yard?

a. Two cut up tank stills, new ones were there in the yard.

q. And he told you Mr. Miller made a case against his brother in laws for making the still?

a. Yes, sir.

q. And they were the ones the Windhams were making?

a. Yes, sir

q. Did you ever find any used equipment that you had destroyed at some other still being put bak in use again?

a. Found any used equipment?

a. Yes, any equipment you destroyed at one still or cut up at one still being put back in operation at another.

a. Well, I noticed a number of these, of these metal drums at this distillery back of Robert lee Gates' had been cut before.

q. That was where Albert Brooks and this King Negro was caught?

a. No, sir. Gates and Cleveland King were caught there.

q. Gates and King instead of Brooks.

a. Yes, sir.

q. And the heads of the barrels or something of the kind were the ones that was at another still you previously cut up?

a. There had been axes struck through quite a few of them, yews, sir, and they had been patched up.

(the witness is excused)

By Mr. Henson: May we inquire whether or not other rebuttal testimony has been offered already to something that some of these witnesses have not already rebutted?

By The Court: You mean what he is now offering?

By Solicitor Wyatt: This is a statement made by the defendant on the commitment trial.

By The Court: Statement of what?

By Solicitor Wyatt: Statement made by the defendant on commitment trial, which would be in rebuttal of the statement he made here.

By Mr. Henson: We object to it, if Your Honor please. He has a right to make any statement he wants to in a commitment trial without it being called to face him in any further trial. It would be unfair, wholly unfair, and they have closed their case, and we have dismissed all our witnesses.

By The Court: Well, I will sustain the objection.

(The case is argued to the jury.)

By The Court: Gentlemen of the Jury, you will observe the instructions which I have given you throughout the trial of this case with reference to discussing this case among yourselves or permitting anyone to discuss it with you or around you. keep your minds open, free, until the case is finally concluded and submitted to you. We will take a recess until one-thirty.

(Recess called at 12:20 p.m.)

After Recess
By The Court: Let the jury come in.

(The jury returns to the box.)

Proceed with the argument.
By Mr. Henson: The Solicitor's statement is entirely unwarranted and

unfair when he said we only called one witness and tested him as to his constitutionality. He knew we did not call others because counsel stated it would be the same thing, and by agreement of State's counsel the determination was made solely on the basis of one that was called, and with the understanding that the other answers would be the same.

By Solicitor Wyatt: I didn't understand that except as to Mr. Mobley and Mr. Sivell.

By The Court: Those were the only two calls, Mr. Mobley and Mr. Sivell.

By Solicitor Wyatt: I didn't understand any agreement about the others.

By The Court: And Mr. Howard represented them.

By Mr. Henson: We decided there was no use to put that test to the others because we were advised by counsel that all the others would be the same.

By The Court: I will let you put that in.

By Mr. Henson: I think that is an unwarranted appeal to ask this jury to please - the publicity that has been pointed at this county, there is only one basis on which they can render the verdict. That is the truth, without respect to what the newspaper people might think about it, or what newspaper might be -- I ask the Court to instruct the jury not to regard that.

By The Court: Gentlemen, you will not give regard to any newspaper publicity, by basing your verdict only upon the evidence in the case.

(Recess called at 2:30 p.m. for 10 minutes.)

After Recess

(Continuation of argument to the jury.)

Charge to the Jury

This is a partial record of the instructions the Judge gave the Jury.

By The Court:

Gentlemen of the Jury, the Grand Jury of this county at the March adjourned term of Court, 1948 returned a true bill of indictment in which they charge John Wallace, Herring Sivell, Tom Strickland and Henry Mobley with the offense of murder.

The State has elected to place on trial at this time John Wallace, and you will not be concerned with any evidence pertaining to the other defendants in the case. They are not on trial. John Wallace is the only defendant on trial.

Now Gentlemen, upon arraignment, the defendant, John Wallace, has filed his pleas of not guilty, and the charge as made in the indictment and his denial of the charge makes the issue that you are to pass upon in this case.

Now Gentlemen, I charge you that the indictment is not evidence and shall not be considered by you as evidence. The only purpose it serves is to bring the charge against the accused into court and the accused, gentlemen, John Wallace, enters upon the trial of his case with the legal presumption of innocence in his favor, and that presumption goes with him throughout the trial until the State has proved him guilty beyond a reasonable doubt.

Therefore, gentlemen, the burden is upon the State to prove each and every material allegation contained in the bill of indictment before you would be authorized to convict the defendant John Wallace, who is on trial, and the material allegations which the State must prove beyond a reasonable doubt are the following:

That John Wallace, who must be identified as the person on trial........ and did unlawfully, wilfully, feloniously and with malice aforethought did kill and murder William H. Turner with a pump shotgun on April 20, 1948 in Coweta county and by beating and striking him with a blunt instrument to the Grand Jury unknown, and thereby inflicting a mortal wound and wounds upon him, from which said wound and wounds then and there died. . . . .

If after considering all of the facts and circumstances of the case, giving the defendant's statement just such weight and credit as you think it entitled to receive, your minds are wavering, unsettled and unsatisfied, then that is the doubt of the law, and you should acquit, but if that doubt does not exist in your minds as to the guilt of the defendant, then you should convict.

If the death of William Turner alias Wilson Turner came from a blow received in Coweta then it does not matter where he died. If the evidence shows he died for other causes that did not occur in Coweta then you should acquit.

The punishment for murder in this State is death by electrocution unless the jury trying the case see fit to recommend mercy.
"We the jury find the defendant John Wallace guilty." A verdict reading that way would mean that the defendant, John Wallace would be put to death by electrocution.

'We the jury find the defendant John Wallace guilty, and recommend him to mercy. A verdict reading that way, would mean the defendant John Wallace would be sent to the penitentiary for and during his natural life.

Before you would be authorized to find the defendant guilty, his guilt should be made plainly and manifestly to appear beyond a reasonable doubt. If you acquit the defendant "we the jury find the defendant John Wallace not guilty.

SENTENCE

The State vs. John Wallace
Coweta Superior Court Indictment and Conviction for Murder

Whereas the jury in the above stated case returned the following verdict
"We the Jury, find the defendant, John Wallace, guilty."

G. Y. Chestnut, foreman
June 18, 1948

It is considered, ordered and adjudged by the Court that the defendant,
John Wallace be taken from the bar of this court to the common jail of
Coweta County, there to be safely kept until his removal to the Georgia
State Prison in Tattnall County for the purpose of the execution of this
sentence in the manner prescribed by law.

It is further ordered and adjudged by the Court that the Sheriff of Coweta
County, or his lawful deputy, together with such deputies as he may deem
necessary (the number of guards to be approved by the presiding Judge, or
the Ordinary of said County_ shall convey the said John Wallace, to the
Georgia State Prison in Tattnall county not more than twenty days and not
less than two days prior to the 30thd day of July 1948 and there deliver
him to the Director of Corrections to be electrocuted as provided by law,
at such Penal Institution as may be designated by said Board.

And it is ordered and adjudged by the Court that the Warden of the
penitentiary of the State of Georgia shall execute the said John Wallace,
by electrocution, as provided herein and by law, in private, witnessed only
by his counsel, relatives, and such clergymen and friends as he may so
desire, within the walls of said institution, on the 30th day of July, 1948,
between the hours of 10:00 o'clock a.m., and 2:00 o'clock pm.
And may God have Mercy on his soul.
This the 18th day of June, 1948

Signed by
L. Wyatt
Solicitor General Coweta Judicial Circuit
and Samuel Boykin
Judge, Superior Court Coweta Judicial Circuit

Request for a New Trial

State vs. John Wallace
Indictment for Murder
Coweta Superior Court May Adjourned Term, 1948

It appearing that the court reporter was unable to furnish counsel a complete record of the testimony in the above-stated case before August 14, 1948, and it further appearing that counsel for movant, John Wallace, was unable to complete the amended motion for a new trial by said date it is hereby ordered that the hearing on the motion for a new trial be and the same is hereby continued until September 10, 1948.
This August 13, 1948

Signed Samuel Boykin
Judge Superior Court Coweta Circuit
....

Coweta Superior Court
Chambers of the Judge:
The recitals of fact contained in the above and foregoing amendment to the original Motion for a New Trial filed in the case and hereby approved as true and correct, and all of the grounds of the Amendment to the Motion for a New Trial are approved and the Amendment is hereby allowed and ordered filed as a part of the record in the case.
This 10th day of September 1948.

Samuel J. Boykin
Judge Superior Court Coweta Judicial Circuit.
....

The motion for a new trial as filed in the above stated case having been heard on the 10th day of September 1948, and was at that time taken under consideration, after considering said motion, including the amendment thereto until the present time.
It is ordered, considered and adjudged by the Court that all of the grounds of the motion, including the amendment, be and the same are overruled and a new trial is denied.
This the 2nd day of October 1948
signed Samuel Boykin
Judge, S.C.C.C.
....

Final disposition

John Wallace to be taken to Georgia State Prison in Tattnall County 11th day of February 1949 to be electrocuted.

So ordered by Judge Samuel Boykin on 28th day of January 1949
....

Atlanta, January 11, 1949
The Honorable Supreme Court met pursuant to adjournment. The following judgment was rendered:

John Wallace VS The State

This case came before this court upon a writ of error from the Superior Court of Coweta County; and after argument had, it is considered and adjudged that the judgment of the court below be affirmed.
All the Justices concur.
....

Extra-ordinary motion for a new trial

Homer Lassetter juror said if he were to serve on the jury that he, regardless of the evidence, would give John Wallace the electric chair. Wright Lipford, Solicitor-General of the Coweta Judicial Circuit affidavits of J. T. carpenter, I. J. Winslett, C. J. Smith, J. Perkins Bailey, H. W. McDonald and R. H. Johnson

Joint affidavit of Frank Odom, E. L. Gross and Mrs. E. L. Gross, which affidavit is as follows:

Coweta county, Georgia
We, the undersigned, are acquainted with Homer Lassetter, who served as a juror in the trial of John Wallace in the Superior Court of Coweta county during the month of June, 1948. We heard Mr. Lassetter state, previous to the trial, that if he was selected to serve on the jury that tried Wallace that he, regardless of the evidence, would give Wallace the electric chair. Mr. Lassetter displayed high prejudice against Mr. Wallace and did state that he was in favor of the extreme penalty before he was selected for jury duty.

Sworn to and subscribed before me this February 22, 1949
G. R. Robertson notary public, Coweta County Georgia.

***The state comes back by saying the statement "is absolutely unfounded, untrue and a falsehood on the part of Frank Odom, E. L. Gross, and Mrs. E. L. Gross.

That he, Homer Lassetter, has never made a statement or statements as set out in the joint affidavit either before or after the trial.

His statement is dated April 26 1949
****
Coweta county, Georgia
Personally appeared before me, the undersigned, an officer duly authorized by law to administer oaths, Lamar Potts, who first being duly sworn deposes on oath and says:

That he is the Sheriff of Coweta County and that he was present throughout the entire trial fo the State Vs. John Wallace charged with the offense of Murder and tried at the March Adjourned Term of the Superior Court of Coweta County on the dates of June 14th, 15th, 16th, 17th, and 18th, in the year 1949.

That deponent is personally acquainted with Tom Strickland, who was indicted jointly with John Wallace and others for the offense of Murder. That during the trial of John Wallace in the Superior Court of Coweta County, Tom Strickland was in the custody of deponent and was available as a witness for the defendant, John Wallace, throughout said trial, and that at no time through the entire trial of the case of The State Vs. John Wallace did John Wallace call as a witness Tom Strickland.

That Tom Strickland, although available as a witness had the defendant seen fit to call him, did not take the witness stand during the trial of the John Wallace case and claim his constitutional right not to testify as his testimony would incriminate him. That counsel, the Hon. Jack Allen of Greenville, Georgia, who represented Tom Strickland did not state to counsel for the defendant in open court that if Tom Strickland was called as a witness for the defendant that Tom Strickland would claim his constitutional right not to testify for fear that his own testimony would incriminate him.

Deponent further states that he makes this affidavit to be used as evidence in the case of John Wallace, Movant Vs. The State of Georgia, Respondent, application for extra-ordinary motion for a new trial
This the 29th day of April, 1949.

Signed: A. L. Potts, deponent

Sworn to and subscribed before me this 29th day of April, 1949.
J. W. Powell

....

Application for commutation of sentence in the above stated case having been filed and a hearing on same having been held on February 24, 1949. Now, in compliance with the authority vested in the Board of Pardons and Paroles of the State of Georgia, it is: Considered, ordered and adjudged that the application for commutation be denied. It is directed that copies of this Order be filed with the Department of Corrections of the State of Georgia and the Clerk of the Superior Court in the county where sentence was imposed.

Given under the hand and seal of the State board of pardons and paroles, this the 18th day of April 1949.

Signed by
Everett, Chairman,
? , member (I couldn't read this name)
Rebecca L. Rainey, member

....

The extraordinary motion for new trial in the above stated case having been presented and after considering the same, it is ordered, that said motion be and the same is hereby overruled on each and every ground, and a new trial is denied.

The Clerk of this Court is hereby directed to immediately notify counsel representing all parties in this case of this order.

This May 7, 1949
Signed Samuel J. Boykin

....

Atlanta, September 13, 1949
The Honorable Supreme Court met pursuant to adjournment. The following judgment was rendered:

John Wallace v. The State.

This case came before this court upon a writ of error from the Superior Court of Coweta County; and after argument had, it is considered and adjudged that the judgment of the court below be affirmed.
All the Justices concur.

....

New execution date set for October 14th, 1949.

A writ of habeas corpus, Habeas corpus. Before Judge Moore. Fulton Superior Court. October 3, 1949.

Judgment affirmed. All the Justices concur.

FEBRUARY 13, 1950. REHEARING DENIED MARCH 15, 1950

Methodist church in Harris county that Wallace and the Stricklands' attended. They also went to the Baptist church upon occasion and some of the stained glass windows were contributed by them.

Chapter Eight

The Cold Hard Facts

The sad truth is that we are never going to know why John Wallace was given the ultimate death penalty. After reading the court record there is major doubt as to John Wallace's intention. He states that the death was an accident and there is every reason to believe that it was. It is also obvious that Turner did not die in Coweta County, Georgia.

We know based on Dr. Herman Jones testimony concerning the lack of blood found in the two vehicles that he did not sustain sufficient injury at the Sunset Tourist Camp to cause his death. In other words, he did not have a fractured skull while in those vehicles or there would have been blood all over the place and it would not have been fresh blood.

We'll never know why Wallace's attorneys didn't act fast the minute Robert Lee Gates said he saw blood around the well. They may have chosen not to ask this man at the time he said it but during the rebuttal they should have asked him. They should have asked him as to how much he saw and they didn't. This is an unexplainable circumstance. In my mind, it is without a doubt that Turner died in Meriwether County. There is no other explanation for the lack of blood found in Sivell and Mobley's vehicles.

We are not given any explanation as to how this particular well was missed in the manhunt that occurred on April 28th. They searched all over Wallace's property and surrounding areas all the way to Warm Springs. Odd, very odd, to say the least and it causes major doubt.

Gates and Brooks were being held in Columbus Georgia jail so that Wallace's counsel could not interview them and find out the portion of the accident that Wallace could not remember. They couldn't find out what had actually happened to the body. If any of their testimony is to be believed and I think the brain tissue found in the well supports the probability that the body was moved. Then Gates and Brooks were the first ones on the scene after Turner's death. The fact that Wallace didn't remember anything that happened after the shooting is supported by the fact that he had to hunt for the well according to these two men.

These two men where also being held on murder charges and they had only Potts and Hancock to communicate with. They were not given an attorney to represent them. They were running scared. Scared of what Potts would do to them if they didn't say what he told them to. We are left not knowing how much of their story to believe if any of it. This detail is very frustrating.

According to cremation experts, we know that the body could not have been burnt to ashes as they stated it was. That story was only concocted so the State could say they had what was left of Turner's body. Although at no time did any expert say that it was Turner's body. They only said it was human bones.

Another point in question is why didn't Wallace's attorneys call any character witnesses on behalf of John? The people in Meriwether may have been too afraid to speak up for him. That would be perfectly understandable with all the murder warrants being thrown around. But this is a fact that we will never know.

Sheriff Potts actions during the case are completely unexplainable.

What would make him step outside of the law and develop a personal interest in the outcome of the case? There are so many possibilities that the mind boggles at it. The fact is that he did, but why he did will remain a mystery. I have given you many possible reasons and it may be a combination of these things or none of them. But there was something!

Why in heavens would the newspapers write against a prominent member of his community and side with a thief and army deserter? It hadn't been that many years back when the people, along with the law enforcement were hanging horse thieves. I don't know what they did with cow thieves but I should think it would be about the same thing. Well, not exactly, horses were used for transportation as well as work so stealing a cow may not have had such dire consequences. In any event, the witnesses state that they did not personally know Wallace so why?

Surely the people of Coweta knew that the army did upon occasion put deserters in front of a firing squad. It had only been three years earlier when such an occurrence happened. So why try and make Turner out to be something that he wasn't? A poor helpless tenant farmer who was beaten and murdered by a big, powerful, arrogant, wealthy plantation owner. It just wasn't the truth.

John Wallace was certainly wrong in his actions. He should have had a little more patience and perhaps justice would have been found in Carroll County in the prosecution of Turner. But at the same time, John Wallace was not a murderer. He didn't intend to kill anyone.

Personal differences should not have played a factor during that trail. The only thing the jury should have been concerned with were the cold hard facts that was presented. They should not have cared about how much land he owned, or how much money they thought he had. The moonshine days were over. Turner had left his land and moved to Carroll County.

Turner came back and began stealing from Wallace, that's what the jury should have focused on. When the Chief of Police in Carroll county said that the gang of cow thieves had been in operation for several months terrorizing the local area why didn't anyone care? The prosecutor kept playing up the moonshine angle, as if that had anything to do with the case at all. The moonshine was over. Turner had left Wallace's land. Until he came back to steal. The facts can't get much clearer than that.

Something was not right in Coweta with the townspeople and we will never know what it was back then that had them so outraged that they were thirsty for more blood. They allowed personal sentiment to get in the way of justice. The horrific accident of Turner's death was not enough. They wanted Wallace dead as well. Even the death of Sheriff Collier didn't satisfy their thirst. They wanted Wallace dead and did everything in their power to make sure that his appeal for a new trial did not get sanctioned. They wrote many, many letters to the editor of their paper encouraging that the motion for a new trial be denied. Why? Were they perhaps afraid that others would hear and know the truth?

John Wallace spoke for six and half hours trying to tell the people on that jury the type man he was. He did this because there was no one else to speak out for him. Everyone who knew any of the facts or details had murder charges filed against them. They were being threatened with the electric chair if they testified.

It was important for Wallace that people know the truth. Therefore it's important to me that people know the truth. At least the best that we can know it.

His motion for a mistrial was denied. His motion for a new trial was denied. All he was asking for was a fair trial where people were free of the prejudices that the Coweta county people had against him but that was denied him, over and over again.

John Wallace was a modest man. He lived a modest life. He didn't have fine, fancy things. He didn't care about fine, fancy things. He cared about making a living. He cared about his family. He cared about his friends.

It is beyond my understanding why the newspapers would persist in parading him around as a wealthy plantation owner. He owned a lot of land. In Tennessee we call that land poor. In Alabama they call it dirt poor. But owning land is not a crime nor does it make a person a cold, heartless, self-centered person. Owning land is the American dream.

I have called Reidsville State Prison and have been unable to confirm what John's last words were. I was told that they are not posted in the museum. We do have a newspaper accounting of his final moments, whether this is correct is anyone's guess. I don't know if Ms. Barnes wrote accurately about his final moments. It is with complete and utter certainty that she concocted the little scene about the Pastor turning to the side and weeping.

John had already said he was sorry for Turner's death. He said that to the jury. He said it was hard to live with himself knowing that he had caused the death of a man. John Wallace was a Christian. I can well believe that he did pray for those who convicted him. Because that was the type man that he was. He had no ill will to any man.

That's the way the Meriwether people remember him and they are after all the ones who knew him. The Coweta county people did not know him yet they hated him. It is really quite unexplainable. Four and a half days for a trial. Seventy minutes for the jury. It is a most bizarre and unbelievable tale yet it is the truth. Three men died so needlessly. If the events were not curtailed in history one could well imagine the story to be a work of fiction. It did happen and three men died, Turner, Collier and Wallace.

I believe the people who knew John Wallace and I believe him. The facts support his story. May his soul rest in peace with the knowledge that his words are out there for anyone who cares to read them.

On the day the lights went out in Georgia for John Wallace, it has been written that he left a will giving property to the Boy Scouts. The fact is that a will was never probated in Meriwether, Harris or Tattnall counties. John Wallace was destitute when he died. His Uncle Mozart had been helping him pay the mounting attorney fees. His Uncle Maynard's wife had given Josephine a place to live for as long as she wanted it.

During the time from 1948 to 1950 the deed books are empty regarding any land transactions for John and Josephine. The quick claim deeds that John supposedly did during his court days do not appear in the deed books. At least the Wallace's are not listed as grantee on any property during that time frame in Meriwether or Harris counties. According to the newspapers he had auctions on the doorsteps of the court house to help raise money for his legal expenses.

How much property he had or did not have shouldn't have been a factor in his case but it was. He was reported as a wealthy plantation owner, over and over again. Why? What possible difference should that have made during his trial?

Let's talk about his terrible temper for a minute. He had difficulty in school as a teenager because of his temper. Anyone who has raised a child can relate to that. Teenage years are not the most pleasant ones to go through. If a person can get their child safely through those teenage years then something wonderful happens. They adjust to the rules and responsibilities of being an adult.

Human beings have emotions. Some that run stronger than others. If you care deeply about anything in this world, then you probably have a temper. Someone, somewhere can push all the right buttons that will throw you into having a hissy fit or a cussing tantrum or however you may react when you get riled up. But we all have emotions that run very deep in regards to certain aspects of our lives. The normal person reigns in their temper and does not physically strike out at someone because we as adults know that as in all things, this too shall pass.

I'm told that Wallace was a happy and jovial man, ninety-nine percent of the time but I'm sure he did have occasions were his temper got the best of him. He had deep emotions. He cared about things. He cared about people, he cared about life. He showed remarkable patience by putting up with Turner for over a year but when a person believes that they have passed one hurdle just to have that person reappear and start stealing from him, well that's a different story all together.

Close your eyes for a minute and picture your most prized possession. Something that you depend on everyday. For John Wallace, it was his cows, he was a dairy farmer but for the rest of us let's say it's our vehicle. We need our vehicle to get to and from work. Now, close your eyes and picture that vehicle either stolen or destroyed. You replace it just to find it stolen or destroyed the next day too. This keeps happening three or four times. Now, be true to yourself. Does that cause you any emotions? If the police caught the person who was doing this and told you they were going to have to turn them loose, how would you feel about that? Now let's say you were bone tired when they gave you this news. How would that make you feel?

Naturally, you would not want to kill anyone but you would want justice to be served. You would want that person to stop annoying you. To get out of your life and leave you in peace. A person does not just sit back` and allow others to continuously steal from them.

I was told recently that John's last wish was to be buried in some blue silk pajamas that he had at the prison with him. I was told that this was not done because his body was so badly fried that they were not able to embalm him. I was told that he remained in a body bag and was throw into a $200 coffin and put in the ground with no vault and the dirt piled in on top of him. This gruesome little story was told to me very smugly with a great deal of satisfaction in the telling of it.

I must have a bit of temper myself because the story riled me up to the point where I called the funeral home to find out if there was any truth to this story. I was told that the financial information was confidential and could not be released. It raises the question as to how this other lady found out it cost $200. I don't know if the above story is true or not but it is a shameful state to know that the people still today hold the same beliefs that they did back in 1948. I have been assured that the pajamas had the prison sent them with the body would have been laid in the coffin with him if they were not put on him.

The purpose of a vault is so the coffin will not be crushed in when the grave is filled in. The fact that his cousin, Pope Davis had some say in the arrangements is a saving grace. There are a lot of people who choose not to have a vault. The body is but an outer shell with his soul having gone to heaven so I don't suppose it matters. But for anyone to take delight in the knowledge is morbid and cruel and certainly does not speak well of the community.

A newspaper accounting of his death, written by Joe Dabney, the Ledger-Enquirer State Editor in 1950, states there were hundreds of relatives, friends and idle curious jammed into the Chipley Methodist church for the funeral. Dr. Charles Allen of Atlanta spoke freely but reverently of the Wallace he knew as a personal friend through the years. "We thank God for every good act of this man. Dr. Allen said, "and there were many. Crowds outside milled with bowed heads around the historic church. "I'm here today at the request of John Wallace, the minister said. "John Wallace told me before he died that 'I put myself in the hands of God and above all else, I love everybody.' The minister continued, "It was a rare and inspiring attitude. Dr. Allen quoted from the last letter which he said Wallace wrote: "I'm going to the home of many mansions . . . don't worry about me.

RECORD OF FUNERAL

Total No. 45   Yearly No. 45   Date of Entry. Nov. 4.

Name of Deceased. John Wallace

Residence. Chipley, Ga. R.F.D.

Charge to May Otey, Carquet & P. Davis

Address. Chipley, Ga.

Order given by. Otey Carquet & Pape Davis

How Secured.

If Veteran, State War.

Occupation.

Employer and Address.

Date of Death 11-3-50 Friday

Date of Birth.

Age. 54

Date of Funeral 11-4-50 Sat. 3 P.m.

Services at Chipley M.E. Church

Clergyman Dr. Paisley Allen.

Religion of the Deceased. M.E.

Birthplace Chambers County Ala.

Resided in the State.

Place of Death. Atmore State Prison.

Cause of Death. Legal Electrocution

Contributory Causes.

...... by J.M. Sughog - Glennville, Ga

Certifying Physician. Dr. J.C. Collins

Its Address. Collins, Ga.

Name of Father.

His Birthplace.

Maiden Name of Mother.

Her Birthplace.

Remains to.

Size of Casket.

Manufactured by. Casket Co.

| Complete Funeral (except outlays) |
| Casket |
| Burial Vault or Box |
| Embalming Body |
| Barber, $ . . . . . Hair Dressing, |
| Dressing Body, $ . . . . Underwear |
| Suit or Dress. |
| Slippers, $ . . . . Hose, $ |
| Folding Chairs, $ . . . . Tarpaulin, $ |
| Candelabrum, $ . . . . Candles, $ |
| Door Spray, $ . . . . Gloves, $ |
| Funeral Car, $ . . . . Ambulance, $ |
| Limousines to Cemetery . . . . @ $ |
| Extra Limousines . . . . @ $ |
| Autos to R. R. Station . . . . @ $ |
| Getting Remains from Atmore, Ga |
| Taking Remains to. |
| Trip to Coroner's Inquest |
| Delivering Box to. |
| Deliver Flowers to. |
| Removal Charges. |
| Procuring Burial Permit. |
| Certif. Copies of Death Certificates N |
| Pall Bearer Service, $ . . . . Use of Clasp |
| Gross Total for Sales Tax. |
| Outlay for Lot. |
| Cremation. |
| Flowers, $ . . . . Palms, $ . . . . Matting |
| Rental of Tent, $ . . . . of Temporary Vau |
| Opening of Grave or Tomb. |
| Lining Grave, $ . . . . Lowering Device |
| Outlay for Shipping Charges. |
| Clergyman, $ . . . . Singers, $ . . . . Organis |
| Railroad or Motor } Tickets, $ . . . . Aeroplane Servic |
| Telegr., Phone, Cable or Radio Charges |
| Cash Advanced. |
| Out of town Undertaker's Charges. |
| Personal Service. |
| Ins. Death Notices in . . . . Papers |
| (Names of Newspapers) |

Lot No.	
Grave No.	Sales Tax
Section No.	Total Footing of Bill
Block No.	Less.
Owner	Balance
	Entered into Ledger, page . . . . or befor

John Wallace stayed true to his beliefs and passions right to the end. It's a shame that William Turner's true identity was not known until after his death. The military would have removed Turner from Wallace's life had it been known and all this would have been avoided. It's tragic to know that the property Wallace owned, reported as 2000 acres with a 40 acre lake, weighed more on the minds of that Coweta county jury than what he had done. He didn't get a fair trial with those people. A body was manufactured by either Potts or by Hancock. Whichever one thought the plan up, is irrelevant, the other party condoned it to the point of causing more death. The entire situation was deplorable and such a waste of human life.

It has been difficult in learning the length that man will go to in order not to admit a mistake. Corruption and greed is never right. Especially not within our legal system. The laws are designed to protect the innocent. They are not to be used to eliminate the competition or for personal vengeance. These things are wrong today, as they were yesterday and since the founding of this great Nation of ours. The Constitution of the United States of America matters. Justice matters.

The lake off John Wallace road.

We find the following poem in a small poetry book entitled:

'Thoughts Written by Josephine Leath Wallace'

Electric Chair and Pardons by Josephine Leath Wallace

Have you been busy recently electric chair?
No! Thank goodness, although I'm shocking and quick at my particular type of
business. I'm always sorry to have anyone sit upon me.

How are the pardons these days?
I'm glad you asked me for I had an average amount to do last year.
It takes a long time to check and recheck all those records, you know.

Her thoughts reflect her sentiments as to what she and her husband are
having to deal with during this time frame.

John, Josephine sitting, her father standing.
Photo provided by a fellow researcher.

Farewell Dear John written by Ivey Nance

Accidents, bad decisions equal terrible consequences for all concerned.
But it does not make you a psychopath, sociopath or a serial killer.
John wasn't a member of the mafia or a threat to our society.
John Wallace was only a man.

Let the truth be told.
Let it ring from the highest tower.
Let it be shouted from the tallest mountain.
May it travel from New York to the Rio Grande.
John Wallace was just a man.

He was a southern gentleman
Only trying to help a fellow man.
He had no way of knowing the depth of the web of lies,
corruption, deceit and even murder in which he'd become entangled.
John Wallace was merely a man.

He killed a man by accident
A man who was stealing cattle from his land.
No one would listen to the truth.
John Wallace was a doomed man.

I have kept the pleasant memory, just rest in peace   JLW